Extending Microsoft 365 for Operations Cookbook

Create and extend real-world solutions using Dynamics 365 Operations

Simon Buxton

BIRMINGHAM - MUMBAI

Extending Microsoft Dynamics 365 for Operations Cookbook

First published: May 2017

Production reference: 1120517

Published by Packt Publishing Ltd.
Livery Place
35 Livery Street
Birmingham
B3 2PB, UK.
ISBN 978-1-78646-713-3

www.packtpub.com

Credits

Author

Simon Buxton

Reviewers

Simon Klingler

Martin Winkler

Commissioning Editor

Aaron Lazar

Acquisition Editor

Denim Pinto

Content Development Editor

Siddhi Chavan

Technical Editor

Dhiraj Chandanshive

Copy Editor

Zainab Bootwala

Project Coordinator

Vaidehi Sawant

Proofreader

Safis Editing

Indexer

Tejal Daruwale Soni

Production Coordinator

Deepika Naik

About the Author

Simon Buxton has worked with Dynamics 365 for Operations since its earliest incarnations, starting out as a consultant and developer in early 1999 when Dynamics 365 for Operations was known as Damgaard Axapta 1.5. He quickly became a team leader at Columbus IT Partners and carried out one of the first Axapta implementations in the UK before joining a new reseller, Sense Enterprise Solutions, as its technical director. Sense Enterprise Solutions enjoyed a global reach through the AxPact alliance, where Simon was placed as AxPact's Technical Lead.

Simon played a major role in growing the company into a successful Microsoft partner and was the Technical Lead on a number of highly challenging technical projects around the world, ranging from the UK, to Bahrain, to the USA. These projects include developing solutions for third-party logistics, multichannel retail, and eventually developing an animal feed vertical, as well as integrating Dynamics 365 for Operations into production control systems, government gateways, and e-commerce solutions, among others.
Now, working with Binary Consultants, he was part of a team that implemented the first Dynamics 365 for Operations implementation with support from Microsoft as part of the Community Technical Preview program (CTP). The knowledge gained as part of this process led to the creation of this book.

Simon has also worked on Mastering Microsoft Dynamics AX 2012 R3 Programming and Microsoft Dynamics AX 2012 R2 Administration Cookbook.

I would like to thank my colleagues at Binary Consultants for their continued support throughout the writing process. I would also like to thank all those who helped review this book, Martin Winkler and Simon Klingler in particular, who put in a lot of effort into reviewing each recipe. A lot of the insight written into this book was only possible by being part of the Dynamics 365 for Operations community technical preview process, and working with Microsoft's R&D team is a true privilege.
Finally, I am told, I have to thank my partner, Evi, for her patience and support as I disappeared for hours each night and weekend working on "yet another book?". Of course, no bio could be complete without mentioning my children, Tyler and Isabella, who seem bemused as to why I would voluntarily do homework.

About the Reviewers

Simon Klingler has been working with Microsoft Dynamics 365 for Operations and its predecessor products (Microsoft Dynamics AX, Axapta) since 2001. He gained experience as a developer, consultant, presales consultant, product manager, and solution architect. He has successfully implemented ERP solutions in national and international projects from 3 to 1000+ users. He was a product manager for several add-ons for Microsoft Dynamics ERP solutions.

He started working on the latest release in its very early days and regularly exchanged experiences, feedbacks, and lessons learned with the author of this book.
Currently, he is working on several cloud and local business data implementation projects as a solution architect.

In 2013, Simon co-founded Semantax, a company providing products and expert consulting services based on Microsoft Dynamics AX. In December 2014, he co-founded the Solutions Factory (`www.sf-ax.com`), a company delivering full-scale Microsoft Dynamics ERP implementations, in stable and long-lasting partnerships with its customers.
He is especially proud of the team that was formed in the course of the last years: the right people with the right attitude, a great mix of experienced advisers and developers, as well as young potentials. The team members motivate each other and unfailingly impress the clients.

Martin Winkler has over 13 years of experience with Microsoft Dynamics 365 for Operations and its previous releases.

After receiving his Master's degree in Mathematical Computer Sciences at Vienna University of Technology, he gained experience as an IT Consultant at Capgemini and later, as a BI Consultant at an Austrian consulting company specializing in CFO-targeted services.

In 2003, Martin joined Solutions Factory, a newly-founded Austrian company that specialized in Microsoft Dynamics 365 for Operations services. Starting as a developer and head of IT, he later became the head of development of up to 10 developers. From 2007 onwards, he additionally built up a team of performance experts. In 2008, the company (then FWI) became the largest Microsoft Dynamics 365 for Operations partner in Austria. While staying in development, he mostly worked as Technical Lead Consultant for several corporate customers with global implementations and with up to 1000 users. He also carried out numerous projects in the areas of performance and Microsoft BI for these customers.

Together with two long-term colleagues, he founded his own company in 2013, Semantax, providing products and expert consulting services based on Microsoft Dynamics 365 for Operations. In 2014, the experts of Semantax teamed up with two further long-term colleagues with vast know-how in industry processes and corporate ERP projects to relaunch the Solutions Factory.

Solutions Factory (www.sf-ax.com) is dedicated to shaping customer processes and to mapping them to Dynamics 365 for Operations in an efficient and optimal way. It follows its vision of contributing to the high competitive capability of European manufacturing companies. During the review of this book, the team was supporting five large customers with their Microsoft Dynamics 365 for Operations implementations.

Over the last decade, Martin has met the author of the book at several technical conferences on Microsoft Dynamics 365 for Operations. He was impressed not only with the author's in-depth technical knowledge, but also with his understanding of the business and process sides of the ERP branch. He enjoyed reviewing the previous books by the same author and was honored to support the author with this book as well. He hopes the readers will enjoy the read as much as he did.

www.PacktPub.com

For support files and downloads related to your book, please visit www.PacktPub.com.

Did you know that Packt offers eBook versions of every book published, with PDF and ePub files available? You can upgrade to the eBook version at www.PacktPub.com and as a print book customer, you are entitled to a discount on the eBook copy. Get in touch with us at service@packtpub.com for more details.

At www.PacktPub.com, you can also read a collection of free technical articles, sign up for a range of free newsletters and receive exclusive discounts and offers on Packt books and eBooks.

https://www.packtpub.com/mapt

Get the most in-demand software skills with Mapt. Mapt gives you full access to all Packt books and video courses, as well as industry-leading tools to help you plan your personal development and advance your career.

Why subscribe?

- Fully searchable across every book published by Packt
- Copy and paste, print, and bookmark content
- On demand and accessible via a web browser

Customer Feedback

Thanks for purchasing this Packt book. At Packt, quality is at the heart of our editorial process. To help us improve, please leave us an honest review on this book's Amazon page at `https://www.amazon.com/dp/1786467135`.

If you'd like to join our team of regular reviewers, you can e-mail us at `customerreviews@packtpub.com`. We award our regular reviewers with free eBooks and videos in exchange for their valuable feedback. Help us be relentless in improving our products!

Table of Contents

Preface

Microsoft Dynamics 365 for Operations is an ERP solution for complex single-site, multi-site, and multi-language global enterprises. This flexible and agile solution provides advanced functionality for manufacturing, retail, public sector, and service sector industries. Not only does this solution provide a strong set of built-in functionality, it also provides an industry-leading integrated development environment, allowing an organization to provide even higher levels of fit. This book should be in the tool belt of any software engineer who works with or is about to embark on a career with Dynamics 365 for Operations.

This provides software engineers and those involved in developing solutions within Dynamics 365 for Operations with a toolkit of practical recipes for common development tasks, with important background information to provide deep insight to allow the recipes to be adapted and extended for your own use. Even for experienced software engineers, this book will provide a good source of reference for efficient software development.

For those moving from Microsoft Dynamics AX 2012, we cover critical changes in how software is adapted, how to use the new extensibility features of Microsoft Dynamics 365 for Operations, and tips on how to use them in a practical way. We also cover the fundamental changes in the physical structure of the application metadata, the application development life cycle, and how we fit in with the new cloud-first development paradigm with Lifecycle services and Visual Studio Team Services. Integration will be a concern to AX developers, and we cover this in detail with working examples of code that can be adapted to your own needs.

In order to facilitate this, the book follows the development of a solution as a means to explain the design and development of tables, classes, forms, BI, menu structures, workflow, and security. We begin at the start of the development process by setting up a Visual Studio Team Services project, integrating Lifecycle services, and explaining new concepts such as Packages, Models, Projects, and what happened to layers. The book progresses with chapters focused on creating the solution in a practical order, but it is written in such a way that each recipe can be used in isolation as a pattern to follow.

The sample solution was designed and developed as the book was written and is available for download. There is a sample Operations project, OData C# integration test project, and a C# project for using web services supplied by Microsoft Dynamics 365 for Operations.

With this comprehensive collection of recipes, you will be armed with the knowledge and insight you need to develop well-designed solutions that will help your organization to get the most value from this comprehensive solution for both the current and the upcoming releases of Microsoft Dynamics 365 for Operations.

What this book covers

Chapter 1, *Starting a New Project*, covers setting up a new Visual Studio Team Service project, integrating with Lifecycle Services, and creating a Microsoft Dynamics 365 for Operations package and model.

Chapter 2, *Data Structures*, contains common recipes for creating data structure elements such as tables, enumerated data types, and extended data types. The recipes are written to patterns, guiding you through the steps you would take when creating the types of table used in Microsoft Dynamics 365 for Operations application development.

Chapter 3, *Creating the User Interface*, explains how to create the user interface elements such as menus, forms, form parts, tiles, and workspaces. This chapter includes recipes for each of the main types of user interfaces used when creating or extending Dynamics 365 for Operations with practical guidance and tips on how to do this efficiently.

Chapter 4, *Application Extensibility, Form Code-Behind, and Frameworks*, helps us step into writing the business logic behind our user interface and understand how to write code designed to be extensible, allowing other parties to extend our code with the over-layering that can version-lock customers. We also cover the SysOperation framework, using which processes are developed, and we'll see how to add a user interface to them.

Chapter 5, *Business Intelligence*, covers the creation of a business intelligence project that can be used to create powerful dashboards in Microsoft Power BI. The recipes in this chapter cover the creation of aggregate dimensions, measures, data entities, and KPIs in a real-world context. This is done using the sample vehicle management application that is created through the course of this book.

Chapter 6, *Security*, explains the security model design in Microsoft Dynamics 365 for Operations and provides recipes for the creation of the elements used in security. The recipes augment the standard documentation in order to provide real-world examples on how to create and model Dynamics 365 for Operations security.

Chapter 7, *Leveraging Extensibility*, shows how extensibility can be said to be one of the biggest changes in Dynamics 365 for Operations. This chapter pays special attention to the key aspects of how to use extend the standard application without becoming version locked in a customized solution.

Chapter 8, *Data Entity Extensibility, OData, and Office*, covers the many ways in which we integrate with the world outside of Dynamics 365 for Operations. This covers how to create and extend data entities, work with Microsoft Office, and use OData to read, write, and update data in Dynamic 365 for Operations from a C# project.

Chapter 9, *Consuming and Exposing Services*, provides recipes for creating a service from within Dynamics 365 for Operations, consuming external services, and also on consuming Dynamics 365 for Operations services in C# using SOAP and JSON. All this is covered using practical examples that should easily translate into your own specific requirements.

Chapter 10, *Extensibility through Metadata and Data Date-Effectiveness*, pushes extensibility even further by showing how we can use metadata stored in data to put more power in the hands of system administrators. We also cover how to make our tables date effective.

Chapter 11, *Unit Testing*, provides recipes to show how to create unit tests and how they are used with the application life cycle. This chapter covers an insight into test-driven development, automated unit testing on the build server, and how to create and use the task recorder to create test cases.

Chapter 12 , *Automated Build Management*, helps us move more into application life cycle management where this chapter provides recipes for setting up and using a build server.

Chapter 13, *Servicing Your Environment*, provides practical recipes that are intended to augment the standard documentation provided by Microsoft in order to provide real-world examples on how we service our Dynamics 365 for Operations environments.

Chapter 14, *Workflow*, covers the development of workflow approvals and tasks in Dynamics 365 for Operations. The recipes are given context by continuing to work with the sample application that is created through the course of this book, effectively explaining state management, which is easily misunderstood.

Chapter 15, *State Machines*, covers state machines, which is another new feature in Dynamics 365 for Operations. This chapter covers all key areas of this new feature, explaining when and how to use this feature appropriately.

What you need for this book

In order to gain access to Microsoft Dynamics 365 for Operations, you need to be either a Microsoft partner or customer. To sign up for a gain access as a partner, you can refer to *Lifecycle Services for Dynamics 365 for Operations partners* at `https://docs.microsoft.com/en-us/dynamics365/operations/dev-itpro/lifecycle-services/getting-started-lcs`.

To sign up for a subscription as a customer, refer to *Lifecycle Services for Dynamics 365 for Operations partners* at `https://docs.microsoft.com/en-us/dynamics365/operations/dev-itpro/lifecycle-services/getting-started-lcs`.

You will need to download or deploy a Dynamics 365 for Operations development VM in Azure. To run the VM locally, you will need at least 100 GB free space available and a minimum of 12 GB free memory, ideally 24 GB. It will run on as little as 8 GB of assigned memory, but the performance will suffer as a result.

The official system requirements are as follows:

- *System requirements* (`https://docs.microsoft.com/en-us/dynamics365/operations/dev-itpro/get-started/system-requirements`)
- *Development system requirements* (`https://docs.microsoft.com/en-us/dynamics365/operations/dev-itpro/dev-tools/development-system-requirements`)

Who this book is for

If you are a software developer new to Dynamics 365 for Operations programming or an experienced software engineer migrating from its predecessor, Dynamics AX, this book is an ideal tutorial to help you avoid the common pitfalls and make the most of this advanced technology. This book is also useful if you are a solution architect or technical consultant, as it provides a deeper insight into the technology behind the solution.

Sections

In this book, you will find several headings that appear frequently (Getting ready, How to do it, How it works, There's more, and See also).

To give clear instructions on how to complete a recipe, we use these sections as follows:

Getting ready

This section tells you what to expect in the recipe, and describes how to set up any software or any preliminary settings required for the recipe.

How to do it...

This section contains the steps required to follow the recipe.

How it works...

This section usually consists of a detailed explanation of what happened in the previous section.

There's more...

This section consists of additional information about the recipe in order to make the reader more knowledgeable about the recipe.

See also

This section provides helpful links to other useful information for the recipe.

Conventions

In this book, you will find a number of text styles that distinguish between different kinds of information. Here are some examples of these styles and an explanation of their meaning.

Code words in text, database table names, folder names, filenames, file extensions, pathnames, dummy URLs, user input, and Twitter handles are shown as follows: "This should have created a folder called `Base Enums`."

A block of code is set as follows:

```
public void modifiedField(FieldId _fieldId)
{
    super(_fieldId);
    switch (_fieldId)
    {
        case fieldNum(ConWHSVehicleServiceLine, ItemId):
            this.initFromInventTable(
                    InventTable::find(this.ItemId));
```

```
            break;
        }
    }
```

New terms and **important words** are shown in bold. Words that you see on the screen, for example, in menus or dialog boxes, appear in the text like this: "In the **Add New Item** dialog, select **Data Model** from the left-hand list and **Query** from the right."

Warnings or important notes appear in a box like this.

Tips and tricks appear like this.

Reader feedback

Feedback from our readers is always welcome. Let us know what you think about this book-what you liked or disliked. Reader feedback is important for us as it helps us develop titles that you will really get the most out of.

To send us general feedback, simply e-mail feedback@packtpub.com, and mention the book's title in the subject of your message.

If there is a topic that you have expertise in and you are interested in either writing or contributing to a book, see our author guide at www.packtpub.com/authors .

Customer support

Now that you are the proud owner of a Packt book, we have a number of things to help you to get the most from your purchase.

Downloading the example code

You can download the example code files for this book from your account at http://www.packtpub.com. If you purchased this book elsewhere, you can visit http://www.packtpub.com/support and register to have the files e-mailed directly to you.

You can download the code files by following these steps:

1. Log in or register to our website using your e-mail address and password.
2. Hover the mouse pointer on the **SUPPORT** tab at the top.
3. Click on **Code Downloads & Errata**.
4. Enter the name of the book in the **Search** box.
5. Select the book for which you're looking to download the code files.
6. Choose from the drop-down menu where you purchased this book from.
7. Click on **Code Download**.

You can also download the code files by clicking on the **Code Files** button on the book's webpage at the Packt Publishing website. This page can be accessed by entering the book's name in the **Search** box. Please note that you need to be logged in to your Packt account.

Once the file is downloaded, please make sure that you unzip or extract the folder using the latest version of:

- WinRAR / 7-Zip for Windows
- Zipeg / iZip / UnRarX for Mac
- 7-Zip / PeaZip for Linux

The code bundle for the book is also hosted on GitHub at `https://github.com/PacktPubl ishing/Extending-Microsoft-Dynamics-365-for-Operations-Cookbook`. We also have other code bundles from our rich catalog of books and videos available at `https://github. com/PacktPublishing/`. Check them out!

Errata

Although we have taken every care to ensure the accuracy of our content, mistakes do happen. If you find a mistake in one of our books-maybe a mistake in the text or the code-we would be grateful if you could report this to us. By doing so, you can save other readers from frustration and help us improve subsequent versions of this book. If you find any errata, please report them by visiting `http://www.packtpub.com/submit-errata`, selecting your book, clicking on the **Errata Submission Form** link, and entering the details of your errata. Once your errata are verified, your submission will be accepted and the errata will be uploaded to our website or added to any list of existing errata under the Errata section of that title.

To view the previously submitted errata, go to `https://www.packtpub.com/books/conten t/support` and enter the name of the book in the search field. The required information will appear under the **Errata** section.

Piracy

Piracy of copyrighted material on the Internet is an ongoing problem across all media. At Packt, we take the protection of our copyright and licenses very seriously. If you come across any illegal copies of our works in any form on the Internet, please provide us with the location address or website name immediately so that we can pursue a remedy.

Please contact us at `copyright@packtpub.com` with a link to the suspected pirated material.

We appreciate your help in protecting our authors and our ability to bring you valuable content.

Questions

If you have a problem with any aspect of this book, you can contact us at `questions@packtpub.com`, and we will do our best to address the problem.

1
Starting a New Project

In this chapter, we will cover the following recipes:

- Creating the Visual Studio Team Services project
- Connecting Visual Studio to your Visual Studio Team Services
- Creating a new Model and Package
- Configuring project and build options
- Creating a Label file

Introduction

Microsoft Dynamics AX 2012 underwent a name change in what would have been version 7. The official name is now **Microsoft Dynamics 365 for Operations**. It isn't just that the version number has been dropped, but it appears to have been adopted into the Microsoft Dynamics 365 product suite. The product is not a component of **Microsoft Dynamics 365**, which is just a way to group Microsoft's various business solutions. We can't, therefore, shorten the name to Dynamics 365, we will refer the product by either its full name or the abbreviation Operations.

New features will be introduced to Operations as both a continual and cumulative process. There are two main types of update, **Platform** and **Application**. Platform updates are similar to the binary updates in prior releases, but also contain AOT elements that are now locked and can no longer be changed. Platform updates can contain changes to the language, and new features have been brought in with each bi-yearly release. When running in the Cloud, Microsoft will periodically release updates to the Platform for you. This is needed, since the it uses Azure SQL Server and they may need to service the platform in order to maintain compatibility to the database server.

Application updates are changes to the other packages that make up the source code of Operations, and can be considered similar to the meta data updates in previous releases of Operations.

This book was started on the May 2016, or Update 1 release and has been updated with each release. The version on publication is Update 5, released in March 2017.

All development work is carried out in conjunction with **Visual Studio Team Services** or **VSTS**. It used to be optional, but the implementation process that is managed through **Lifecycle Services** (**LCS**) requires that we have a VSTS project linked to it to function to its fullest. This is not just for source control and work management, but it is also used when performing code upgrades.

Please see the following links for further reading on Microsoft Dynamics 365 for Operations:

- For more information on LCS, please see the link, `https://lcs.dynamics.com/Logon/Index`
- An overview of Microsoft Dynamics 365 for Operations for Developers and IT Pros is available at `https://docs.microsoft.com/en-us/dynamics365/operations/dev-itpro/`
- To obtain an evaluation copy of Microsoft Dynamics 365 for Operations, please see the link, `https://docs.microsoft.com/en-us/dynamics365/operations/dev-itpro/dev-tools/get-evaluation-copy`

All development work in Operations is either performed on a development virtual machine hosted in **Azure**, or a local virtual machine. Each developer will use their own virtual machine. Azure hosted virtual machines are deployed through LCS under your own Azure subscription, and can be used to development, learning, and demonstration. Once, as a customer, a cloud hosted subscription has been bought, you are provided 3 environments as part of that subscription under Microsoft's subscription. These are Build, Sandbox, and Production. The build sever is a OneBox server (all in one virtual machine) that is also labelled Development, but it should always be used as a build server and not for development. The sandbox server is a full environment, with multiple servers using a separate Azure SQL Server. The production environment is the environment that you (as a customer) will go live with. All code must first be deployed to the sandbox before it is applied to live, which this is enforced by LCS - no more 'quick fixes' directly into live, and no access to SQL server for the production environment.

The on premise version of Operations may allow us to bypass some of these rules, but we shouldn't try - these practices of forcing code through a full testing cycle are very important. Waiting a couple of days for a needed feature may be inconvenient, but regression is perceived very negatively by users. During the implementation we ask a lot of the users, they are already busy with their jobs and are being asked to also help with testing new software, so user buy-in to the project is a critical factor, and regression is the most efficient way of eroding the initial excitement of delivering new software.

For local development virtual machines that are often the cheapest option, we will download the virtual machine from **Microsoft Connect**. This is a website used for many programs at Microsoft, and access is provided to partners and customers.

Creating the Visual Studio Team Services project

The terms Visual Studio Team Services and **Team Foundation Server** (TFS) are often used interchangeably. In Visual Studio, the user interface states that we are connecting to a Team Foundation Server. However, we are actually connecting to VSTS, which is an online service. VSTS is required for Operations development, and that is what we will use.

The project is normally created under the end-user's VSTS site, unless the work is being written as an ISV solution (or a personal development or learning project). The reason for using the client's VSTS system is that LCS is associated with the VSTS site, and support calls created through **Cloud-powered support** are generated within the associated VSTS. Cloud powered support is an online support solution within LCS that is exposed to the Operations client, allowing users to log support issues with their internal support team.

For up to five users, VSTS is free, and the customer can create many accounts with limited access without charge. These accounts as called stakeholder accounts, and allows the user access to work items, which also allows the users the ability to log support calls from within Operations. For those with an MSDN subscription, the five user limit is not counted.

This process is normally performed as part of the LCS project creation. If this were an implementation project type, the project is created when the customer signs up for Operations. The customer would then invite their **Cloud solution provider** (Partner) to the project. If this were an internal development project, such as a new vertical solution by an ISV, a `Migrate, create solutions,` and `learn Dynamics 365 for Operations` project type would be used.

In either case, we will have an LCS project, which will usually have an Azure VM deployed that acts as a build server.

For simplicity, and to keep the focus on software development, a project of type `Migrate, create solutions,` and `learn Dynamics 365 for Operations` was created for the purpose of the example of the book.

Getting ready

Before we get started, we will need an LCS project and a VSTS site. The VSTS site can be created through the following link:

```
https://www.visualstudio.com/en-us/products/visual-studio-team-services-vs.a
spx
```

Once we have the site created, we can then create our project.

How to do it...

To create the project, follow these steps:

1. Navigate to your VSTS site, for example,
   `https://<yourdomain>.visualstudio.com/.`
2. Under **Recent projects & teams**, click on **New**.
3. Complete the form as shown as follows:

Field	Value
Project name	Unique name, careful to name the projects for easy recognition, and how they are ordered. This is more important for ISVs who may have many projects.
Description	Short description of the project
Process template	Agile
Version control	Team Foundation Version Control

4. Press **Create project**.

5. Once complete, you can then navigate to your project and work with VSTS in order to plan your project.

6. To authenticate with LCS, we will need to generate a personal access token; to set this up, click on the control panel (cog) icon, as shown in the following screenshot:

7. This takes you to the control panel, again, on the top-right click on your name and choose **Security**, as shown in the following screenshot:

8. The personal access tokens option is selected by default; on the right-hand pane, click on **Add**.

9. On **Create a personal access token form**, enter a short description, for example, the LCS project name. Set the **Expires in** field based on how long you would like it to last for.

10. Leaving the **Accounts** and **Authorized scopes** fields as default; press **Create token**.

11. Finally, copy the resultant access code into a safe place; we will need it when we link VSTS to LCS. If we don't, we will have to create a new access token as you can't see it after the web page is closed.

Next, we will need to link the project to our LCS project. If an LCS project is not currently linked to a VSTS project, we get the following message on the left hand side, as shown in the following screenshot:

To configure VSTS for the LCS project, follow these steps:

1. To authenticate with LCS, we will need to generate a personal access token, so from within VSTS.

2. Click on the **Setup Visual Studio Team Services** button in the **Action center** dialog box.

3. On the **Enter the Visual Studio Team Service** site page, enter the URL of our VSTS site into the **Visual Studio Team Services site URL** field; for example, `https://<mysite>.visualstudio.com/`.

4. Enter the personal access token generated earlier into the **Personal access token** field.

5. Press **Continue**.

6. On the **Select the Visual Studio Team Service project** page, select the project from the **Visual Studio Team Service** list.

7. You are then shown the **Workitem type mapping** list. This allows you to select how to **LCS Workitem Type / LCS Workitem Sub Type** elements to **VSTS Workitem Type** elements. Leave this as the default and press **Continue**.

8. On the final **Review and save** page, press **Save**.

9. This takes us back to the main project page and the action center will ask you to authorize the project; click on **Authorize**.

10. You will be warned about being redirected to an external site; click on **Yes**.

11. You may be asked to log on; if so, do it with the account you use for VSTS, which might be your **Microsoft account**.

12. This will open the Authorize application page from within VSTS, and you will be told that you are allowing **Microsoft Dynamics Lifecycle Services** to access the VSTS and the specific permissions it will receive. Press **Accept**.

How it works...

Operations uses VSTS for its source control, work, and build management. The only steps here that we technically must perform are step 1 through step 5, but without performing the previous steps, we lose the ability to integrate LCS. If our project was for a customer implementation, we should consider it mandatory to integrate VSTS with LCS.

See also...

For more information on VSTS and LCS, please check out the following links:

- *AX Dev ALM usage guide and resources*
  (https://blogs.msdn.microsoft.com/axdevalm/)
- *LCS for Microsoft Dynamics 365 for Operations customers*
  (https://ax.help.dynamics.com/en/wiki/how-lifecycle-services-for-microsoft-dynamics-ax-works-lcs/)
- *Developer topology deployment with continuous build and test automation*
  (https://ax.help.dynamics.com/en/wiki/developer-topology-deployment-with-continuous-build-and-test-automation/)

The next link is useful background knowledge, but a lot of this is one for you when using an implementation LCS project:

- *Set up technical support for Microsoft Dynamics 365 for Operations*
  (https://ax.help.dynamics.com/en/wiki/ax-support-experience/)

This link is for when we have a customer implementation project and demonstrate some of the synergy of leveraging VSTS and LCS with Operations.

Connecting Visual Studio to Visual Studio Team Services

Each developer has their own development VM, hosted either in Azure or locally. This is by design and is part of the application lifecycle process. Each developer would get the latest code from source control, and then check in their changes according their organization's development methodology. As part of this check in they can link the check-ins. This allows a build to then be created, and we gain a level of traceability since each work item (user story, feature, bug, and so on.) is linked to the check-ins in that build. This also allows test projects to be automatically executed when the build is generated.

Getting ready

Once the virtual machine has started, ensure that it has Internet access, and that you have used the admin user provisioning tool to associate your O365 account with the administrator account of Operations.

Before you start this, especially when working in a team, we must rename the VM to make it unique across our team; see the *There's more...* section for details on this.

How to do it...

To connect Visual Studio to VSTS, follow these steps:

1. Create a folder for your projects, and underneath a subfolder with your initials, or others that make the folder unique, within your team; in my example, I chose `C:ProjectsTFS`.
2. Start Visual Studio.
3. You will be presented with the licensing page. Use the page to log in to the account used to create the project within VSTS. Which could be either your Microsoft account, or Work (O365) account.
4. On the top toolbar, select **Team** and then **Manage connections**.
5. The Team Explorer will open, under default layout, on the right-hand side. On this pane, select **Manage Connections** | **Connect to Team Project**:

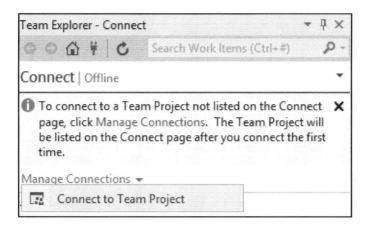

6. This will open the **Connect to Team Foundation Server** dialog, in the **Select a Team Foundation Server** drop-down list and select your VSTS site.

7. Select your project in the lower portion of the dialog, as shown in the following screenshot:

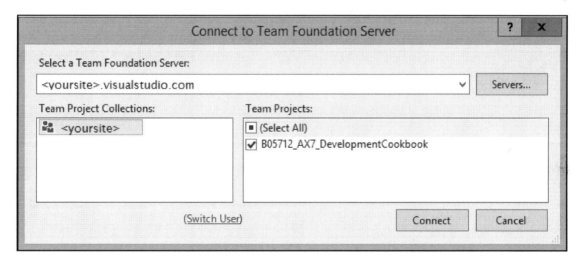

8. After pressing**Connect**, Visual Studio is connected to your project.

9. We have one final step before we continue; we have to configure our workspace so Visual Studio knows which folders are under source control and how they map to VSTS. On Team Explorer, click on **Configure workspace** under the **Project** section. This will show the **Configure Workspace** section at the top of the Team Explorer.

10. Do not press **Map & Get**.

11. Press **Advanced...**.

12. The **Edit Workspace** dialog will look similar to the following screenshot:

Name:	WIN-33FS1TD8OB2	
Working folders:		
Status	Source Control Folder ⌃	Local Folder
Active	$/B05712_AX7_DevelopmentCookbook	C:\Users\Administrator\Source\Workspaces\B0
	Click here to enter a new working folder	

For Operations development, we will need to map a projects folder and the Operations local packages folder (the application source code, or metadata as it is often referred to) to two different folders in VSTS. The `Projects` folder is the one we created earlier, which was `C:ProjectsSB` in my case. The Operations local packages folder is `C:AOSServicePackagesLocalDirectory`.

> If you look around the local packages folder, you can see how the relationship between package and Model is actually stored.

13. In my case, the project is `B05712_AX7_DevelopmentCookbook`, so I will configure the dialog as shown in the following screenshot:

Name:	WIN-33FS1TD8OB2	
Working folders:		
Status	Source Control Folder ⌃	Local Folder
Active	$/B05712_AX7_DevelopmentCookbook/Projects	C:\Projects\SB
Active	$/B05712_AX7_DevelopmentCookbook/Metadata	C:\AOSService\PackagesLocalDirectory

14. Press **OK**.
15. You will then be told that the workspace has been modified, and if you want to get the latest code. Either option has no effect if we are the first developer, but it is a good habit to always press **Yes**.

How it works...

Source control in Operations has come a long way in this release, mainly because our development tool is now Visual Studio and that the source files are now actual files in the file system. Operations no longer needs special code to integrate with a **Team Foundation Server**.

The reason we have two folders is that our projects don't actually contain the files we create when writing code. When we create a file, such as a new class, it is created within the local packages folder and referenced with in the project. This also means that we can't just zip up a project and e-mail it to a co-worker. This is done by connecting to the same VSTS project or using a project export feature.

There's more...

When working with multiple developers, one often overlooked task is to rename the virtual machine. This has gotten easier with each update, and the steps we take at the current release are as follows:

1. Use Computer management to rename the machine. Use something like project ID and your initials for this; for example, B05712SB.
2. Restart the virtual machine.
3. Use the SQL Server Reporting Services configuration utility so that it references the correct server name.

See also

- *Renaming a VM*
  (https://ax.help.dynamics.com/en/wiki/visual-studio-online-vso-machine-renaming/)
- *Configuring your VSTS mapping after a code upgrade*
  (https://ax.help.dynamics.com/en/wiki/configuring-your-vso-solution/)

 In this link, it suggests using the default visual studio folder; however, for local development VMs, this will always be Administrator. For this reason, using a folder such as C:ProjectsTFS is better in terms of ease of use.

Creating a new Model and Packages

When creating a new project, it is usually a new Package and a new Model. This keeps things simple, and there is usually no benefit in separating them. You may wish to create a test project in a different Model in the same solution, but you may not wish to deploy the test projects to live.

There are two types of projects: an extension project and an over-layer project. Over-layering means modifying the source code of Operations, and requires a code upgrade for each application hotfix. Extension projects work on delta changes to the standard object, or using delegates to affect code execution. Extension projects shouldn't need a code upgrade when application hotfixes are applied. Avoidance of over-layering cannot be overstated, in the time this book was being written Platform and Foundation have been locked, meaning that the over-layering must be removed. The ability to write good code through extension has been improved with each release, and with clever design the need to over-layer has been significantly reduced.

We will use extension projects exclusively, in order to to avoid conflicts with future upgrades. They make it possible to service the environment without having to deploy a new build of the custom solution. This is very exciting for ISV solutions, but also very important for VAR and end-user customers.

See the *There's more...* section for information on the relationship between packages, models and projects.

Getting ready

Startup Visual Studio and ensure that we are correctly connected to VSTS. As of the current release, you must start visual studio as an administrator.

How to do it...

To create the project, follow these steps:

1. Under the **Dynamics 365** menu, choose **Model Management** | **Create model...**
2. The Model name is named as we would in AX 2012, and should be named like a new type, such as `<prefix><area/module><ShortName>`.
3. Complete the first steps as follows:

Field	Value
Model name	In our case, our company is called Contoso, so our prefix will be `Con`, the area of change is an existing module (`WHS`) and it is for general extensions (extending standard objects without customization). It is therefore named `ConWHSGeneralExtensions`. You should use your own prefix and prefixes, and the name for explained further in the *There's more...* section.
Model publisher	Your organization's name.
Layer	As follows: ISV / vertical solution / add-on: `ISV` VAR / Partner solution / add-on: `VAR` Customer solution / add-on: `CUS` or `USR` The customer layers were traditionally used to segregate a customer's global solution layer from the requirements of each country implementation. The layer technology is processed very differently for the extension projects, and has lost some significance in this release.
Version	Leave as `1.0.0.0` You can update this to maintain a version of the model. This does not auto-increment and is usually left as default.
Model description	A full description of the model for other developers to read.

Model display name	Leave as default, which should be the Model name.

4. Press **Next**.
5. In the Select package page, choose **Create new package**.

> If you choose **Select existing package**, it will mean that your model will be placed under the package and is intended to over-layer the elements in in that package. You cannot over-layer elements in extension projects, but unless we absolutely must over-layer, always choose **Create new package**.

6. Press **Next**.
7. We are now offered a list of packages that we can reference, these are listed as package's name and the models that the package contains, check **ApplicationSuite** and press **Next**.

> Most of the elements in Operations are in `ApplicationSuite`; so, unless our package doesn't need any standard, type this will always be selected. The others we would select based on the elements we know we will use. We can add more package references later, but if we know which elements we will use, it saves some time..

8. The two check boxes, **Create new project** and **Make this my default model for new projects**, should both be checked.
9. Press **Finish**.
10. This opens the **New Project** dialog. The project name is usually the same as the package and Model name; then, enter the package name in the **Name** field.
11. The **Location** field must be changed; it will create the project in the default project folder, but we linked `C:Projects<initials/username>` to source control. The project must be created under this folder. So, in my case, **Location** must be `C:ProjectsSB`.
12. The **Solution name** field should be left as the project name.
13. Ensure that both **Create directory for solution** and **Add to source control** are checked.
14. Press **OK**.

How it works...

To see what we just did, we can simply look at the results. Use Windows explorer to navigate to the local packages folder, which is usually, `C:AOSServicePackagesLocalDirectory`. There, you will see the following structure, for the example package, `ConWHSGeneralExtensions`:

Folder	Description
`ConWHSGeneralExtensions`	This is a package folder
`+ ConWHSGeneralExtensions`	This is a model folder with a subfolder per type
`+ Descriptor`	This contains a descriptor file for each model
`+ XppMetadata`	This system managed folder for the Xpp metadata for all models in the package. This holds compiler metadata information about each element, not the actually source code. This includes the methods in a class, the type of method, the parameters, and so on.

We would never normally change anything here, but there are exceptions:

- If two developers create a different package at the same time, they can both get the same model ID, in which case, bad things start to happen. The solution is to check out the model's descriptor xml file in the Source Control Explorer and manually change the ID to the next number.
- You may decide that a standard package should be deleted, such as the tutorial or the sample fleet management solution. You can do this by simply deleting the package folder. Should you want to remove a standard model, you can delete the model folder, but you must also delete the relevant model descriptor file from the package's `Descriptor` folder. Obvious care needs to be taken, as you can't get it back!

The first point about can be solved by nominating a person to create packages and models.

If you look in the Source Control Explorer in Visual Studio, you will only see that the Projects folder has been added. This is correct. The `Metadata` folder will only appears when we create new elements.

There's more...

When a solution is designed, it will be done by breaking the solution into packages of functionality. This is a normal design paradigm that has now been implemented (and, to an extent, enforced) within Operations. This means that our solution design will now define the various packages, and how they depend on each other. In the case of Operations, the **package** is a deployable unit that becomes a distinct DLL.

We can make a hotfix to a package and, technically, deploy it separately to other packages in the solution. Although this is possible, we would normally create a release of packages as a **Deployable package**. A Deployable package is a collection of one or more packages that contains both the built package code of one or more packages, and the routine required to install them. This process is simplified using a build server that performs the build process for us, executes any tests, and creates Deployable packages that we can then apply to our test environment.

There is a further level within Operations, which is a **Model**. A Model is a subset of elements, such as classes, within a package and can be used to move code from one development system to another, for example. A Model can only belong to one package, and a Package can contain one or more Models. Each package becomes a DLL, that has to have references added in order to 'see' elements in order packages. Because of this we should use a limited number of packages. As a guide we tend to have one package for the main stream, and one for reporting and business intelligence. To simplify management of development tasks, we tend to have a project per specification / **Technical Design Document (TDD)**, all within the main or reporting packages, simplifying multi-developer projects. Just like working on complex C# projects, we can perform code merges, branching, and shelving within VSTS.

Layers has been a core part of prior releases from its first release, but is no longer that significant. As a partner we still use the VAR layer, and recommend the same guidelines as before to customers as before, but since we avoid over-layering this feature will not be covered in this book.

 The dependencies are defined against the Package, not the Model. When we create a project, the project is associated with a Model. It is typical, and desirable, to keep this structure simple and only have one Model (or limited to a few Models) for each package and to give both entities the same name.

The following diagram shows a typical Package, Model, and Project structure:

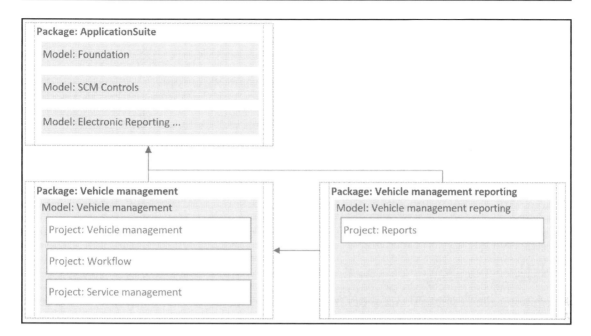

 The `ApplicationSuite` package is a standard package that we normally always reference, as it contains the majority of the types that we usually need. The arrows indicate the reference direction, showing that it is not possible for the Vehicle management package to see the elements created in the Vehicle management reporting package.

Prefixes and naming conventions

Operations does not use namespaces. Neither packages nor models equate to a namespace. A model simply implies a scope, but all types must be globally unique; even in different models and packages. A name space would allow a class to have the same name as another class in a different namespace.

Therefore, every element must be globally unique by type; this includes models, packages, and every element in the application metadata. So, we will still need prefixes. Even if we create an extension of an element, such as a form, we must change the name so that it is guaranteed to be globally unique.

For example, if we wanted to create an extension of the `WHSLoadTable` table, it will call the `WHSLoadTable.extension` object by default. As our customer might want an add-on that also adds fields to this table, we need a want to ensure that the element is unique.

The best way to do this would be to use our prefix, which is Con in our case. To make it obvious of where the element is used, we use the package name as the suffix, for example, WHSLoadTable.ConWHS. There is no official best practice available for this, but the point to remember is that all elements of a type must be globally unique - and extensions are no exception.

Configuring project and build options

Before we can get stuck into writing some code, we need to set up some parameters. Many settings described here are good for all projects, but some you may wish to change, depending on the scenario.

Getting ready

This follows the previous recipe, but can apply equally to any Operations project. Just load up Visual Studio and the project you wish to configure.

How to do it...

This will be split into two parts: generic options for all projects, Operations options; and project specific parameters.

Before we do either, we should always have the Application Explorer open, which is hidden by default. This is the **Application Object Tree** (**AOT**) of prior versions. This is opened from the **View** menu.

Dynamics 365 for Operations' options

To configure the generic options for all projects, follow these steps:

1. Select **Options** from the **Dynamics 365** menu.

> The form is actually the Visual Studio options dialog, but it takes you to the section specific to Operations.

2. The default option in the left-hand tree view is **Debugging**; the options here are usually fine. The **Load symbols only for items in this solution** option affects debugging and should be left checked for performance of the debugger. We would uncheck this if we want to trace code that calls code outside of the current package.

3. Select the **Projects** option on the left and check **Organize projects by element type**. When adding new elements to the project, it will automatically create a sub folder in the project for the element type. This makes organization much easier to maintain.

4. The other two options should be left blank. Although the **Synchronize database on build for newly created project** option can be useful, this database synchronization takes time, and it is usually preferable to do this as required. That is, before you run it.

5. The **Best practices** node lets you choose which best practice checks you wish to be executed on build. This detail is beyond the scope of this book as the checks required are case specific.

The project-specific parameters

These are usually fine as default for development, but we often want to test our code using the sample data that comes with the virtual machine.

To set up the common parameters, follow these steps:

1. Right-click on the project in **Solution Explorer** and choose **Properties**.

2. To save time whilst debugging, you select which object you wish to start with. To start with the form `SalesTable`, set the **Startup Object Type** option to `Form`, and **Startup Object** to `SalesTable`.

3. Set **Company** to `USMF` or any other company you wish to start with when debugging.

4. Leave **Partition** as `initial`. These are now only supported for certain unit test scenarios.

5. If you wish to always synchronize the database on build, you can set **Synchronize Database on Build**. My advice is to do this manually, as required after the build completes.

There's more...

You may notice that we can change the Model in the project's parameters. Our advice is, don't do it. To change the project's Model also means that the folders have to be moved in the local packages folder.

Creating a Label file

Most projects have some kind of user interface, and therefore we need to display text to the user other than the field names. The best practice method to do this is to use a label file. The label file contains a language specific dictionary of label IDs and the translation.

Standard elements tend to have the legacy label IDs of an @ symbol, followed by a three-digit label ID and a number. This format worked well for the past 15 years, but the prefix was potentially limiting, especially to aid ISVs. Labels are no longer restricted to three digits, which helps Microsoft attain one of its goals of making ISV add-ons easier to write, maintain and adopt.

The choice of how many and which packages need a label file depends on the solution design.

It isn't a terrible idea for an end user customer solution to have one package just for labels that are re-used by each package. This does mean that we run the risk of using a label out of context. You may choose to use a standard label for `Name` on personal record, only for the label to be changed by the original developer to something specific to the original context, for example, `Product name`.

We tend to create a label file for each package as this ensures that the package can correct and change labels without worrying about regression in other Models.

Getting ready

To get started, open Visual Studio, and the project in question, in my case I will continue with the `ConWHSGeneralExtensions` project.

How to do it...

To create the label file, follow these steps:

1. Right-click on the project and select **Add** | **New item...** or use the keyboard shortcut, *Ctrl + Shift + A*.
2. Choose **Labels and Resources** from the **Operations Artifacts** list.
3. From the list on the left, select **Label File**.
4. In the **Name** field, enter a short, but unique label name, in my case `ConWHS`. I want it to be as short as possible, but be completely sure it will be globally unique, regardless of any future add-on we may choose to install.
5. Press **Add**.
6. In the **Label file** wizard, leave **Label file ID** as default.

> It seems that we can specify a different name in this step, but the previous only called this wizard with a suggested file name. The **Label file ID** field contains both the ID and the file name that will be created.

7. Press **Next**.
8. In the language selection, move the languages from the left-hand list into the right-hand list using the buttons. Only leave languages selected that you will maintain. This involves creating a label in each language file.

> This also applies to language with subtle differences, such as English and Spanish. Even though the label will often be the same, we still need to manually maintain each language file. Currently this also means we have to be careful to ensure we give them the correct ID.

9. Press **Next**.
10. Check that the **Summary** page is correct, and press **Finish**.

How it works...

The creation is straightforward. The process creates a text file on the disk that contains a tab-separated list of label IDs and translations.

When a label is selected against a control, it will be given a label file ID that ensures it is unique. In our example, the label file ID was `ConWHS`. As we create a label, it will be given the IDs in the sequence `@ConWHS:ConWHS1`, `@ConWHS:ConWHS2`, and so on.

In our example, the label IDs given to the control will be `@ConWHS:ConWHS1`. This seems needlessly long. Since, we can actually specify the label ID manually, we can choose to enter a shorter ID per label, generating a label such as `@ConWHS:L001`, or enter a memorable name as an ID, where the ID would then become `@ConWHS:ItemNotExists`.

There's more...

Currently, the maintenance of labels can be time consuming, in that, we do not have a translation list per label ID as we did in Dynamics AX 2012, but a separate file per language. This is targeted for improvement, and may change by release. The concept, however, will remain the same.

When writing labels for variants of the same or similar languages, we can copy and paste the labels between files. Expand the label file to the lowest node to the file with a `.txt` extension, and right click on it to select **Open With...**. Choose **Notepad** from the list.

Each label will have two lines, one for the label, and the other for the comment, as shown in the following extract from an en-gb label file:

```
ConWHS1=Vehicle type
  ;ConWHS
ConWHS2=The type of vehicle
  ;ConWHS
VehTransComplete=Complete inspection
  ;ConWHS
VehTransCompleteHT=Complete, and finalise the vehicle inspection
  ;ConWHS
```

You can than translate to the desired language and paste it into the target label file, again by opening the txt file in **Notepad**. You must do this from within Visual Studio, otherwise the file may not be checked out from source control. Be careful, as it will not validate that there aren't duplicates or file formatting errors.

If you intend to write add-ons, you should always maintain the en-us language file. You will get compilation warnings that the label ID does not exist, if you do not. If you are to release the software to a region with a variant of a language (en-au, en-gb, en-ie, en-us, and so on), please use the correct translation, as not only will it make your add-on more professional and global, but some terms have completely different meanings. For example, stock means inventory in en-gb, but means financial share holdings in en-us.

2

Data Structures

In this chapter, we will cover the following recipes:

- Creating enumerated types
- Creating extended data types
- Creating setup tables
- Creating a parameter table
- Creating main data tables
- Creating order header tables
- Creating order line tables

Introduction

In this chapter, we will cover the tasks required to write the data dictionary elements commonly used within Operations development.

Data structures in Operations are not just tables and views, but also include the ability to define a data dictionary. This is now called the Data Model in Operations. The data model hasn't changed much in structure since AX 2012, but is much more refined with many more features to aid development and minimize the footprint when extending standard tables and types.

This chapter does not cover creating extensions of standard types, but it does cover how to create types that allow your structures to be extensible. Extensibility is covered in *Extending standard tables without customization footprint* section of `Chapter 7`, *Leveraging Extensibility* .

Most development in Operations is based on patterns, even if we are not aware of it. For example, the Vendor and Customer lists are very similar, and are called `Main` tables. Purchase orders and Sales orders are also very similar, which are `Worksheet` tables; in this case, order header and lines.

Tables in Operations have a property that defines the type of table, and each type is associated with a particular style of form for the user interface. We could therefore consider these types as patterns. If we think of them as patterns, it is far easier to apply the recipes to our own development.

The following list is of the common table types, listed with the usual form design and their typical usage:

Table group	Form design pattern	Usage
Miscellaneous		This is essentially 'undefined' and shouldn't be used, other than for temporary tables.
Parameter	Table of contents	This is used for single-record parameter forms.
Group	Simple list Simple list and Details - List Grid	This is used for the backing table for drop-down lists. The Simple list design pattern is suitable for when only a few fields are required; otherwise, the Simple list and Details patterns should be used so the fields are presented in a useful way to the user.
Main	Details Master	This is used for main tables, such as customers, suppliers, and items.
Transaction Header Transaction Line	Simple List and Details with Standard tabs	This is used for datasets, such as the invoice journal form, that contain posted transactional data with a header and lines.
Transaction	Simple List and Details w/Standard tabs	This is used for tables, such as the `Inventory transaction` form, that contain posted transactional data, but at a single level.

Worksheet header Worksheet line	Details Transaction	This is used for data entry datasets, such as the purchase order, where the dataset is made up of header and line tables. The pattern has two views, a list view of header records, and a detail view where the focus is the lines.
Worksheet	Details master	This is a single-level data entry dataset, which is rarely used in Operations.

In this chapter, we will create types and tables for the common types of table, but we will complete the patterns when we cover the user interface in Chapter 3, *Creating the User Interface*.

Creating enumerated types

Enumerated types are called **Base Enums** in Operations, which are similar to enumerated types in C#. They are commonly referred to as Enums. It is an integer referenced as a symbol, which can be used in code to control logic. It can also be used as a field on a table that provides a fixed drop-down list to the user. When used as a field, it has the ability to provide user-friendly labels for each symbol.

 Base Enums are usually only used as a drop-down list if we need to understand, in code, what each value means. They should contain a small number of options, and when used as a field, the list cannot be searched or extended by the user.

All Enums have to be defined in the data model before we use them and can't be defined within a class or method.

 Base Enums are given the ability to be extensible in this release; the mechanics of this is covered in more detail in the *There's more...* section.

Getting ready

The following tasks continue the vehicle management project, ConWHSVehicleManagement, which was created in Chapter 1, *Starting a New Project*, although, this is not a prerequisite. We just need an Operations project that was created as an extension project.

How to do it...

In order to create a new Enum, follow these steps:

1. Either right-click on the project (or any subfolder in the project) and choose **Add | New item...**.

 Always try to use keyboard shortcuts, which are displayed next to the option. In this case, try *Ctrl + Shift + A*.

2. This will open the **Add New Item** window. On the left-hand list, select **Data Types**, which is under the **Operations Artifacts** node.
3. This will filter the available options on the right-hand list. From this list, choose **Base Enum**.
4. Enter a name, prefixed appropriately. In this example, we are creating an Enum to store the type of vehicle; so, we will enter ConWHSVehicleType as **Name** and press **Add**.

 This should have created a folder called Base Enums, or added the new Enum to the folder if it already existed. This is regardless of the folder we selected when the Enum was created. If this did not happen, the **Organize projects by element type** setting in **Dynamics 365 | Options** was not checked.

5. We will now have a new tab open with our empty Enum. Before we continue, we must create labels for the **Label** and **Help** properties. Double-click on the label file so we can add a new label.

 This was created in the previous chapter; if you don't have a label file, one must be created before we continue.

6. This will add an empty line for us. On this empty line, click on **Label ID** and enter the next number, for example, 1, and press *Tab*. This will change the number so that it is prefixed with the label file ID; in our case, ConWHS1.
7. Enter Vehicle type in the **Label** column and ConWHS in the comment: this is to provide context to other developers, in case it is reused.

8. Press **New** and repeat for the next label and enter the text `The type of the vehicle` for the **Label** property.

> Repeat these for each label file language we created; if we support US and British English and Norwegian Bokmål, we will need to create a label with the same ID for `ConWHS.en-us.label.txt`, `ConWHS.en-gb.label.txt`, and `ConWHS.no-no.label.txt`.

9. Reselect the tab for the Enum. If we don't have a property sheet open, which is usually on the lower right of the screen, right-click on the Enum inside the tab and select **Properties**.
10. In the property sheet, fill in the **Label** property as `Vehicle type`.
11. Press the lookup button for this property, select our label, and press **Paste label**.
12. Repeat this process for the **Help** property, which should be `The type of vehicle`.

> These properties do not have to be populated, but it will cause a best practice deviation warning when the project is built and these properties are left empty.

13. The **Use Enum Value** property should always be `Yes`, as it allows us to set the numeric value of each symbol we created.
14. The **Is Extensible** property should usually be `False`. This alters the way the numeric value is assigned, and is described later.
15. Next, we will add the elements to the Enum. There must always be an element with 0, as this is the default on new records. Also consider that having a default is desirable. If you wish to force the user to select an option, make the first element "Undefined". Since 0 is classed as empty by the system, making the field mandatory will force the user to select an option. The options we will add should be created as follows:

Name (Symbol)	Enum Value	Label
Bike	0	Motorbike
Car	1	Car
Truck	2	Truck

The **Label** column in the preceding table shows the literal to use, the actual value will be the label Id, such as @ConWHS:Motorbike or @ConWHS:ConWHS2 if you are using numbers for label IDs.

16. To add each symbol, or element as it is referred to in the editor, right-click on the Enum and choose **New Element**, as shown in the following screenshot:

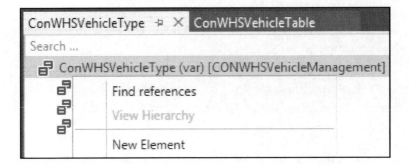

17. Complete the property sheet as per the table, and repeat for each required element.
18. You can reorder the elements using the *Alt* + up key and *Alt* + down key, but this will only affect how they are displayed in the editor. You must also change **Enum Value**.
19. Press the **Save** or **Save all** buttons in the toolbar.

How it works...

Enums are stored as integers in the database, and we can assign an integer value to a field based on an Enum.

When the values of the Enum are shown to the user, Operations will look this up using the Enum's definition from the field in the user's language. If a label is not defined for the user's language, the label ID, and not the symbol, is shown to the user. If a label was not defined, the symbol is shown.

For standard, non-extensible Enums, the following lines of code are effectively the same:

```
InventTable.ABCRevenue = 1;
InventTable.ABCRevenue = ABC::B;
```

Of course, we would never write the first option - we use enumerated types specifically to avoid having to remember what each number means. If the Enum was created as extensible, the values associated with the symbol are not assigned at design time. They are installation specific. Extensible Enums are implemented as a class, and we therefore have a slight performance hit as with are no longer dealing with numbers.

We use Enums for many purposes, ranging from table inheritance (different fields are relevant to a type of vehicle) to providing an option list to a user, and even controlling which type of class is created to handle logic specific to the vehicle type.

There's more...

Base Enums are therefore a great way to provide a link between logic and the user interface. However, there are limitations; the options are defined in code and the user cannot add to the list. The problem with making the options user-definable is that we can't use the values in code, unless we want to add the options to a parameter form, which is not very extendable!

What we can do is use the code pattern exemplified in the `Item model group` form. Here, we have a user-definable list, with an Enum that determines the Inventory model that the items will use.

Using Enums for comparison and status

It is very common to use an Enum to define the status of a record, and we will cover state machines in `Chapter 15`, *State Machines*. When defining an Enum for status, we will order the elements so that we can compare them in code.

In the case of the `SalesStatus` Enum, the elements are as follows:

Symbol	Value
None	0
Backorder	1
Delivered	2
Invoiced	3
Canceled	4

This way, we can select all sales orders, which are not yet invoiced, using the following code lines:

```
select SalesId, SalesName
    from salesTable
    where salesTable.SalesStatus < SalesStatus::Invoiced
```

Sometimes, we will need to reverse the order. In the case of the `InvenTrans` table, there are two status fields: `StatusIssue` and `StatusReceipt`; one is for issue transactions, such as sales orders or positive inventory adjustments, and the other for receipts. When the transaction is an issue, `StatusReceipt` will hold a value of 0 (None), and vice versa.

This method of using comparisons on extensible enums cannot be used. They will probably be numbered in order of the elements that are listed in the enum's definition, but we cannot assume that. It is possible for them to differ.

The first three elements of `StatusIssue` are as follows:

Symbol	Value
None	0
Sold	1
Deducted	2

The first three elements of `StatusReceipt` are as follows:

Symbol	Value
None	0
Purchased	1
Received	2

The reason the status appears to be reversed is to allow us to form a query such as the following piece of code:

```
select sum(Qty), ItemId
    from inventTrans
    where inventTrans.StatusIssue <= StatusIssue::Sold
    && inventTrans.StatusReceipt <= StatusReceipt::Purchased
```

This will sum the `Qty` field for all the `InventTrans` records that were financially issued or received.

Extensibility in Base Enums

One confusion that occurs in Operations is the terms extend and extension. **Extend** is the term used where a type, such as a class, table or EDT, extends a parent of the same type. **Extension** or **extensible** is used where we can alter an element in another package without modifying the original. When this is done and used correctly, the original author can publish revisions to the package without forcing their customers to merge and update their code, allowing end-user customers more flexibility and enabling them to efficiently stay up to date with updates.

We will cover the extensibility of each type throughout this book, with a particular focus in Chapter 7, *Leveraging Extensibility*. There is a big difference with Enums; in that, the author of the Enum decides whether or not this is allowed. For other types that are extensible, the objects are all extensible.

A common view is to just make all Enums extensible, but this has a drawback, specifically in terms of an overhead when the type is loaded. Standard Enums are compiled to CLR enumerations, in the same way that C# enumerations are, and are exceptionally quick. If we make an Enum extensible, they are compiled to a class with static methods for each element in the enumeration. The actually numeric values are installation-specific, and we can't use them for status fields where we want to compare; for example, `SalesTable.SalesStatus < SalesStatus::Invoiced` makes no sense in this case.

In terms of refreshing databases between environments this has been considered. The actual value is stored in a table within the Operations database, which is created when the database is synchronized. It will not change after that point, and this means that the values are moved with the database.

Creating extended data types

Extended Data Types are commonly referred to as **EDTs**. They extend base types, such as `Strings` and `Integers` by adding properties that affect the appearance, behavior, data (size), and table reference/relationships. This means that we can have types like `Customer account` that have a label, size, table relation information, and other properties that provide consistency and greater understanding within the data model.

Another example of an EDT is `Name`. Should we change the `StringSize` property of this field, all fields based on this EDT will be adjusted; and if we reduce the size, it will truncate the values to the new size.

All fields should be based on an EDT or an Enum, but they are not just used to enforce consistency in the Data model, but are used as types when writing code.

The EDT in this example will be a primary key field for a table that we will use later in the chapter.

Getting ready

We just need to have a Operations project open in Visual studio. To look at standard examples, ensure that **Application Explorer** is open by selecting **View | Application Explorer**.

How to do it...

We will create an EDT for the vehicle number. A vehicle table is of a similar pattern to customers and vendors, and we will extend the `AccountNum` EDT for this type.

To create the EDT, follow these steps:

1. Creating an EDT starts in the same way as all new Operations artifacts: by pressing *Ctrl* + *Shift* + *A* or right-clicking on a folder in the solution explorer and choosing **Add | New Item**.
2. Select **Data Types** in the left-hand list, and then select **EDT String**.
3. In the **Name** field, enter `ConWHSVehicleId` and press **Add**.
4. Next, we will need to complete the property sheet; the main properties are covered in the following table:

Property	Value	Description
Label	Vehicle ID	This is the label that will be presented to the user on the user interface when added as a field to a table.
Help Text	The vehicle number	This is the help text shown to the user when this field is selected or the mouse hovers over the controls based on this EDT.
Extends	AccountNum	This is completed for most fields, as we are usually following a pattern, such as ID, Name, and grouping fields. This is explained in the *There's more...* section.

Size		This will be read-only, as we have based this EDT on another EDT. This is under the Appearance section, but it does control the size of the associated fields in the database.
Reference Table		For types used as a primary key field on a table, this property should be populated. Along with the Table references, it can be used to create the foreign key relation on child tables.

 As always, remember to create labels for the **Label** and **Help Text** properties for each of your supported languages.

5. If this EDT is to be used as a primary key field, we will need to populate the **Table References** node.

 We will complete this later in the chapter, but you can see a good example by looking at the standard `AssetId` EDT. Navigate **Application Explorer** to **AOT** | **Data Types** | **Extended Data Types**, right-click on **AssetId**, and select **Open designer**.

6. Press **Save** or **Save all** in the toolbar to save the changes.

How it works...

There is a back and forth element to EDT creation when we are creating a primary key field. We can't create the field without the EDT, yet we can't complete the EDT with the field being on the table.

EDTs are types. Therefore, they must be globally unique amongst all other types, such as tables, views, data entities, enums, classes, and other EDTs. The EDT's properties aren't just defaults, but they control behavior too. Should we add an unbound control to a form based on an EDT, the EDT can use the `Table Reference` property to provide a drop-down list, and the contents will be taken from a field group on the table.

There's more...

EDTs can also extend other EDTs; although, these child EDTs can only affect appearance properties. This is useful when we want to enforce physical storage attributes of a range of types, but have a different label depending on context. If we change the size of a base EDT, all EDTs that extend it will be affected and, consequently, all of the fields that are based on them.

We often extend specific EDTs when creating an EDT for certain types of fields.

The typical EDTs we used for this are as shown in the following table:

EDT	Type	Size	Reason
SysGroup	String	10	This is used for the primary key fields for group tables. Group tables are those used for backing tables for drop-down lists. They may provide further definition to a record, or just be used for reporting. Examples include the following: • Item group • Customer group • Item model group
Num	String	20	This is used for primary keys on worksheet tables, such as the sales order table (SalesTable). These fields are usually numbered based on a number sequence, which must have a string size of 20 characters. Examples include the following: • Sales order number • Purchase order number
AccountNum	String	20	This is used for primary key fields for main tables, such as the Customer table. These tables are also, usually, based on a number sequence. Examples include the following: • Customer account • Vendor account
Name	String	60	All name fields should be based on this EDT, such as vehicle name, customer name, and so on. This EDT can be used as is, unless we wish to specify a label and help text.
Description	String	30	This is used as the description field on group tables. This EDT is usually used as is, and isn't usually extended.

AmountMST	Real		All monetary value EDTs that store the amount in local currency should be based on this EDT. MST stands for Monetary Standard.
AmountCur	Real		All monetary value EDTs that store the amount in the transaction's currency should be based on this EDT.
Qty	Real		All fields that store a quantity should be based on this EDT.

There are many more, and rather than listing them all here, a good practice is to locate a pattern used in standard Operations and follow the same pattern.

Creating setup tables

In this section, we will create a group table. A group table is used as a foreign key on main tables, such as the customer group on the customer table and the vendor group on the vendor table; the customer and vendor tables are examples of main tables. Group tables have at least two fields, an ID and a Description field, but can contain more as required.

In this case, to aid flow, we will create the group table first.

Getting ready

We just need a Operations project open in Visual Studio.

How to do it...

We will create a `Vehicle group` table. We don't have much choice on the name in this as it has to start with our prefix, and end with Group; therefore, it will be `ConWHSVehicleGroup`. To create this table, follow these steps:

1. Using the recipe for creating EDTs, create a Vehicle group EDT using the following parameters:

Property	Value
Name	ConWHSVehicleGroupId
Label	Vehicle group
Help Text	The vehicle group id

Extends	SysGroup

2. Save the EDT, but don't close the designer.
3. From within the project, choose to create a new item.
4. Choose **Data Model** from the left-hand list and select **Table** from the right.
5. Enter ConWHSVehicleGroup in the **Name** field and press **Add**.
6. This opens the table designer in a new tab. From the project, drag the ConWHSVehicleGroupId EDT on top of the **Fields** node in our table, as shown in the following screenshot:

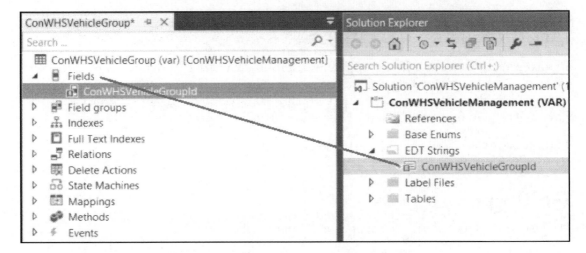

7. This creates the field with the same name as the EDT. As this is our table, we should remove the prefix and name it VehicleGroupId.
8. We can now complete our EDT, open the ConWHSVehicleGroupId EDT (or select the tab if it is still open), and enter ConWHSVehicleGroup in the **Reference Table** property.
9. Right-click on the **Table References** node and select **New | Table Reference**.
10. In the property sheet, select the **Related Field** property and then select **VehicleGroupId** from the drop-down list.

If the dropdown is blank, it is likely that the Reference Table property on the table was mistyped.

11. Save the EDT and close its designer. This should make the active tab the `ConWHSVehicleGroup` table designer; if not, reselect it.

12. From **Application Explorer**, which is opened from the **View** menu, expand **Data Types** and then expand **Extended Data Types**.

13. Locate the **Description** field, and drag it onto the **Fields** node of our table.

> This can be done by selecting the first EDT in the list and typing description until you can see it in view.

14. We will now need to add an index; even though this table will only have a few records, we will need to ensure that the ID field is unique. Right-click on the **Indexes** node and choose **New Index**.

15. With the new index highlighted, press *F2* and rename it to `GroupIdx`. Change the **Alternate Key** property to `Yes`. All unique indexes that will be the primary key must have this set to `Yes`.

> At the time of writing, this property still needs to be set to yes in order to support certain data import and export scenarios and may be removed. You will get a best practice deviation warning should the primary key not have this property set.

16. Drag the **VehicleGroupId** field on top of the new index.

> The defaults for indexes to create a unique index, so they are correct in this case. Indexes will be discussed later in this chapter.

17. Open the field's properties and set the **Mandatory** property to **Yes**, **AllowEdit** to **No**, and leave **AllowEditOnCreate** as **Yes**.

> Since we will leave **AllowEditOnCreate** as **Yes**, we can enter the ID, but not change it after the record is saved; this helps enforce referential integrity. The **Mandatory**, **Allow Edit**, and **Allow Edit On Create** field properties only affect data manipulated through a form. These restrictions aren't enforced when updating data through code.

18. We can now complete the table properties, select the table node in the table design (the table name), and complete the property sheet as follows:

Property	Value	Comment
Label	Vehicle groups	This is the plural name that appears to the user.
Title Field 1	VehicleGroupId	This appears in the title of forms.
Title Field 2	Description	
Cache lookup	Found	**None**: no caching is fetched from the DB every time. **NotInTTS**: Fetched once per transaction **Found**: Cached once found, not looked up again **EntireTable**: Entire table is loaded into memory The cache is only invalidated when records are updated or flushed.
Clustered Index	GroupIdx	This index is created as a clustered index. Clustered indexes are useful as they include the entire record in the index, avoiding a bookmark lookup. This makes them efficient, but the key should always increment, such as a sales order id, otherwise it will need to reorganize the index when records are inserted. This table is small, so it won't cause a performance issue. It will also sort the table in Vehicle Group order.
Primary Index	GroupIdx	This defines the primary index and is used when creating foreign key joins to this table.
Table Group	Group	Setup tables should always be Group tables.

Created By Created Date Time Modified By Modified Date Time	Yes	This creates and maintains the **Created by** tracking fields and is useful if we want to know who created and changed the record, and when.
Developer Documentation	The ConWHSVehicleGroup table contains definitions of vehicle groups.	This is required for best practice and should contain anything that other developers should understand about the table.
Form Ref	ConWHSVehicleGroup	This should be left blank until we have created the form, and resulting menu item. This allows the user interface to know which form to open when viewing details via a foreign key. The pattern states that this should be the same name as the table.

Remember that **Label**, **Help Text**, and **Developer Documentation** require a label in each of your supported languages.

19. We will now need to create a field group; as we will use a `Simple list` design pattern for this type of table, we will only need one. Right-click on the **Field groups** node and select **New Group**.

Field groups are used mainly in the user interface. We can add the group to the user interface and the controls will match the fields in the field group. All visible fields must be in a field group.

20. Select **New group** and rename the group to `Overview` by pressing *F2*.
21. Create a label for `Overview`.

As we use some labels in many contexts, type in Overview for the label ID. The label ID that we use for the field group's Label property will be `@ConWHS:Overview`. For common labels, this makes them easier to remember and read without having to open the label editor.

22. In the property sheet, enter `Overview` as the **Label** property and click on the **lookup** button to locate the label we created in the previous step.

 We can reuse existing labels, and this is fine if we are sure that the context is correct. If we chose a label called Overview, we will run the risk that Microsoft may rename to Financial overview, for example. Also, only reuse @SYS labels--you may find that you have used a label in a sample application that isn't shipped to the production environment.

23. Drag the two fields onto the group and order them so that `VehicleId` is first in the list.

24. In order for any automatic lookups to this table to show both ID and Description fields, add both fields to the `AutoLookup` field group.

25. We can skip to the **Methods** node, where best practice dictates we need to provide the `Find` and `Exist` methods.

 Methods in Operations have changed the naming convention, in that they should now start with a capital letter. You will find many standard methods still start with a lowercase letter, as they have not been refactored.

26. Right-click on the **Methods** node and chose **New Method**.

 This opens the code editor. Elements that contain code, such as tables and forms, can be opened in both designer and code editors.

27. The code editor has changed in this release so that all methods are shown in the same editor. We are given a method stub, as shown here:

```
/// <summary>
///
/// </summary>
private void Method1()
{
}
```

We can see that the first line in the editor is `public class ConWHSVehicleGroup extends Common`. All methods are created inside the two out braces.

28. Remove the XML documentation comment section and create the `Find` method as follows:

```
public static ConWHSVehicleGroup Find(
    ConWHSVehicleGroupId _groupId,
    boolean _forUpdate = false)
{
    ConWHSVehicleGroup vehGroup;

    vehGroup.selectForUpdate(_forUpdate);

    select firstonly * from vehGroup
        where vehGroup.VehicleGroupId == _groupId;

    return vehGroup;
}
```

29. Create a blank line above the method declaration and type three slashes (///), which causes Operations to create the XML documentation based on the method declaration. Fill in this documentation as follows:

```
/// <summary>
/// Returns a record in <c>ConWHSVehicleGroup</c>
/// based on the _groupId parameter
/// </summary>
/// <param name = "_groupId">
/// The Vehicle group ID to find
/// </param>
/// <param name = "_forUpdate">
/// True if the record should be selected for update
/// </param>
/// <returns>
/// The <c>ConWHSVehicleGroup</c> record
///</returns>
```

Should the supplied vehicle group not be found, it returns an empty buffer (where the system `RecId` field is zero). The `_forUpdate` parameter is explained in the *There's more...* section.

30. Now, to create the `Exist` method, go to the end of our `Find` method and create a new line after the method's end brace and just before the final brace for the table, and type as follows:

```
/// <summary>
/// Checks if a record exists in <c>ConWHSVehicleGroup</c>
/// </summary>
/// <param name = "_groupId">
/// The Vehicle group ID to find
/// </param>
/// <returns>
/// True if found
/// </returns>
public static boolean Exist(
                    ConWHSVehicleGroupId _groupId)
{
    ConWHSVehicleGroup vehGroup;
    if (_groupId != '')
    {
        select firstonly RecId from vehGroup
            where vehGroup.VehicleGroupId == _groupId;
    }

    return (vehGroup.RecId != 0);
}
```

 These methods are very similar, and it is better to write the Find method and copy it in order to create the Exist method.

31. We will have two tabs open, the code editor and the table designer. Since the code editor will be open, close this first, saving the changes. Then close and save the table designer.

32. Finally, we will need to synchronize the database so that the table is created within the SQL Server. Before we do this, we will need to build the model by following these steps:
    1. From the menu, select **Operations** and then **Build models....**
    2. Check **ConWHSVehicleManagement** from the list and press **Build**.

33. To synchronize the database with the table definitions, right-click on the project in the Solution Explorer and choose **Synchronize ConWHSVehicleManagement with Database**.

34. This will start the process and will be visible in the **Output** window. We will only need to do this when we need to either run unit tests or tests within our environment.

How it works...

Creating a table creates a definition that Operations will use to create the physical table in the SQL Server. The tables are also types that contain a lot of metadata at application level.

When creating the fields, we didn't specify the label, size, or type. This comes from the EDT. We can change the label, give it specific context, but the size and type cannot be changed.

The relations we created are used at application level and not within SQL. They are used to generate drop-down lists and handle orphan records. Within the client, you can navigate to the main table. It determines the table via the relation and uses the **FormRef** property on the main table to work out which form to use.

The `Find` and `Exist` methods are a best practice rule, and should always be written and used. For example, although `Select * from PurchLine where PurchLine.InventTransId == _id` may appear to be correct as `InventTransId` is a unique key, it would be wrong as there is now a field on `PurchLine` to flag whether it is marked as deleted. Using `PurchLine::findInventTransId` would only find a record if it was not marked as deleted.

There are also many methods that we can override to provide special handling. When overriding a method, it creates a method that simply calls the `super()` method. The `super()` method calls the base class' (Common) method, which for `update`, `insert`, and `delete` a special method that starts with `do`. The `do` methods cannot be overridden, but can be called directly. The do method is a method on a base class called `xRecord` that performs the database operation.

The methods for validation, such as `validateField`, `validateWrite` and `validateDelete`, are only called from events on a form data source; this is covered in the next chapter.

Creating a parameter table

A parameter table only contains one record per company. The table contains a list of fields, which can be defaults or company-specific options used in code to determine what should happen. The parameter table is usually created first, and the various fields that act as parameters are added as we create the solution.

This follows directly from the *Creating setup tables* recipe.

How to do it...

To create the parameter table follow these steps:

1. Create a new table called `ConWHSVehiclePararameters`; again, the prefix and suffix is based on practice. Usually, the name will only be `<Prefix>+<Module>+Parameters`.
2. Set the table's parameters as follows:

Property	Value
Label	Vehicle management parameters
Cache lookup	Found
Table Group	Parameter
Created By Created Date Time Modified By Modified Date Time	Yes
Developer Documentation	The ConWHSVehicleParameters table stores the parameters for the Vehicle management solution

3. Drag the `ConWHSVehicleGroupId` EDT onto the **Fields** node and rename it to `DefaultVehicleGroupId`.
4. Drag the `ParametersKey` EDT from the Application Explorer to our **Fields** node.
5. Rename it to `Key` and change the **Visible** property to `No`.

This is only used as a constraint to limit the table to only having one record. All visible fields need to be in a field group.

6. Create a field group called `Defaults` and set the **Label** property. Use the lookup to locate a suitable label.

 The label `@SYS334126` has a description indicating that we can use this for a defaults field group. You will see other examples that are clearly unsuitable by reading the **Description** field.

7. Drag the `DefaultVehicleGroupId` field to the new **Defaults** field group.

 We will use this on the parameter form so that it has the heading as `Defaults`. This is why we don't need to change the field's label to specify context.

8. Right-click on the **Relations** node and select **New | Foreign Key Relation**.
9. Complete the parameters as follows; if not specified, leave as default:

Parameter	Value	Comment
Name	`ConWHSVehicleGroup`	The name of the relation is usually the name of the table, unless we have two foreign keys to the same table.
Related Table	`ConWHSVehicleGroup`	The table to which our foreign key relates.
Cardinality	`ZeroOne`	There will be either one or no parameter record relating to the vehicle group record. A one-to-many relationship would use **ZeroMore** or **OneMore**.
Related Table Cardinality	`ZeroOne`	The value is not mandatory, so we can therefore relate to zero vehicle group records, or one.
Relationship Type	`Association`	The parameter record is associated with a vehicle record. Composition would be used in header/lines datasets, where deleting the header should delete the lines records.

On Delete	Restricted	This will prevent a vehicle group record from being deleted, if it is specified on this table. See the There's more section for more information on delete actions.
Role		This is the role of the relation, and it must be unique within this table. If **UseUniqueRoleNames** is Yes, we will only need to specify this if we have two foreign key relations to the same table.

10. Right-click on **Relation** and choose **New** | **Normal**.
11. In the **Field** property, specify the foreign key (the field in this table), DefaultVehicleGroupId.
12. In the **Related Field** property, specify the key in the parent table: VehicleGroupId.
13. Create a new index called KeyIdx and add the Key field to it. It is unique by default, so it acts as a constraint index.
14. We can now create the Find and Exist method. There is a difference for parameter tables, in that the Find method creates a record in a particular way. Create the Find method as shown in the following piece of code:

```
public static ConWHSVehicleParameters Find(
        boolean _forupdate = false)
{
    ConWHSVehicleParameters parameter;

    parameter.selectForUpdate(_forupdate);

    select firstonly parameter
        index Key
        where parameter.Key == 0;

    if (!parameter && !parameter.isTmp())
    {
        // Create the parameter
        Company::createParameter(parameter);
    }

    return parameter;
}
```

15. We will use a slightly different select statement where we can write the select statement inline, which means that we don't have to declare the type as a variable; write the `Exist` method as follows:

```
public static boolean Exist()
{
    return (select firstonly RecId
                from ConWHSVehicleParameters).RecId != 0;
}
```

16. We want to ensure that the record cannot be deleted. So, we will override the `Delete` method. Press **Return** at the start of the `Find` method to create a blank line at the top. Right-click on this blank line and choose **Insert Override Method | Delete**. Change the method so that it reads as follows:

```
public void delete()
{
    throw error("@SYS23721");
}
```

This method is called whenever we try and delete a record, either through the UI or in code. The call to `super()` that we removed, calls `doDelete()`, which in turn tells the kernel to delete the record.

17. We set the **Table Cache** property to `EntireTable`. Whenever this table is updated, we will need to flush the cache so that the system uses the updated values. Override the `update` method as follows:

```
public void update()
{
    super();
    flush ConWHSVehicleParameters;
}
```

We want to tell Operations to write the record, and then flush the cache. This is why `super()` is the first line.

There's more...

The build operation will validate and compile the package into a DLL. This must be done before we synchronize the database. This can fail, and at this stage, it is normally due to missing references. Within the Application Explorer, each element shows the package to which it belongs. We must ensure that our model references for all types that we use within our project. If we don't, we will get build errors like this:

Description
⊗ The underlying type 'Description ' or its base type for table 'ConWHSVehicleGroup' field 'Description' does not exist.
⊗ The name 'Description' does not denote a class, a table, or an extended data type.

To add the required references, we can follow these steps:

1. Locate the type with the error in Application Explorer.
2. Note the package it is in, which is in square brackets.
3. Navigate to **Dynamics 365 | Model Management | Update model parameters....**
4. Select the **ConWHSVehicleManagement** model.
5. Click on **Next**.
6. Check if the required package is checked, and then press **Next**.

 We would normally reference the `ApplicationPlatform`, `ApplicationFoundation`, and `ApplicationSuite` packages anyway, as we would often use elements from these packages.

7. Press **Finish**.
8. Navigate to **Dynamics 365 | Model Management** and select **Refresh models**.
9. Try the build operation again; you may need to repeat this as one error can mask another.

Copying and pasting methods to save time

Be careful when copying the `Find` and `Exist` methods to other tables as a template. As they are static, the methods can technically be on any class or table - that is, check the return type. This can cause some confusion when they behave strangely. As EDTs can be used interchangeably, we won't get a type error unless the base type of the EDT is different. This means that you could pass a variable of type `ConWHSVehicleGroupId` to `InventItemGroup::Find()`, and it would simply return a record (or empty buffer) of type `InventItemGroup`. So, if we copied the `Find` method from `InventItemGroup`, to our table the following scenarios are possible:

Code	Result
`ConWHSVehicleGroup    group;` `group =    ConWHSVehicleGroup::Find(<val>);`	This will cause a compilation error, as you can't assign an object of type `InventItemGroup` to type `ConWHSVehicleGroup`.
`ConWHSVehicleGroup::Find(<val>).Description;`	This will compile without error, but it will try to find `value` in the `InventItemGroup` table.

Optimistic concurrency and selectForUpdate

The record in Operations contains at least four system fields:

Field	Description
DataAreaId	This is the company ID if the Save Data Per Company is set to Yes. This filters, at application level, the data in forms and select statements to be data just in the current company.
RecId	This is a system-maintained record ID.
Partition	This is used to filter data at kernel level; it is largely deprecated, except for testing scenarios.
RecVersion	This is used to determine if the record has changed since it was read.

Optimistic concurrency (OCC) is enabled by default on new tables. We select a record "for update" by adding a `forUpdate` clause to a `select` or `while select` statement, or by using the `selectForUpdate(true)` method that exists on all tables.

When we select a record for update, a physical lock is not placed on the record and it is therefore possible for two different processes to select the same record for update.

As the record or records are read, they are read from the database into an internal record buffer. When the record is written back, it will check that the value of the RecVersion field in the physical table is the same as when the record was fetched into the internal buffer.

If RecVersion is different, an exception will be thrown. If this is thrown whilst editing data, the user is given a message that the record has changed and asked to refresh the data. If the error is thrown within code, we will get an update conflict exception that can be caught. Should the update succeed, the RecVersion field will be changed to a different number.

If we are using OCC, we can make the call to selectForUpdate() even after the record has been fetched from the database.

See also

The following documentation (*Table Relation Properties [AX 2012]*) is for AX 2012, but the details are still correct for Operations:

- *Table Relation Properties [AX 2012]* (https://msdn.microsoft.com/en-us/library/hh803130.aspx)
- *Table properties* (https://ax.help.dynamics.com/en/wiki/table-properties/)

Creating main data tables

In this section, we will create a main table, similar to the customer table. The steps are similar to the vehicle group, and we will abbreviate some of the steps we have already done. The pattern described in this recipe can be applied to any main table using your own data types.

The table in this example will be to store vehicle details. The table design will be as follows:

Field	Type	Size	EDT (: indicates extends)
VehicleId	String	20	ConWHSVehicleId : Num
VehicleGroupId	String	10	ConWHSVehicleGroupId

| RegNum | String | 10 | ConWHSVehRegNum |
| AcquiredDate | Date | | ConWHSAcquiredDate : TransDate |

Getting ready

In order to follow these steps, the elements created earlier in this chapter must be created.

How to do it...

To create the vehicle table, follow these steps:

1. Create the `ConWHSVehicleId` string EDT with the following properties:

Property	Value
Name	ConWHSVehicleId
Extends	Num
Label	Vehicle Id
Help Text	The vehicle id

2. Create the `ConWHSVehRegNum` string EDT with the following properties:

Property	Value
Name	ConWHSVehRegNum
Size	10
Label	Registration Add a comment that this is a vehicle registration number
Help Text	The vehicle registration number
Change case	UpperCase

3. Create the `ConWHSAcquiredDate` date EDT, remembering that we will need to create the EDT as an EDT date. Use the following properties:

Property	Value

Name	ConWHSAcquiredDate
Extends	TransDate
Label	Date acquired
Help Text	The date that the vehicle was acquired.

 Although we created this EDT as a date, this is mainly for the way it appears. It is created in the database as a date time, and compiles to a CLR date time type.

4. Create a new table, and name it `ConWHSVehicleTable`. The convention is that it starts with our prefix, followed by the entity name as a singular noun, and suffixed with `Table`.

5. Drag the EDTs to the table in this order:
   - ConWHSVehicleId
   - Description
   - ConWHSVehicleGroupId
   - ConWHSVehicleType
   - ConWHSVehRegNum
   - ConWHSAcquiredDate

 The reason for the order, is specifically for the ID, description, and group fields. These are usually placed as the first 3 fields, and the ID field is usually first.

6. Remove the `ConWHS` prefix from the fields as they are on our table.

7. On the `VehRegNum` field, change the **AliasFor** property to `VehicleId`.

 The **AliasFor** property allows the user to enter a registration number in the `VehicleId` field in foreign tables, causing Operations to look up a vehicle and replace the entry with `VehicleId`. This concept is common on most main tables.

8. Save the table and open the `ConWHSVehicleId` EDT. Complete the **Reference Table** property on the **Table References** node.

9. Close the designer table for the EDT and navigate back to the table designer.

10. Change the `VehicleId` fields' properties as an ID field as follows:

Property	Value
Allow Edit	No
Allow Edit On Create	Yes
Mandatory	Yes

The preceding properties only affect the way the field behaves on a form.

11. A main table's `GroupId` field usually has an impact on logic, and is usually mandatory. Even if it does not, we should still make the `VehicleGroupId` field mandatory.

Careful consideration must be taken when deciding on whether the field is mandatory or when it can be edited. In some cases, the decision on whether it can be changed is based on data in other fields or tables. This can be accomplished in the `validateField` event methods.

12. Do not make the `VehicleType` field mandatory.

Enums start at 0, and increment by one each time. Operations validates this using the integer value, which would make the first option invalid. As Enums always default to the first option, the only way to force a selection from the list would be to make the first element called `NotSet`, for example, with a blank label.

13. Create a unique index called `VehicleIdx` with the `VehicleId` field.
14. Group fields are often used for aggregation or search queries, so we should create an index called `VehicleGroupIdx` and add the `VehicleGroupId` field to it. The index must not be unique.
15. Complete the table's properties as follows:

Property	Value
Label	Vehicles
Title Field 1	VehicleId

Title Field 2	Description
Cache lookup	Found
Clustered Index	VehicleIdx
Primary Index	VehicleIdx
Table Group	Main
Created By Created Date Time Modified By Modified Date Time	Yes
Developer Documentation	ConWHSVehicleTable contains vehicle records.
Form Ref	This is blank until we have created the form

16. Create a field group `Overview`, labelled appropriately, and drag in the fields you wish to show on the main list grid on the form.

17. Create a field group, `Details`, and find an appropriate label. Drag in the fields that should show on the header of the form when viewing the details of the vehicle.

It is usual to have many more fields than we have on this table, which necessitates that several field groups are needed. When the form is created, the form designer will use these field groups to create the form. The designer will usually have several fast tabs (collapsible regions) and place one or more field groups into them.

18. Main tables are usually referenced in worksheet tables, and Operations will create a lookup for us based on the relation on the foreign table. To control the fields in the automatic lookup, drag the fields you wish to see into the **AutoLookup** field group, and ensure that `VehicleId` is first.

19. Create a foreign key relation for the `VehicleGroupId` field using the following properties:

Parameter	Value
Name	ConWHSVehicleGroup
Related Table	ConWHSVehicleGroup

Cardinality	OneMore The field is mandatory
Related Table Cardinality	ZeroOne
Relationship Type	Association
On Delete	Restricted

20. Add a normal field relation to the relation, connecting the `GroupId` fields.

21. It is common to initialize main tables from defaults, held in parameters. The `initValue` method is called when the user creates a new record. Right-click on the **Methods** node and select **Override | initValue**.

22. In the code editor, adjust the code so that it reads as follows:

```
public void initValue()
{
    ConWHSVehicleParameters parm;
    parm = ConWHSVehicleParameters::Find();

    super();

    this.VehicleGroupId = parm.DefaultVehicleGroupId;
}
```

23. Next, add the `Find` and `Exist` methods using the table's primary key field as usual.

24. Finally, we will add a field validation method to ensure that the acquisition date is not before today. Override the `validateField` method and add the following code between code the `ret = super();` line and `return ret;`:

```
switch (ret)
{
    case fieldNum(ConWHSVehicleTable, AcquiredDate):
        Timezone clientTimeZone =
            DateTimeUtil::getClientMachineTimeZone();
        TransDate today =
            DateTimeUtil::getSystemDate(clientTimeZone);
        if(this.AcquiredDate < today)
        {
            // The acquisition date must be today or later
            ret = checkFailed("@ConWHS:ConWHS29");
        }
        break;
}
```

25. Create a label for the error message returned by `checkFailed` and replace the literal with the label ID.
26. Once complete, save and close the table code editor and designer tab pages.

How it works...

We have introduced a couple of new concepts and statements in this recipe.

The `switch` statement should always be used on the `validateField` method, even if we only ever intend to handle one case. An `if` statement might seem easier, but it will make the code less maintainable. This goes for any check like this, where the cases have the possibility to increase.

The next new concept is that we can now declare variables as we need them. This helps with scope, but shouldn't be over used. The `initValue` and `validateField` methods are good examples of explaining where the code should be declared.

The AX 2012 `systemGetDate()` function is deprecated in this release. `DateTimeUtil` provides better handling for time zones. The date can be different across time zones, and can differ between the client's machine (the browser) and the server where Operations is hosted.

In the `validateField` method, we will allow the standard code to run first; the standard call will validate the following:

- The value valid for the type, such as a valid date in a date field
- If the field is a foreign key, does the value exist in the parent table?
- If the field is mandatory, check that it is filled in, or that it is not zero for numeric and Enum fields

There's more...

Every element (table, table field, class, form, and so on) has an ID. Tables and fields are commonly referenced by their ID and not by their name. The `validateField` method, for example, uses the field id as the parameter and not the field's name. As we can't know the ID, Operations provides intrinsic functions, such as `tableNum` and `fieldNum` to assist us. The peculiar nature of these functions is that they do not accept a string, they want the type name.

Other intrinsic functions, such as `tableStr`, `fieldStr`, and `classStr`, simply return the type as a string. The reason is that these functions will cause a compilation error should the type be typed incorrectly. If we don't use them, not only do we fail a best practice check, but we make any future refactoring unnecessarily difficult.

More on indexes

Table indexes are a physical structure that are used to improve read performance, ensure uniqueness of records, and for ordering of data in the table. When records are inserted, updated, or deleted, the index is also updated. We must therefore be careful when adding indexes, as they can carry a performance hit when writing data back to the table.

A typical index is an ordered collection of keys and a bookmark reference to the actual data. Finding a record matching a given key involves going to the appropriate location in the index where that key is stored. Then, you will have to follow the pointer to the location of the actual data. This, of course, requires two Operations: an index seek and a lookup to get the actual data.

When we search for a record, the SQL Server is able to determine the best index, or indexes, to use for that particular query. If we realize that we often require the same set of fields from a specific query, we can create an index that contains the keys we wish to search on, and the fields we wish to fetch. This improves performance considerably, as SQL will use that index and can then simply return the values that already exist in the index.

We can improve this further by marking the fields we simply wish to return as `IncludedColumn` (a property of the fields in a Operations index). So, in our case, we may wish to select the description from the vehicle table where the vehicle group is `Artic`, for example.

Therefore, a solution can be to add the `Description` field to our `VehGroupIdx` index and mark it as `IncludedColumn`. However, there is a better solution in this case, which is to use clustered indexes.

A clustered index is similar to this, but the clustered index will contain the entire record, avoiding a lookup in the data for any field in the table. Clustered indexes are sorted by their keys; as the index contains the entire record, it can add a significant load to the SQL Server if records are inserted, as opposed to being appended at the end of the table.

For setup tables, where the number of records is small and changes infrequently, this isn't a problem, and the read benefit far outweighs any drawback. For transactional tables, we must be careful. We should always have a clustered index, but the key must be sequential and the records must be added at the end of the table.

An example of this is the sales order table, which has a clustered index based on `SalesId`. This is a great choice as we will often use this key to locate a sales order record, and the field is also controlled by a number sequence; records should always be appended at the end. However, should we change the number sequence so that records are inserted "mid-table," we will experience a delay in inserting records and we will be adding unnecessary load to the SQL Server.

See also

The following is based on AX 2012, but the content is still relevant in Operations:

- *Intrinsic Functions [AX 2012]* (`https://msdn.microsoft.com/en-us/library/aa 626893.aspx`)

This link goes a little beyond what we have done in this chapter, but has some very useful information about types.

- *X++ variables and data types* (`https://ax.help.dynamics.com/en/wiki/xpp-vari ables-and-data-types/`)

The following link focusses on modelling aggregate data, but also includes important information about **Non-Clustered Column Store Indexes** (**NCCI**), which are in memory indexes used for analysing aggregate data.

- *BIR100: Modeling and using aggregate data* (`https://ax.help.dynamics.com/en/w iki/modeling-and-using-aggregate-data/`)

Creating order header tables

Order and line tables are used whenever we need a worksheet to enter data that is later acted upon. Once they have been processed, they should no longer be required. Reports should act upon the transactions that the order created, such as inventory transactions, sales ledger transactions, invoices, and more.

Getting ready

Although we will be using the tables created earlier, the pattern can be followed with your own solution.

How to do it...

We will first create the worksheet header table, which will be a vehicle service order table:

1. Create a new table named ConWHSVehicleServiceTable.
2. Create a primary key EDT, ConWHSVehicleServiceId; this time, extend Num. Complete the Label and Help Text properties with appropriate labels.
3. Drag the EDT from Solution Explorer to the **Fields** node of our table, and rename it to ServiceId.
4. Complete the ServiceId field as an ID field: **Mandatory** = Yes, **Allow Edit** = No, **Allow Edit On Create** = Yes.
5. Complete the relation information on the EDT.
6. Create the primary key index as ServiceIdx with ServiceId as the only field.
7. Set the **Clustered Index** and **Primary Index** properties as ServiceIdx.
8. Drag the ConWHSVehicleId EDT to our table and rename it to VehicleId.
9. Make the VehicleId field mandatory. The decision to make the field editable depends on the associated logic (referential integrity) and the business requirement.
10. Create a foreign key relation for ConWHSVehicleId to ConWHSVehicleTable.VehicleId.

 The cardinality should be OneMore as it is mandatory. On Delete should be Restricted on foreign key relations to main tables.

11. Drag the Description EDT onto our table from the Application Explorer.
12. Create a new Base Enum for the service status, as defined here:

Property	Value
Name	ConWHSVehicleServiceStatus
Label	Status (for example @SYS36398)

Help	The service order status
Is Extensible	True Remember that we can't use > or < comparisons in code with this set.

Elements	Label
None	<empty>
Confirmed	Confirmed
Complete	Complete
Cancelled	Cancelled

13. Drag `ConWHSVehicleServiceStatus` to our table as `ServiceStatus`.

14. Save and drag the new Enum to our table and rename it to `ServiceStatus`.

15. Make the `ServiceStatus` field read only. `Allow Edit` and `Allow Edit On Create` should be `No`. Status fields should be controlled through business logic.

16. Create date EDTs `ConWHSVehicleServiceDateReq` `'Requested service date'` and `ConWHSVehicleServiceDateConf` `'Confirmed service date'`. The dates should extend `TransDate`. Label appropriately and drag to the new table.

17. Rename the fields to `ServiceDateRequested` and `ServiceDateConfirmed`.

18. Complete the table properties as shown here:

Property	Value
Label	Vehicle service orders
Title Field 1	ServiceId
Title Field 2	Description
Cache lookup	Found
Clustered Index	ServiceIdx
Primary Index	ServiceIdx
Table Group	WorksheetHeader
Created By Created Date Time Modified By Modified Date Time	Yes

Developer Documentation	ConWHSVehicleServiceTable contains vehicle service order records.
Form Ref	Blank until we have created the form

19. Create the field groups as follows:

Group / fields	Label
Overview • ServiceId • VehicleId • Description • ServiceStatus	Overview
Details • ServiceId • VehicleId • Description • ServiceStatus	Details
ServiceDates • ServiceDateRequested • ServiceDateConfirmed	Service dates

20. Create the now usual `Find` and `Exist` methods using `ServiceId` as the key.

21. You can also create your own validation on the service dates.

22. Finally, we will introduce the `validateWrite` method. This is to enforce the requirement that only service orders at status confirmed or less can be changed; the method should be written as follows:

```
public boolean validateWrite()
{
    boolean ret;
    ret = super();
    ret = ret && this.CheckCanEdit();
    return ret;
}
public boolean CheckCanEdit()
{
    If (!this.CanEdit())
    {
        //Service order cannot be changed.
        return checkFailed("@ConWHS:ConWHS33");
```

```
        }
        return true;
    }
    public boolean CanEdit()
    {
        switch (this.ServiceStatus)
        {
            case ConWHSVehicleServiceStatus::None:
            case ConWHSVehicleServiceStatus::Confirmed:
                return true;
        }
        return false;
    }
```

23. Finally, we will write a method that initializes the defaults from the main table record, that is, vehicle, when it is selected. Write the following method:

```
public void InitFromVehicleTable(ConWHSVehicleTable _vehicle)
{
    this.Description = _vehicle.Description;
}
```

24. Then, override `modifiedField` as follows:

```
public void modifiedField(FieldId _fieldId)
{
    super(_fieldId);
    switch(_fieldId)
    {
        case fieldNum(ConWHSVehicleServiceTable,
                VehicleId):
            this.InitFromVehicleTable(
                ConWHSVehicleTable::Find(
                        this.VehicleId));
            break;
    }
}
```

25. Save the table and close the editor tabs.

How it works...

There are few new concepts here, and I'll start with the code structure at the end of the step list.

The most important part of this code is that we didn't write `this.ServiceStatus <= ConWHSVehicleServiceStatus::Confirmed`. This is an extensible enum, and we can't be sure of the numeric value that the symbols have.

The other part is that we have split what may seem to be a simple if statement in `validateWrite` into three methods. The reason is reusability. It is nicer to make a record read-only in the form than it is to throw an error when the user tries to save. So, we can use `CanEdit` to control whether the record is editable on the form, making all controls greyed out.

Check methods are written to simplify the validation methods where they are used, and also to make the checks reusable, ergo consistent. Check methods are expected to return a silent true if the check passes, or to display an error should the check fail. The error is sent to the user using the `checkFailed` method, which does not throw an exception.

The next is the `InitFrom` method. This is a very common technique and should always be used to initialize data from foreign tables. The odd thing is that we don't check that it exists first.

This is deliberate. Records in Operations initialize so that all the fields are empty, or zero (depending on the field's type). So, if the record is not found, the values that are initialized will be made to be empty, which is desirable. Also, `modifiedField` occurs after the field is validated. So, the method won't be triggered should the user enter and invalid vehicle ID. If the vehicle is not mandatory, we may find the vehicle ID is empty; however, again, this is fine.

There's more...

The **On Delete** property for table relations is similar to the functionality controlled by the **Delete Actions** node on the table. The difference is that the Delete Action is placed on the parent table. This is a problem if the parent table is a standard table, and we are trying to avoid over-layering. Using the **On Delete** property is therefore controlled in a much better location, even though the result is the same.

We have the following options for both **Delete Actions** and the **On Delete** property:

- None
- Restricted
- Cascade
- Cascade + Restricted

None has no effect, and effectively disables the delete action; this is useful if you want to specifically state "Do nothing" so someone else doesn't try to correct what seems to be an omission.

Restricted will prevent the record from being deleted, if there are records in the related table that match the selected relation. This occurs within the validateDelete table event, which is called by the validateDelete form data source event.

Cascade will delete the record in the related table based on the relation; it is no use having a sales order line without a sales order. This is an extension to the delete table event.

Cascade + Restricted is a little special. In a two-table scenario, it is the same as Restricted; it will stop the record from being deleted if a related record exists. However, if the record is being deleted as part of a cascade from a table related to it, the records will be deleted.

Creating order line tables

This recipe continues from the previous order header table recipe. The example in this recipe is that we will have service order lines that reflect the work required on the vehicle. The concepts in this recipe can be applied to any order line table; to follow exactly, the previous recipes should be completed first.

How to do it...

To create the order line table, follow these steps:

1. Create a new table named `ConWHSVehicleServiceLine`.
2. Drag the following EDTs onto the table:
    - ConWHSVehicleServiceId
    - LineNum
    - `ItemId` (you may receive an error if you haven't referenced `Application Suite`)
    - ItemName
    - ConWHSVehicleServiceStatus

3. Remove the `ConWHSVehicle` prefixes.
4. The `ServiceId` and `LineNum` fields are usually controlled from code, so make them read-only and mandatory (this ensures that the code that sets them has run before the user saves the line).

 The `LineNum` field is usually used to order the lines and can be made not visible if this isn't to be displayed in the user interface. All visible (non-system) fields should either be in a field group or made not visible.

5. Make `ItemId` mandatory and only allow it to be edited on creation.
6. Create a unique index called `ServiceLineIdx` and add the `ServiceId` and `LineNum` fields. We will use this as a clustered index as it will naturally sort the lines on the form.
7. Add a relation to `ConWHSVehicleServiceTable`, but service lines are contained within a service order record, so complete it as follows:

Parameter	Value
Name	ConWHSVehicleServiceTable
Related Table	ConWHSVehicleServiceTable
Cardinality	ZeroMore
Related Table Cardinality	ZeroOne
Relationship Type	Composition
On Delete	Cascade

8. Add a relation to `InventTable` on `ItemId` as follows:

Parameter	Value
Name	InventTable
Related Table	InventTable
Cardinality	OneMore
Related Table Cardinality	ExactlyOne
Relationship Type	Association
On Delete	Restrict

9. Create an `Overview` group to control what appears on the lines and add all fields. In our case, this is sufficient. We would usually have many more fields on a line, and we would organize the fields into logical groups that are used in the form design.

10. Update the table's properties as follows:

Property	Value
Label	Vehicle service order lines
Title Field 1	ItemId
Title Field 2	ItemName
Cache lookup	Found
Clustered Index	ServiceLineIdx
Primary Index	SurrogateKey (default)

Table Group	WorksheetLine
Created By Created Date Time Modified By Modified Date Time	Yes
Developer Documentation	ConWHSVehicleServiceLine contains vehicle service order line records.

11. The `Find` and `Exist` methods will need two keys in this case, `ServiceId` and `LineNum`. The `select` statement clause should be written as follows:

```
select firstonly * from serviceLine
    where serviceLine.ServiceId == _id
        && serviceLine.LineNum == _lineNum;
```

12. Finally, we will need to initialize the `ItemName` field from the item table; first, create the `initFromInventTable` method. We will follow the same pattern as we did earlier and write the following lines of code:

```
public void initFromInventTable(InventTable _inventTable)
{
    this.ItemName = _inventTable.itemName();
}
```

13. Override the `modifiedField` method and call the preceding method as shown here:

```
public void modifiedField(FieldId _fieldId)
{
    super(_fieldId);
    switch (_fieldId)
    {
        case fieldNum(ConWHSVehicleServiceLine, ItemId):
            this.initFromInventTable(
                        InventTable::find(this.ItemId));
            break;
    }
}
```

14. Once complete, save and close the editors.

How it works...

The first new concept is the use of the clustered index to control the order that the records are displayed in grid controls. This is simply using the fact that SQL will return records in the order of the clustered index. Composite keys are fine for this purpose, but we just wouldn't usually use them as a primary key.

We also touched on Surrogate keys, which we have so far avoided. The explanation requires a little bit history to understand. These were introduced in AX 2012 as a performance aid and allowed features like the ledger account lookup when entering general ledger journals. The problem is that they are hard wired to be `RecId`. So, when we added foreign key relations, the field created contained an unhelpful `RecId`. To solve this, an alternate key was added, which is a property on the index definition. This allows a more meaningful relation to be used for a foreign key. The primary key could only be unique indexes that had the **Alternate Key** property set.

The other type of key introduced was the Replacement key. The Replacement key is a way to show a meaningful key, other than the numeric `RecId` based `SurrogateKey`.

What `SurrogateKey` still allows us to do is to use `RecId` as the foreign key, but shows meaningful information from a `Field Group` on the parent table. An example is that we could add a foreign key relation to `ConWHSServiceOrderLine`, which should use `SurrogateKey`. When we add the foreign key, containing the meaningless number, we add a `ReferenceGroup` control that can display fields from a field group on the `ConWHSServiceOrderLine` table; the user is oblivious to the magical replacement that is going on behind the scenes.

The final point brought out in this recipe is in the `initFromInventTable` method. The pattern is straightforward, but the call to `inventTable.itemName()` is a method, hence the parentheses. The declaration for the method is `publicItemNameDisplay itemName([Common])`. As all tables derive from `Common`, we can pass in any table, which is as true as it is pointless. If we look at the method, it can actually only handle `InventDim`.

Reading through the methods is always a good investment, taking time to understand the reason why the code was written that particular way.

See also

For the history of the Surrogate key, see
https://msdn.microsoft.com/en-us/library/hh812105.aspx.

3
Creating the User Interface

In this chapter, we will cover the following recipes:

- Creating the menu structure
- Creating a parameter form
- Creating menu items
- Creating setup forms
- Creating details master (main table) forms
- Creating a details transaction (order entry) form
- Creating form parts
- Create tiles with counters for the workspace
- Creating a workspace

Introduction

In this chapter, we will many of the tasks when creating a user interface. This continues on from Chapter 2, *Data Structures*. As discussed in Chapter 2, *Data Structures*, we usually create tables and forms as part of the same process; so, the recipes in this chapter will involve completing a few properties in the data model.

When creating forms, we must provide consistency to the users, and to aid with this, we will use form design patterns. The form design pattern is determined by the table group, as stated in Chapter 2, *Data Structures*. There are special cases when we can have variations but, for the main part, we should stick to the patterns suggested in this chapter.

Creating the menu structure

The menu structure is carried over from the user interface concepts in AX 2012. In Operations, the menus have the same structure, but are opened from the 'burger' menu button just below the Office 365 logo on the top left of the page, as shown in the following screenshot:

Each menu appears under the **Modules** option, as shown in the following screenshot:

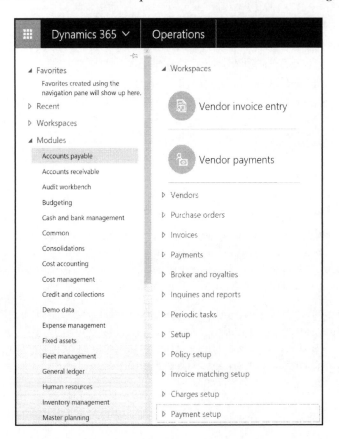

All menu items for forms, reports, and processes must be placed in the menu structure, even if we later create a workspace.

The menu structure may seem to have been relaxed slightly from thee rigid structure recommended in Dynamics AX 2012. In Dynamics AX 2012, we always have the following main headings in a menu: Common, Inquiries, Reports, Periodic, and Setup. If we look at the `AccountsPayable` menu in the **Application Explorer**, we can see that the old structure has been flattened, as shown in the following screenshot:

The actual structure is now organized as follows:

- **Workspaces**: `VendInvoiceWorkspace`, `VendPaymentWorkspaceTile`.
- **Details Master (Main) tables**: `Vendors`
- **Details Transaction (Worksheets)**: `PurchaseOrders`, `VendorInvoices`
- **Journals**: `Payments`
- **Inquiries and Reports**: `VendPackingSlipJournal`, `VendTransList`, `VendAccountStatementInt`
- **Periodic tasks**: `PeriodicTasks`
- **Set up and configuration**: `Setup`, `PolicySetup`, and so on

The menu still needs a common structure in order to make it easier for users to find the options more easily, but we aren't constrained to a rigid structure. You may argue that the menu does not have a workspace node, this is because this was added through a menu extension, as shown in the following screenshot:

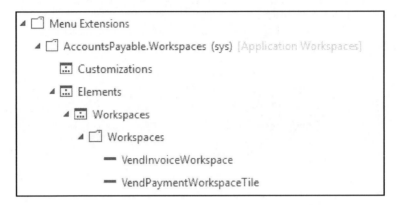

Getting ready

We will just need our project open in Visual Studio.

How to do it...

To create the menu structure, follow these steps:

1. Add a new item to the project (select a folder node and press Ctrl + Shift + A).
2. Select **User Interface** from the left-hand list and then **Menu** from the right.
3. Type `ConWHSVehicleManagement` in the **Name** field and press **OK**.
4. In the designer, create a label for `Vehicle management` and enter this as the menu's **Label** property.
5. Right-click on **new menu** in the designer and choose **New** | **Submenu**.
6. Complete as follows for the following submenus:

Name	Label
Workspaces	`@SYS:Platform_Menu_ColHeading_Workspaces`
Vehicles	`Vehicles` (new label)

ServiceOrders	`Service orders` (new label)
PeriodicTasks	`@SYS76406`
InquiriesAndReports	`@SYS3850`
Setup	`@SYS333869`

7. We can add more submenus to help organize the structure, should this be required.
8. Save and close the menu designer.
9. We will now need to extend the main menu so that we can navigate to our menu.
10. In the **Application Explorer**, navigate to **AOT** | **User Interface** | **Menus**.
11. Right-click on **MainMenu** and choose **Create extension**.

 This creates an extension to the **MainMenu** menu, but does not over-layer it, allowing our change to sit nicely alongside the other extension of the same element without having to do a code merge.

12. Rename the new item in our project from `MainMenu.Extension` to `MainMenu.ConWHSVehicleManagement`.

 Leaving the name, as it is given automatically, is a common omission and is a mistake; all menu extensions must have a unique name. Many partners will insist we prefix extension, such as `ConWHSMainMenu.Extension`. The point of the name is to make it easy to find in Application Explorer and that it is unique.

13. Open `MainMenu.ConWHSVehicleManagement`.
14. Right-click on the root node and choose **New** | **Menu reference**.
15. Set the **Name** and **Menu Name** properties to `ConWHSVehicleManagement`.
16. Save and close the designer.

How it works...

This is a structure to which we will add the various menu items. This structure is present as the user opens the menu from the left-hand menu button from within the client-user interface.

This becomes more apparent as we complete the user interface.

Creating a parameter form

Parameter forms show settings grouped into field groups and tabs using a table of contents style form. They are also used to show the number sequences set up for that module. Number sequences are covered in Chapter 4, *Application Extensibility, Form Code-Behind, and Frameworks*. We are following our vehicle management sample solution, but this pattern can be applied to any parameter table.

How to do it...

To create the parameter form, follow these steps:

1. Drag the ConWHSVehicleParameters table from the project onto the **Data Sources** node in the top-left pane of form designer.
2. Name the form as per the table's name; in this case, ConWHSVehicleParameters.
3. Select **User Interface** from the left-hand pane and **Form** from the right-hand pane.
4. Choose to add a new item to the project.
5. Data sources provide additional options of how this table should behave on this form. We don't want the user to be able to delete and create records, so change the following properties to No:
   - Allow Create
   - Allow Delete
   - Insert At End
   - Insert If Empty

6. The form designer is broken into three areas: The **Form** pane, **Design** pane, and **Preview/Pattern** conformance pane, as shown in the following screenshot:

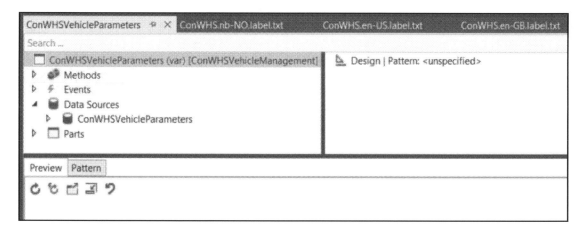

7. Let's apply some basic properties for the form, which are held against the **Design** node, as shown here:

Property	Value	Comment
Caption	Vehicle management parameters	This is shown in the title of the form and is usually the table's name.
Data Source	ConWHSVehicleParameters	Child nodes in the form will use this as the default Data Source property.
Title Data Source	ConWHSVehicleParameters	This form will use the title field properties from the table and display them on the form.

8. The **Design** node states that a pattern is not specified, which we must do. To apply the main form pattern, right-click on the **Design** node and choose **Apply Pattern | Table of Contents**.

9. The lower pane changes to the **Pattern** tab and shows the pattern's required structure, as shown in the following screenshot:

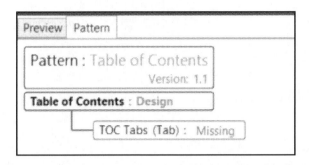

We will refer to each node in the pattern structure as a pattern element and, to aid ease of design, name the controls based on the pattern element's name.

10. This enables us to add a `Tab` control, so right-click on the **Design** node and choose **New | Tab**.

11. The error is removed from the **Pattern** pane, but shows that we have no tab pages within the **TOC Tabs (Tab)** pattern element.

12. First, rename the new control to `ParameterTab`, and then add a new Tab Page by right-clicking on it in the **Design** pane and selecting **New Tab Page**.

13. The first tab is usually a general settings tab, so name this new control `GeneralTabPage`.

14. Find a suitable label for `General` and enter that into the **Label** property.

15. As we alter the design, the designer will continually check that we are conforming to the pattern. It has found the following issues with the tab page control:

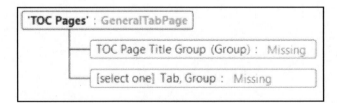

16. We must add two `Group` controls, one for title fields that provide help to the user, and the other for the fields we wish to show in this page.

17. Right-click on the **GeneralTabPage** control and select **New | Group**.

 Once this is done, reselect the **GeneralTabPage** control and note that the pattern conformance pane has changed from a red error to a yellow warning. This means that that the controls below this level have pattern conformance errors.

18. Rename the new group control to `GeneralTitleGroup`.

 All controls must be unique, and naming in a way that helps us navigate to the control easily will help us greatly. should we get a build error later on.

19. The pattern conformance pane shows we must have a `StaticText` control for the main title, and 0 or 1 `StaticText` controls for a secondary title. Right-click on **GeneralTitleGroup** and choose **New | Static Text**.

20. Rename the new `StaticText` control to `GeneralTitleText`.

21. Create a new label for the text `General parameters` and enter the ID into the **Text** property.

22. Reselect the **GeneralTitleGroup** control and check if the pattern errors are gone.

23. Reselect **GeneralTabPage**, as we now have one pattern error for a missing group. Add a new **Group** control.

24. The new group control knows that it must also have a pattern applied, indicated by the **Pattern: <unspecified>** text after the control's name. Right-click on the control and choose **Apply Pattern | Fields and Field Groups**.

25. Rename the control to `GeneralFields`.

26. On the form pane, expand **Data Sources**, **ConWHSVehicleParameters**, and then **Field Groups**.

27. Drag the field group, **Defaults**, onto the **GeneralFields** control in the design pane, as shown in the following screenshot:

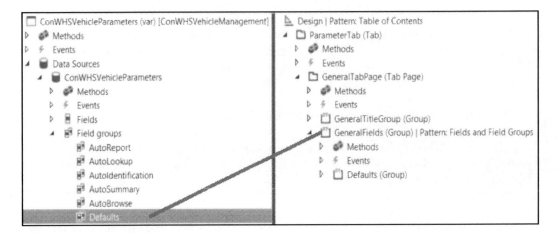

 We can manually create groups and then add the appropriate fields. However, using a field group, any new fields added to the group will get automatically added to the form, and the **Label** property will be set based on the field group's label.

28. Check each node for pattern conformance errors.
29. Finally, we will have a special task for parameter forms; to ensure that at least one record exists, click on the **Methods** node and choose **Override | init**.
30. Create a blank line before the call to `super()` and enter the following line of code:

```
ConWHSVehicleParameters::Find();
```

 We don't care about the return value in this case. We are using the fact that the `Find` method for `Parameter` tables will automatically create a record if the table is empty.

31. Save and close the code editor and form designers.

How it works...

When we specify the form design's main pattern, we are then guided as to the controls we should add and where. This helps us ensure that the forms we design follow a best practice user-interface design, which in turn makes our forms easier to use, quicker to train, and less prone to user error.

We can still opt out of the pattern using the `Custom` pattern; this allows us to add any control in any order. This should be avoided, and the form design should be redesigned so that it uses standard patterns.

There's more...

The form is based on the `FormRun` class. We can see this by opening (double-click) `classDeclaration` for the `CustGroup` form:

```
public class ConWHSVehicleParameters extends FormRun
```

 This differs from AX 2012, where the declaration was `public class FormRun extends ObjectRun`, which was probably a little more honest, as the form is not a type; this is why it can have the same name as a table.

This is actually a definition file that `FormRun` instantiates with in order to build and execute the form.

Once the system has built the form design using `SysSetupFormRun`, it will perform the initialization tasks and run the form. The key methods in this are `Init` and `Run`. These can be overridden on the form in order to perform additional initialization tasks.

One of `FormRunInit` method's key tasks is to construct the form's data sources; these aren't table references but `FormDataSource` objects constructed from the tables listed under the `Data Sources` node.

In the case of the `ConWHSVehicleParameters` form, the system creates the following objects from the `ConWHSVehicleParameters` data source for us:

- `ConWHSVehicleParameters` as type `ConWHSVehicleParameters`(table)
- `ConWHSVehicleParameters_DS` as type `FormDataSource`
- `ConWHSVehicleParameters_Q` as type `Query`
- `ConWHSVehicleParameters_QR` as type `QueryRun`

We aren't normally concerned with the `Query` and `QueryRun` objects as we can access them through the `FormDataSource` object anyway.

The data sources are declared as global variables to the form and provide a layer of functionality between the form and the table. This allows us to control the interaction between the bound form controls and the table.

Let's override the `init` method on the data source, and then override the `modifiedField` event on a field; the code editor will present the change as follows:

```
[Form]
public class ConWHSVehicleParameters extends FormRun
{
    public void init()
    {
        ConWHSVehicleParameters::Find();
        super();
    }

    [DataSource]
    class ConWHSVehicleParameters
    {
        public void init()
        {
            super();
        }
        [DataField]
        class DefaultVehicleGroupId
        {
            public void modified()
            {
                super();
            }
        }
    }
}
```

It adds the data source as a class within the form's class declaration, and then adds the field as a class within the data source class. This is the only place in Operations where this occurs. If the data source class were a class, it would have to extend `FormDataSource`. The `Form`, `DataSource`, and `DataField` attributes are a clue as to what's going on here. As all executable code compiles to CLR types, the compiler uses these attributes in order to create the actual types. The structure is written as such for our convenience as a presentation of code.

Let's take the modifiedField method. This is an event that occurs after the validateField event returns true. The call to super() calls the table's modifiedField method. We may wonder why the call to super() has no parameter. This happens behind the scenes, and it is useful that this is handled for us.

This pattern is followed for the following methods:

DataSource method	Calls table method
validateWrite	validateWrite
write	write (in turn, insert or update)
initValue	initValue
validateDelete	validateDelete
delete	delete
DataField.validateField	validateField(FieldId)
DataField.modifiedField	modifedField(FieldId)

The table's initValue, validateField, modifiedField, validateWrite, and validateDelete methods are only called from form events; the write method does not call validateWrite.

From this, we have a choice as to where we place our code, and this decision is very important. The rule to follow here is to make changes as high as possible: table, data source, and form control.

 It is critically important that code on a form must only be written to control the user interface and should not contain validation or business logic.

We can go further with this and write form interaction classes that allow user interface control logic to be shared across forms; for instance, controlling which buttons are available to a list page and the associated detail form.

See also

The general form guidelines
(https://ax.help.dynamics.com/en/wiki/general-form-guidelines/).

Creating menu items

Menu items are a reference to an object that we wish to add to a menu. We have three types of menu items: Display, Output, and Action. Display is used to add forms, Output is used for reports, and Action is used for classes.

Menu items are also added as privileges to the security system. Users that aren't an administrator will not be able to see the menu items unless they are assigned a role, duty, or privilege that gives them access to the menu item's required access level.

Getting ready

We will just need a form, report, or class that we need to create the menu item for.

How to do it...

1. Choose to add a new item to the project.
2. Select **User Interface** from the left-hand pane and **Form** from the right-hand pane.
3. Name the menu item to be the same as the form; in this case, ConWHSVehicleParameters.
4. Enter the label @SYS7764 as the **Label** property; this is the lowest @SYS label that has no specific context described.
5. Create a help text label for Maintains the vehicle management settings and number sequences. Assign the ID to the **HelpText** property.
6. Enter ConWHSVehicleParameters to the **Object** property.
7. The **ObjectType** property is Form by default, so this is correct.
8. Save the menu item and open the ConWHSVehicleParameters table, and then enter ConWHSVehicleParameters to the **Form Ref** property.
9. Finally, open the ConWHSVehicleManagement menu and drag the ConWHSVehicleParameters menu item on top of the **Setup** node.

10. Save and close the open tabs.

How it works...

Although this recipe is listed in isolation, it should always be done as part of the process. For example, the process of creating a `Parameter` table involves four main steps:

1. Create the table
2. Create the form
3. Create the menu item
4. Add the menu item to the menu

Nearly all of the tables that we create in Operations will have a form that is used to maintain it. So, the last part of the table's design is to tell the table design which form is used for that purpose. This is how the `View details` option works in the client. The foreign key is used to determine the table, and the table's **Form Ref** property is used to determine the form to be used. The foreign key details are then used to filter the form. All this happens automatically based on the metadata.

Menu items for forms and reports trigger the system to build and execute the form or report definition. The form is rendered in the browser using some very clever JavaScript that interfaces with server, and reports are essentially rendered using SSRS. Classes must either have a static entry point method in order to be called. This is covered in `Chapter 4`, *Application Extensibility, Form Code-Behind, and Frameworks*.

Creating setup forms

This follows a similar pattern to the Parameter form. Using the table in `Chapter 2`, *Data Structures*, we know we should use `Simple list` or `Simple list and Details – List Grid` patterns. Our table has two fields, so we will use the `Simple list` form design pattern. This follows the pattern of creating a table of type `Group`.

How to do it...

1. Choose to add a new item to the project.
2. Select **User Interface** from the left-hand pane and **Form** from the right-hand pane.

3. Name the form as per the table's name; in this case, ConWHSVehicleGroup.
4. Drag the ConWHSVehicleGroup table from the project onto the **Data Sources** node of the form designer.
5. Use the same label as the table for the **Caption** property of the **Design** node.
6. Set the **Title Data Source** and **Data Sources** properties to the table name, ConWHSVehicleGroup.
7. Apply the **Simple List** pattern to **Design** (right-click and choose **Apply Pattern** | **Simple List**).

> We will use the pattern conformation errors as our to-do list. If we don't conform to the pattern, the project will not build. However, just conforming to the pattern may not be enough; the build will also spot some errors in properties, which are stated as mandatory by the pattern.

8. Add an **ActionPane** control; rename to FormActionPaneControl as there will only be one on this form.

> We don't need to specify the **Data Source** property, as this will default from the **Design** node.

9. Reselect the **Design** node. The pattern highlights that we need a Custom Filter Group, which is a **Group** control. So, add a new control of type Group.
10. Rename the control to CustomFilterGroup, for ease of reference.

> Apart from navigating form build errors, this becomes more important for complicated patterns, as we will be able to see if the pattern is using the correct control. The name is not how the pattern knows which controls map to the pattern's structure.

11. We can see that the new group control needs a pattern; assign **Custom and Quick Filters**.
12. We will now have more to do for this control. The pattern highlights that we must have one QuickFilterControl. Right-click on the **CustomFilterGroup** control and choose **New** | **QuickFilterControl**.

We will need to link this to a Grid control, so we will complete this control a little later.

13. Right-click on the **Design** node and select **New** | **Grid**.
14. We can rename the control to `FormGridControl` as there will only be one grid control with this pattern.
15. The **Data Source** property does not inherit from the parent node, and we must specify this as `ConWHSVehicleGroup`.
16. We created an `Overview` field group for this table, so set the **Data Group** property to `Overview`.

Rename the container controls before adding fields to them, or setting the **Data Group** property, as the fields will be prefixed with the container control's name.

17. Go back to the `QuickFilter` control and set **Target Control** to the grid control's name and **Default Column** to the desired default control of the target control.
18. Double check that pattern pane for errors, and then save the form.
19. Next, create a menu item using the same name as the form and the same label as we used in the **Caption** property.
20. Complete the table's **Form Ref** property with the menu item name.
21. Finally, add the menu item to the setup menu so it lies under the **Parameters** menu item.

How it works...

The steps were similar to the parameter form, although there were just a few more to complete. We can see that the pattern is actually a to-do list, although pattern errors will prevent the project from being built.

There's more...

If you want to actually test the form, you can do so by following these steps:

1. Build the package using **Dynamics 365** | **Build Models**; select the package from the list.

2. If we added tables or fields since the last database synchronization, synchronize the databases by right-clicking on the project and choosing **Synchronize <your project name> with database**.
3. Open the project's properties.
4. Set the **Startup Object Type** option to **MenuItemDisplay**.
5. Set the **Startup Object** option to the menu item to open, for example, ConWHSVehicleGroup.
6. Specify **Initial Company**; USMF is a useful company for when we are using the developer VMs that use Microsoft's demo data.
7. Close the property form and press *F5*.

This is also how we debug code, and should a break point be encountered, Visual Studio will move to the fore and allow us to debug the code.

Creating details master (main table) forms

For those that are used to Dynamics AX 2012, this style of form replaces the List page and separates the Details form used for main tables, such as Products and Customers. List pages are effectively deprecated for this purpose. It may seem a little confusing at first, as we are developing two views of a form at the same time. However, once we have done this a few times, it becomes more automatic.

The pattern pane will be our guide in this recipe, helping us simplify the process, and reminding us when we have forgotten a key step. We are continuing the form design for the main table, ConWHSVehicleTable. However, this recipe can be used as a pattern for any main table.

How to do it...

To create the details master form, please follow these steps:

1. Choose to add a new item to the project.
2. Select **User Interface** from the left-hand pane and **Form** from the right-hand pane.
3. Name the form as per the table's name; in this case, ConWHSVehicleTable.
4. Drag the ConWHSVehicleTable table from the project onto the **Data Sources** node of the form designer.

5. Select the `ConWHSVehicleServiceTable` data source and set the **Insert If Empty** and **Insert At End** properties to `No`.

 Insert If Empty will create a new record if there are no records, which is undesirable for main table and order header tables. The **Insert At End** property can also be undesirable; if the user presses the down arrow key on the last record, a new empty record will be created.

6. Use the same label as the table for the **Caption** property of the **Design** node.
7. Set the **Title Data Source** and **Data Sources** properties to the table name, `ConWHSVehicleTable`.
8. Apply the **Details Master** pattern to the **Design**.
9. As required by the pattern, add an `Action Pane` control named `FormActionPane`.
10. Add a `Group` control called `NavigationListGroup`. This section is used in the details view so that the user can change records without going back to the list view.

 The tasks for `NavigationListGroup` are similar to the `Simple List` pattern, so the steps will be summarized.

11. Under the `NavigationListGroup` control, create a `Quick Filter` control and name it `NavgationQuickFilter`.
12. Then, create a `Grid` control named `NavigationGrid`.

 There will be another grid and quick filter added later, and control names must be unique.

13. Set the **Data Source** property of the grid control to `ConWHSVehicleTable` and add the `VehicleId` and `Description` fields by dragging them from the **Fields** node of the data source.

 We can add whichever fields we like here, but keep the number of fields to just a few.

Creating the User Interface

14. Complete the quick filter control with **Target Control** as the grid control and **Default Column** as desired.

15. Checking the nodes on and under the **Design** node, we will now need to create a **Tab** control for the **Panel Tab**. Create a new `Tab` control as follows:

Property	Value
Name	PanelTab
Arrange Method	Vertical

You can see here that we have a tab page for the details panel and the list panel. The system controls the pages that are visible for us.

16. Add a tab page named `DetailsPanelTabPage` first, and then `ListPanelTabPage`.

The pattern seems to make a mistake as we add `DetailsPanelTabPage` and thinks that we are adding the list panel. It corrects itself once we have created the second tab page control.

17. Let's complete the `ListPanelTabPage` control first. As required by the pattern, under this control, add a **Group** control named `ListQuickFilterGroup` and a `Grid` control named `ListGrid`.

18. Complete the grid control's **Data Source** property and use the `Overview` field group for the **Data Group** property.

19. We will complete `ListQuickFilterGroup` in the same way as we did for the Simple List pattern. Apply the `Custom and Quick Filters` pattern to the control. Then, add a `Quick Filter` control and name it `ListQuickFilter`. Complete the control by referencing it to the grid control we named `ListGrid`.

20. The pattern now states that we will need **Main Grid Default Action**, which is a `Command Button` control. Add `Command Button` to `ListPanelTabPage`, setting the properties, as shown in the following table:

Property	Value
Name	ListGridDefaultButton
Command	DetailsView

You may notice there are many commands we could use, so we must be careful which command is selected!

21. On the `ListGrid` control, enter `ListGridDefaultButton` to the **Default Action** property.
22. Moving on to the **Details Panel** pattern element, reselect the `DetailsPanelTabPage` control and add a group control named `DetailsTitleGroup`.
23. Add a `String` control for the header titles, as shown here:

Property	Value
Name	DetailsHeaderTitle
Data Source	ConWHSVehicleTable
Data Method	TitleFields
View Edit Mode	View
Skip	Yes

The `titleFields` method is a system-provided data method that uses the title field properties from the table. We can write our own, should we prefer.

24. Checking our progress against the pattern pane, we will see that we need to add the **Details Tab (Tab)** pattern element. Add a new `Tab` control to the `DetailPanelTabPage` tab page control, setting the properties as follows:

Property	Value
Name	DetailsTab
Arrange Method	Vertical

We will now create a tab page to organize the various fields onto the form, and each tab page can be a list of fields or something more elaborate. The `VendTable` form is a good example of a more complicated form.

25. Add a new tab page name `DetailsTabGeneral` and apply the **Fields and Field Groups** pattern.

    The first tab page is customarily a tab page labelled `General`.

26. In this case, we can simply drag the `Details` field group from the `ConWHSVehicleTable` data source, but feel free to reorganize the fields into more appropriate groups.

     Should new field groups (or fields) be added, you can refresh the data source by right-clicking on the data source and choosing **Restore**.

27. We will need to create the menu item using the same label as the table's, but we will need to default **Form View Option** to `Grid` so we can get the list view when the form is opened.

28. Next, complete the **Form Ref** property of the `ConWHVehicleTable` table.

29. Finally, add the menu item to our menu.

How it works...

The concept is the same as for any form, we just have more features. The peculiar part of this form is that we have two views--one for the list view and the other to edit or view the details of the form.

This is done by showing and hiding the detail and list tabs. It knows which control to show or hide, because we followed the pattern--this is one of the reasons why a pattern conformation error will result in the compilation, should we try and build the project.

To test this on the development VM provided by Microsoft, build the project and use the following URL:

```
https://usnconeboxax1aos.cloud.onebox.dynamics.com/?cmp=usmf&mi=ConWHSV
ehicleTable
```

You can use this pattern to open any display menu item.

Creating a details transaction (order entry) form

These worksheet forms are the most complicated in terms of the steps required, as we now have three states to design: list, header, and lines views. To familiarize yourself with the end result, open and use the All purchase orders form from **Accounts Payable | Purchase orders | All purchase orders**.

The first part of the pattern is very similar to the `Details Master` pattern, so we will summarize slightly. We will continue the vehicle service order table, but again, the recipe is written so that it can be applied to any worksheet table.

How to do it...

To create the form, follow these steps:

1. Choose to add a new item to the project.
2. Select **User Interface** from the left-hand pane and **Form** from the right-hand pane.
3. Name the form as per the table's name; in this case, `ConWHSVehicleServiceTable`.
4. Drag the `ConWHSVehicleServiceTable` table from the project onto the **Data Sources** node of the form designer.
5. Select the `ConWHSVehicleServiceTable` data source and set the **Insert If Empty** and **Insert At End** properties to `No`.
6. Drag the `ConWHSVehicleServiceLine` table to the **Data Sources** node.
7. Select the `ConWHSVehicleServiceLine` data source and set the **Join Source** property to `ConWHSVehicleServiceTable`.

> We don't specify and join information beyond the name, as it will use the foreign key relation defined in the child table.

8. Override the `initValue` method on `ConWHSVehicleServiceLine` so that we can set the `ServiceId` field as this is not set for us. Use the following code:

```
public void initValue()
{
```

```
                    super();
                    ConWHSVehicleServiceLine.ServiceId =
                                    ConWHSVehicleServiceTable.ServiceId;
          }
```

9. Close the code editor and go back to the form designed tab.
10. Set the properties as follows:

Property	Value
Caption	Use the label from the table
Data Source	ConWHSVehicleServiceTable
Title Data Source	ConWHSVehicleServiceTable

 This is so that the header will use the current line for the header section. This isn't mandatory, and is done here to demonstrate that we have a choice.

11. Apply the **Details Transaction** pattern to the **Design** node.
12. Add an `Action Pane` control named `HeaderActionPane` and then a `Group` control called `NavigationListGroup` under the **Design** node.

 We will have two `Action Panes`, one for the header and one for the lines.

13. Add a `Quick Filter` control to the `NavigationListGroup` control named `NavgationQuickFilter`.
14. Then, create a `Grid` control named `NavigationGrid`.
15. Set the **Data Source** property of the grid control to `ConWHSVehicleServiceTable` and add the `ServiceId` and `Description` fields from the `ConWHSVehicleServiceTable` data source.
16. Complete the quick filter control with **Target Control** as the grid control and **Default Column** as desired.
17. Under the **Design** node, create a **Tab** control for **Panel Tab**. Create a new `Tab` control and name it `MainTab`. Set **Arrange Property** to `Vertical`.
18. Add a tab page named `DetailsPanelTabPage` first, and then `GridPanelTabPage`.

The names differ from the **Details Master** pattern. We will name our controls after the text control descriptions in the **Pattern** pane.

19. We will complete the GridPanelTabPage control first. Under this control, add a **Group** control named GridPanelQuickFilterGroup and a Grid control named ListGrid.
20. Complete the grid control's **Data Source** property and use the Overview field group for the **Data Group** property.
21. For GridPanelQuickFilterGroup, apply the Custom and Quick Filters pattern to the control. Then add a Quick Filter control, and name it ListQuickFilter. Complete the control by referencing it to the grid control we named ListGrid.
22. The pattern now states we need **Main Grid Default Action**, which is a Command Button control. Add Command Button to GridPanelTabPage called MainGridDefaultAction.
23. Set the **Command** property to DetailsView.

You may notice that there are many commands, and we must be careful which command is selected!

24. On the MainGrid control, enter MainGridDefaultAction to the **Default Action** property.
25. To complete the **Details Panel (TabPage)** pattern element, reselect the DetailsPanelTabPage control and add a group control named DetailsPanelTitleGroup.
26. Add a String control, setting the properties as follows:

Property	Value
Name	DetailsPanelHeaderTitle
Data Source	ConWHSVehicleServiceLine
Data Method	titleFields
View Edit Mode	View
Skip	Yes

Optionally, create a group under the DetailsPanelTitleGroup control called DetailsPanelStatusGroup, and then drag the ServiceStatus field from the ConWHSVehicleServiceTable table. Rename the field control to DetailsPanelTitle_ServiceStatus.

27. We will now need to complete the **Header and Line Panels (Tab)** pattern element. Add a new Tab control to DetailPanelTabPage, as follows:

Property	Value
Name	HeaderAndLinePanelTab
Arrange Method	Vertical

28. Add a new tab page for Lines Panel using the following properties:

Property	Value
Name	LinesPanelTabPage
Style	DetailsFormDetails

 The **Style** property adds more information to the pattern in order to control presentation and behavior.

29. Add a second tab page control, shown as follows: HeaderPanelTabPage.

Property	Value
Name	HeaderPanelTabPage
Style	DetailsFormDetails

30. Add a new **Tab** control to the LinePanelTabPage control named LineViewTab.
31. We will now add three tab pages to this control.
32. Add the **Line View Header Details (TabPage)** pattern element using the following properties:

Property	Value
Name	LineViewHeaderTabPage

Label	Vehicle service order header
Pattern	Apply the **Field and Field Groups** pattern

33. Add the **Line View Lines (TabPage)** pattern element using the following properties:

Property	Value
Name	LineViewLines
Label	@SYS9664

34. Add the **Line View Line Details (TabPage)** pattern element using the following properties:

Property	Value
Name	LineViewLineDetailsTabPage
Label	Vehicle Service order lines
Data Source	ConWHSVehicleServiceLine

35. Add an **Action Pane** control to the `LineViewLinesTabPage` control named `LinesActionPane`, and under that, an **Action Pane Tab** control named `LineActionRecordActions`.

36. Right-click on the new `LineActionRecordActions` control and select the **New Button Group** control under this named `LineActionRecordActionsGroup`.

For this action pane, we will need to add buttons to add and remove lines. These are only added automatically in the main header `Action Pane` control.

37. Under the `LineActionRecordActionsGroup` button group, add a **Command** button named `LineActionAddLine`.

38. This is to allow the user to add lines to the lines grid. Set the following properties:

Property	Value	Description
Normal Image	Delete	This adds a waste bin symbol

| Label | @SYS135131 | Remove |
| Command | New | This triggers the new record task for the data source |

39. Then, add a second **Command** button named `LineActionRemove`, setting the properties as follows:

Property	Value	Description
Normal Image	Add	This adds a simple plus symbol
Label	@SYS319116	Add line
Command	DeleteRecord	This triggers the delete record task
Save Record	No	We want to allow records that are not yet saved to be deleted

40. Under this button group, we will need a grid for the lines. Add a new **Grid** control, setting the following properties:

Property	Value
Name	LinesGrid
Data Source	ConWHSVehicleServiceLine
Data Group	Overview

 As we usually have many more fields that can realistically fit in the grid, we have a tab control that allows the user to see these fields grouped in a logical order using tab pages.

41. Create a **Tab** control under `LineViewLineDetailsTabPage` and set the following properties:

Property	Value
Name	LineViewDetailsTab
Label	@SYS23823
Data Source	ConWHSVehicleServiceLine
Arrange Method	Vertical

42. We would add one or more tab pages but, in our case, we will only need one.

43. Add a **Tab Page** control named `LineViewDetailsTabDetails` and set the **Label** property to `@ConWHS:Details`.

44. Drag `Identification` and `Details` from the `ConWHSVehicleServiceLines` data source.

45. We will now need to complete the header view of the form, which is governed by the **Header Panel** pattern element. Right-click on `HeaderPanelTabPage` and choose **New | Tab**, and complete as follows:

Property	Value
Name	HeaderDetailsTab
Arrange Method	Vertical
Data Source	ConWHSVehicleServiceTable

46. We would usually have many field groups to add but, in this case, we will just need one. Create a new `Tab Page` control named `HeaderDetailsTabDetails`. Set the **Caption** property to `@ConWHS:Details`.

47. Drag the `Details` and `ServiceDates` field groups from the `ConWHSVehicleServiceTable` data source, but rename them, prefixed with `HeaderDetailsTabDetails`.

48. We will need to create the menu item using the same label as the table's, but we will need to default **Form View Option** to `Grid` so we can get the list view when the form is opened.

49. Then, complete the **Form Ref** property of the `ConWHVehicleServiceTable` table.

50. Finally, add the menu item to our menu.

How it works...

The process, albeit extended, is the same as the `Details Master` pattern. There are some additional properties to set in this case to help with the form's behavior. There are a lot of steps, and it is easy to get lost and potentially set the wrong property. This is why we name the controls after the pattern element name.

This form pattern was deliberately as simple as it can be, and once we are comfortable with the process, it should be straightforward to expand this to more complicated data structures.

Creating form parts

Form parts are used for two purposes. One is to provide a popup form as you hover over a foreign key, such as the popup when you hover the Product number when entering sales or purchase orders. This is great for users, as it means they don't necessarily have to navigate away from the task they are performing.

Another use is to create a reused form part that we can place within other forms. We could have a form part that contains product information, which we could add to the product and sales order forms. We can specify a link when we add the form part, making them easy to implement.

Getting ready

We will create a simple form part, which is a list of vehicle service orders, so we will only need a table created from which the data will be displayed.

How to do it...

To create a form part for open vehicle service orders, follow these steps:

1. Create a new form called `ConWHSVehicleServiceOpenPart`.
2. Drag the `ConWHSVehicleServiceTable` table to the **Data Sources** node.
3. Set the properties of the data source as follows:

Property	Value
Allow Edit	No
Allow Create	No
Allow Delete	No
Insert If Empty	No
Insert At End	No

4. Set the properties on the **Design** node as follows:

Property	Value

Data Source	ConWHSVehicleServiceTable
Show Delete Button	No
Show New Button	No

5. Apply the **Form Part Section List** pattern.

 You can use any of the patterns starting with **Form Part**, each of which is for a different style; for instance, **Form Part Factbox Card** is useful to apply to the **Preview Part** property of a table in order show a nice popup when the user hovers over a foreign key.

6. Add a new group control named `HeaderGroup` and apply the **Filters and Toolbar - inline** pattern.

7. Add a group to this called `FilterGroup` and add a **Quick Filter** control to this.

8. Reselect the `HeaderGroup` control and add an **Action Pane** control called `ToolbarActionPane`.

9. Add a **Button Group** control named `ToolbarButtonGroup`.

10. Drag the `ConWHSVehicleServiceTable` Display Menu Item onto the button group and set the properties as follows:

Property	Value
Name	ActionNew
Label	@SYS2055 (New)
Normal Image	New
Form View Option	Details
Open Mode	Edit

11. Drag the menu item a second time but, this time, set the properties as follows:

Property	Value
Name	ActionDetails
Label	@ConWHS:Details
Normal Image	Details
Needs Record	Yes

Save Record	No
Copy Caller Query	Yes
Form View Option	Details
Open Mode	New

12. Create a new grid control under the **Design** node named `ContentGrid`.

13. Set the **Data Source** property to `ConWHSVehicleServiceTable` and drag the fields, as desired, from the data source to the grid.

 You could consider creating a field group for this purpose. The fields on a form part will be less than the list view of the details form as they should only occupy a third of the width of the screen.

14. Set the **Default Action** property of the grid to `ActionEdit`.

15. Create a menu item using the same name as the form part, that is, `ConWHSVehicleServiceOpenPart`.

How it works...

Form Parts are just forms, but the pattern forces us to design in accordance with how the form part will be used; which is why there are four types of form part patterns.

We will use the preceding part when creating the workspace form later. **Form Part FactBox Card** is also very useful and easy to create. Just use the pattern to create the form part, create a menu item from it, and complete the table's **Preview Part Ref** property.

Later, we will use queries and composite subqueries to apply filters to forms. We can use the technique of specifying a query, or one of the query's composite queries, to a menu item. This means that we can have one form part, but the menu item can be used to apply a filter to the form.

Create tiles with counters for the workspace

Tiles are used as an entry point to a form whilst having the ability to show information about the data. It can act as a prompt to action and is presented on a tile section of a workspace, as shown in the following screenshot:

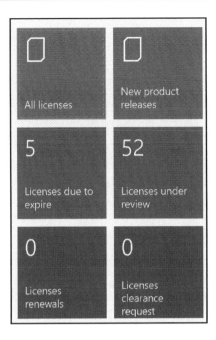

The page that opens when you first sign into Operations is also a list of Tiles, and each opens a workspace. The workspace will have an image resource that we would design; a key guideline is that all graphics are minimalistic. All solutions should look and feel as if they were part of the standard solution.

Getting ready

This recipe can be used to create a tile for any form, and is usually done for Details Master and Details Transaction to show both all records and commonly used subsets of data.

In this case, we will create a tile for all vehicles, and then a tile for a type of vehicle.

How to do it...

To create a tile, follow these steps:

1. We will first create a query that the tile will use. Create a new operations artifact and select **Query** from the **Data Model** artifacts.
2. Set **Name** to ConWHSVehicleTableAll and press **Add**.

3. Drag the `ConWHSVehicleTable` table to the **Data Sources** node.
4. Change the **Dynamics Fields** property to `Yes`.

This will ensure that the query always references all the fields in the table, which is important when it will be used with a form.

5. Save and close the query.
6. Choose to add a new **Operations Artifact** and select **Tile** from the **User Interface** node.
7. Change **Name** to `ConWHSVehiclesAllTile` and press **Add**.
8. Set the following properties:

Property	Value
Query	ConWHSVehicleTableAll
Label	All vehicles
Menu Item Name	ConWHSVehicleTable
Normal Image	GenericDocument
Copy Caller Query	Yes

Next, we will create a tile for bikes. We will create a composite query, which will allow us to use a base query and add ranges to it.

9. Create a new artifact, and choose **Composite Query** from the **Data Model** node.
10. Set **Name** to `ConWHSVehicleTableBikes` and press **Add**.
11. In the **Query** property, enter `ConWHSVehicleTableAll`.
12. Right-click on the **Ranges** node and select **New Composite Query Range**.
13. In the **Data Source** property, select `ConWHSVehicleTable`.
14. Set the **Field** property to `VehicleType`.
15. We will enter the criteria by entering the enum's symbol in the **Value** property; so, enter `Bike` in the **Value** property.

You may also enter the numeric value, but this can only be used for non-extensible enums.

16. Create a new tile called `ConWHSVehicleBikesTile`.
17. Complete the properties of the Tile as follows:

Property	Value
Query	ConWHSVehicleTableBikes
Label	Bikes
Menu Item Name	ConWHSVehicleTable
Normal Image	<Blank>
Copy Caller Query	Yes
Type	Count

18. Save and close all designer tabs.

How it works...

Tiles have two basic properties, the source query and the target form's menu item. When the tile is clicked, the query is applied to the target form, filtering the data. The **Copy Query Caller** property is important here, and should the filter not appear to work, it is nearly always because this property was not set.

This technique of applying queries can also be applied to menu items, and we can create menu items that will open the vehicle table filter based on the query. This is done by specifying the **Query** and **Copy Caller Query** properties on a duplicate of the menu items.

When experimenting with filters, don't filter based on data that the user can change; a tile for a particular vehicle group would be a very good example of a bad idea.

There's more...

A good tile is a tile that takes you to service orders due tomorrow, so we will need to filter based on a function.

In the query range's **Value** property, we can also enter query functions. The standard functions are defined in the `SysQueryRangeUtil` class. So, to filter on today's orders, you will enter `(currentDate())` in the query range's **Value** property.

We used to modify this class to add new functions in Dynamics AX 2012, but since overlayering is discouraged, we have a better way to do this in Operations.

Create a new class and call it `ConWHSQueryRangeUtil`. The name is not important. To create a method that returns a date a number of days from today, use the following code:

```
[QueryRangeFunction]
public static date RelativeDate(int relativeDays = 0)
{
    utcdatetime   currentDateTime;

    currentDateTime = DateTimeUtil::applyTimeZoneOffset(
                    DateTimeUtil::getSystemDateTime(),
                    DateTimeUtil::getUserPreferredTimeZone());

    return DateTimeUtil::date(
                DateTimeUtil::addDays(
                    currentDateTime, relativeDays));
}
```

To use the preceding function to return tomorrow's date, add a new range for the required date field and enter `(ConWHSQueryRangeUtil::RelativeDate(1))` in the `Value` property. To filter records on or before tomorrow, use `..(ConWHSQueryRangeUtil::RelativeDate(1))`.

Creating a workspace

The workspace provides an area for everything a user will need for a task or group of tasks. The workspace should be able to display all of the key information without scrolling, and is structured as a horizontal space with the following sections:

- Tiles
- Tabbed lists of key data
- Charts (Optional)
- Power BI (Optional)
- Related information, for example, links to key forms

The dashboard is normally created once we have completed most of the solution; otherwise, we will have nothing to add. The pattern can be easily transposed to your own requirement.

How to do it...

To create the workspace, follow these steps:

1. Create a new form and name it `ConWHSVehicleWorkspace`.
2. Apply the **Workspace Operational** pattern to the **Design** node.

 You can also use the Workspace, which provides a simpler design where we will only show tiles and links.

3. Complete the **Caption** property as `Vehicle management workspace`.
4. Add a **Tab** control and call it `PanoramaTab`, following the idea that we will name controls along the lines of the pattern element we are creating.
5. Create a new tab page, named `PanoramaSectionTiles`, and apply the **Section Tiles** pattern.
6. Set the following properties on the new tab page:

Property	Value
Caption	Summary
Extended Style	panoramaItem_backgroundNone

7. For the tab page, create the **Tile Button** controls for each of our tiles. Use the following properties as a guide:

Property	Value
Name	ConWHSVehiclesAllTile
Tile	ConWHSVehiclesAllTile
Copy Caller Query	Yes

8. Add a new tab page to the `PanoramaTab` control, named `PanoramaSectionList`, and apply the **Section Tabbed List** pattern.
9. Provide **Caption**, such as `Service orders`.

10. Add a **Tab** control named `TabbedListTab`.

11. To the `TabbeListTab` control, add a tab page and name it
    `TabbedListPageOrders`.

12. Complete the **Caption** property as `Orders`.

13. Add a new **Form Part** control, specifying the following parameters:

Property	Value
Name	ConWHSVehicleServiceOpenPart
MenuItemName	ConWHSVehicleServiceOpenPart
Run Mode	Local

14. Right-click on the `PanoramaTab` control and select **New Tab Page**.

15. Apply the **Section Related Links** pattern.

 Here, we will add links to forms that are needed for the workspaces
task; these can include set forms, and other links that the user will use.

16. Rename the control to `PanoramaSectionLinks` and set the **Caption** property to
    `Links`.

17. Create a new group and call it `LinksSetupGroup`. Set the **Caption** property to
    `Setup`.

18. Drag the menu items `ConWHSParameters` and `ConWHSVehicleGroups` to the
    new group.

19. Save and close the design tabs.

20. Create a menu item for the form, setting the **Label** property to `Vehicle
    management workspace`.

21. We will need a Tile to add to the main navigation workspace; create the Tile as
    follows:

Property	Value
Name	ConWHSVehicleWorkspaceTile
Menu Item Name	ConWHSVehicleWorkspace
Normal Image	Workspace_PurchaseReceiptAndFollowup (this is a cheat, more on resources later)

Size	Wide
Tile Display	BackgroundImage

22. Locate the `navpanemenu` menu in Application Explorer, and right-click on it. Choose **Create extension**.
23. Rename it to `navpanemenu.ConWHS`.
24. Open the menu extension. Right-click on the root node and choose **New** | **Submenu**.
25. Rename the new submenu to `ConWHSMenu`.
26. Right-click on the submenu and choose **New** | **Menu Element Tile**.
27. Complete the **Tile** property as `ConWHSVehicleWorkspaceTile`.
28. Save and close all windows and perform a build.

How it works...

The form design here is just like the other forms, and much simpler than the Details Master and Transaction patterns. The clever part of this is that we are thinking task-based. We are creating a workspace based on what the user does. The traditional form design from Dynamics AX 2012 was to provide all the features that the user could want, which resulted in a lot of features that most users never used. With workspaces, the concept is that most of the workspace is used regularly. The user shouldn't have to change workspace to locate a form for that task. It is also OK for a user to use more than one workspace. We want to provide everything the user needs, but without clutter.

There's more...

For more inspiration on workspaces, investigate the `ReqCreatePlanWorkspace` form. Specifically, look at the way it handles the way the filter controls the tiles.

4
Application Extensibility, Form Code-Behind, and Frameworks

In this chapter, we will cover the following recipes:

- Creating a handler class using the application extension factory
- Hooking up a number sequence
- Creating a create dialog for details transaction forms
- Creating a SysOperation process
- Adding an interface to a SysOperation framework

Introduction

In this chapter, we will get straight into writing code. The recipes chosen for this chapter are common tasks that will be used on many development projects.

As we progress through the chapter, references to code placement is made. Code placement is critical to a maintainable and extendable solution. We will see that code can be written on the form, in a class, or in a table. The rule of thumb here is that we must place code as low in the stack as possible. If we write code on a form, that code is only available to that form and cannot be reused. This is fine when we are hiding a button, but data (validation, and other data specific code) logic usually belongs to a table. As the code on the form or table gets more complicated, the code should be moved to a class.

The `SalesTable` form and table is an example. In this case table events are handled by the `SalesableType` and `SalesLineType` classes and form logic is handled by the `SalesTableForm` class. The reason here is that there can be different types of sales order, and the best solution was to have a base class for the base code and a specialized class to handle the different requirements of each order type.

Creating a handler class using the Application Extension factory

Form handler classes have a role in more complicated forms, such as `Details Transaction` (order entry) forms. These are the two main reasons why we would consider developing a form handler class:

- We intend to create a separate form for the creation of the record, which is common on order entry forms
- The user interface logic is particularly complicated, or varies by type of record

We can also have table handler classes, for similar reasons. The table handler will have code that is record-specific, wherever the data is presented. The code in the form handler is form specific. The placement of code is therefore important. Code that determines whether a field is editable will be in the table handler class, and the form handler class will use that method in order to make the control editable.

We may not always have a table handler class, and these methods can be placed directly on the table; although we can't change the method declarations of public methods after release (in case other parties have used them), we can change the internal logic with impunity.

In this example, we will control which fields on the vehicle service table are enabled, based on the service status. It is a simple example in order to demonstrate a pattern that can be used to abstract complicated scenarios, simplifying code creation, and maintenance. We will create a table and form handler class using a standard pattern. We will then create the table handler using the `SysExtension` pattern. This allows the code to be extended by other parties without over-layering.

Getting ready

We should have a table and form created to the `Design Transaction` pattern for this recipe. In our case, we will use `ConWHSVehicleServiceTable`.

How to do it...

Let's create the table handler class first, since we will need this in order to complete the form handler class. To use the `SysExtension` pattern, we will need at least two classes: the attribute class and the class that will be constructed using the pattern.

1. To create the attribute class, choose to add a new item to the project, select the **Code** node, and then choose **Class** from the artifact list.

2. Enter `ConWHSVehicleServiceStatusAttribute` in the **Name** field and press **Add**.

3. Alter the class declaration to be as follows:

```
class ConWHSVehicleServiceStatusAttribute
    extends SysAttribute
    implements SysExtensionIAttribute
{
}
```

4. We will need to store the attribute we are handling as a variable in the class, so declare the service status as follows:

```
ConWHSVehicleServiceStatus status;
```

5. Override the new method so it constructs using the `status` field, as shown in the following lines of code:

```
public void new(ConWHSVehicleServiceStatus _status)
{
    status = _status;
}
```

6. If we save the changes so far, the compiler will complain that certain methods aren't implemented; the quick way to solve this is to click inside the `SysExtensionIAttribute` text and press *F12*.

7. This opens the code editor for the interface, copies the `parmCacheKey` methods and `useSingleton` into your class, so it reads as follows:

```
public str parmCacheKey()
{
  // you can't cast an extensible enum directly
  // to an int, the following warning will be given
  // by the compiler:
  // Cast from extensible enum 'Extensible
  // Enumeration(ConWHSVehicleServiceStatus)' to 'int'
  // potentially harmful and deprecated.
  return classStr(ConWHSVehicleServiceStatusAttribute)
    +';'+int2Str(enum2int(status));
}

public boolean useSingleton()
{
  return false;
}
```

Read the method documentation for these methods, with specific thought to whether the class will be immutable. Returning `false` is safe as it won't construct from a cached instance, but will have an impact on performance. Before making this true, you must ensure that it is immutable.

8. Next, we will create the table handler classes. Create a new class named ConWHSVehicleServiceTableType.

This naming convention is important so that we know that the class is a handler class for a table and which table it handles.

9. We will construct the instance from ConWHSVehicleServiceTable and will, therefore, store this as a global variable on the class; add this as follows:

```
class ConWHSVehicleServiceTableType
{
  ConWHSVehicleServiceTable serviceTable;
}
```

10. In order to construct the class, we will need to be able to set the value of serviceTable using an accessor method (a way to get and set internal variables), which is called a Parm method in Operations:

```
public ConWHSVehicleServiceTable
  ParmConWHSVehicleServiceTable(
  ConWHSVehicleServiceTable
```

```
    _serviceTable = serviceTable)
{
  serviceTable = _serviceTable;
  return serviceTable;
}
```

11. We will write the constructor so that it uses the `SysExtension` pattern to return the class based on the value of the `ServiceStatus` field. This could simply be a `switch` statement in the construct method, but the following method is naturally extensible:

```
public static ConWHSVehicleServiceTableType Construct(
  ConWHSVehicleServiceTable _serviceTable)
{
  ConWHSVehicleServiceTableType tableHandler;

  tableHandler =
    SysExtensionAppClassFactory::getClassFromSysAttribute(
    classStr(ConWHSVehicleServiceTableType),
      new ConWHSVehicleServiceStatusAttribute(
      _serviceTable.ServiceStatus));
      tableHandler.ParmConWHSVehicleServiceTable(
        _serviceTable);
  return tableHandler;
}
```

You can also use the `getClassInstanceListFromSysAttribute` method to check if the attribute is being handled.

12. We will now need to create a method on the table that returns the preceding class; the method is always called `type`. Open the code editor for the `ConWHSVehicleServiceTable` table and create the following method:

```
public ConWHSVehicleServiceTableType Type()
{
  return ConWHSVehicleServiceTableType::Construct(this);
}
```

13. The standard pattern for table handler classes is that all table events are moved to the class. Ensure that all of the following table events are overridden on the `ConWHSVehicleServiceTable` table:

- `insert`
- `update`

- `delete`
- `validateField`
- `validateDelete`
- `validateWrite`

14. To handle the insert and update methods, we can write two methods that are called either side of the `super()` call. Create place holder methods for `Insert`, `Delete`, and `Update` using the following pattern:

```
public void InsertPre()
{
}

public void InsertPost()
{
}
```

Please see the *How it works...* section for details on why this differs from other table handlers.

15. For the rest, the quickest way is to copy all table event methods to the class and refactor them, as shown in the following piece of code:

```
public boolean ValidateWrite()
{
    boolean ret = true;

    ret = ret && this.CheckCanEdit();
    // more checks can be added using the same pattern
    return ret;
}

public void ModifiedField(FieldId _fieldId)
{
    Switch (_fieldId)
    {
        case fieldNum(
                ConWHSVehicleServiceTable, VehicleId):
            serviceTable.InitFromConWHSVehicleTable(
                ConWHSVehicleTable::Find(
                    serviceTable.VehicleId));
            break;
```

```
        }
    }

    public boolean ValidateDelete()
    {
        return true;
    }

    public boolean CheckCanEdit()
    {
        If (!this.CanEdit())
        {
            //Service order cannot be changed.
            return checkFailed("@ConWHS:ConWHS33");
        }
        return true;
    }

    public boolean CanEdit()
    {
        switch (serviceTable.ServiceStatus)
        {
            case ConWHSVehicleServiceStatus::None:
            case ConWHSVehicleServiceStatus::Confirmed:
                return true;
        }
        return false;
    }
```

Do not be tempted to call `serviceTable.validateWrite()` in the `Insert` or `Update` methods, or `validateDelete()` in the `Delete` method. The form's `FormDataSource` object must do this.

We will now complete the changes required to `ConWHSVehicleServiceTable`.

1. Remove the `CheckCanEdit` and `CanEdit` methods from the table; `Can` or `May` methods should always be on the handler class if one exists.
2. Alter the table's event methods so that they use the handler class instead; to insert, update, and delete, use the following pattern:

```
    public void insert()
    {
        this.type().InsertPre();
        super()
        this.type().InsertPost();
    }
```

When overriding insert, delete, or update consider performance, this
will force the operation to be done one at a time, and not as a set. So
`delete_from`, `update_recordset` and `insert_recordset`
commands will no longer be a set based operation, significantly
affecting performance. Also, if you remove `super()` from the call, the
table event delegates will not fire.

3. For the validate and modified methods, use the following piece of code:

```
public boolean validateField(FieldId _fieldIdToCheck)
{
    boolean ret = super(_fieldIdToCheck);
    if(ret)
    {
        ret = ret &&
            this.type().ValidateField(_fieldIdToCheck);
    }
    return ret;
}

public boolean validateWrite()
{
    boolean ret = super();
    if(ret)
    {
        ret = this.type().ValidateWrite();
    }
    return ret;
}

public boolean validateDelete()
{
    boolean ret = super();
    if(ret)
    {
        ret = this.type().ValidateDelete();
    }
    return ret;
}

public void modifiedField(FieldId _fieldId)
{
    super(_fieldId);
    this.type().modifiedField(_fieldId);
}
```

4. We now need to control whether or not the `VehicleId`, `ServiceDateRequested`, and `ServiceDateConfirmed` fields can be edited. Create three methods on the `ConWHSVehicleServiceTableType` class, as shown here:

```
public boolean CanEditVehicleId()
{
    return true;
}
public boolean CanEditServiceDateRequested()
{
    return true;
}
public boolean CanEditServiceDateConfirmed()
{
    return true;
}
```

5. Each of the child classes will override the preceding methods, return the correct status for the status, and create four classes, which are named as follows:
    - `ConWHSVehicleServiceTableTypeNone`
    - `ConWHSVehicleServiceTableTypeConfirmed`
    - `ConWHSVehicleServiceTableTypeCompleted`
    - `ConWHSVehicleServiceTableTypeCanceled`

6. For each class, add `extends ConWHSVehicleServiceTableType` to the class declaration:

```
Class ConWHSVehicleServiceTableTypeNone
    extends ConWHSVehicleServiceTableType
```

7. Override the `CanEdit` methods in each class so that the following result will be achieved:

Status / action	None	Confirmed	Completed	Canceled
`CanEdit`	True	True	True	False
`CanEditVehicleId`	True	True	False	False
`CanEditServiceDateRequested`	True	False	False	False
`CanEditServiceDateConfirmed`	True	False	False	False

8. Repeat this pattern for each of the other three classes.

You may also notice that the code in `ConWHSVehicleServiceTableType.CanEdit()` is now redundant, and we should just return true (or false, as desired). It may seem that the current code isn't doing any effective harm, but it looks like it is doing something, and it should be changed.

9. The final step is to decorate the four classes with the `ConWHSVehicleServiceStatusAttribute` attribute class, but we will need to build the project first. *Ctrl + Shift + B* may suffice in this case, if we have built recently. Also, in order to allow intellitype to work for the new attribute, restart Visual Studio.

10. Add the following line, changing the enum value as appropriate, to the very top of each of our four classes:

```
[ConWHSVehicleServiceStatusAttribute(
    ConWHSVehicleServiceStatus::Cancelled)]
```

This completes the table handler for now, so we can move on to the form handler class:

1. Create a new class named `ConWHSVehicleServiceTableForm`.

Again, the naming convention is important so that we know that the class is a handler class for a form and which form is being handled.

2. This is the base class and will contain code common to all classes that extend it, which we will construct from a `FormDataSource` object that the form will have constructed automatically (in our case, `ConWHSVehicleServiceTable_DS`). We will, therefore, need to store this as a variable global to the call, as shown here:

```
class ConWHSVehicleServiceTableForm
{
    protected FormDataSource serviceTableDS;
}
```

We are declaring this as protected to show that we are deliberately making the variable available to this class and all classes that extend it.

3. We will also need a way to set this method, which could be done directly if it was made public; so, we will need to provide an accessor method. In Operations, these are called the `parm` methods and are created as follows:

```
public FormDataSource ParmServiceTableDS(
  FormDataSource
  _serviceTableDS = serviceTableDS)
{
    serviceTableDS = _serviceTableDS;
    return serviceTableDS;
}
```

In this case, there is little difference between making the variable public and using it as a property directly. However, once we make something public, we may not be able to undo it, especially if it is used in other packages or by other parties.

4. Although we won't use this method until later, we should write it now. One of the main reasons to write a form handler class is to handle the interaction between a create dialog and the main details form. This is done by adding an accessor method to the handler class so that the new record can be passed between the dialog and the details form. Define the variable and `Parm` methods, as shown here:

```
public ConWHSVehicleServiceTable ParmServiceTableCreated(
    ConWHSVehicleServiceTable
        _serviceTable = serviceTableCreated)
{
    serviceTableCreated = _serviceTable;
    return serviceTableCreated;
}
```

You may notice that this method is written in other parts of Operations without the `Created` suffix, but this can lead to confusion and the variable can be used for the wrong purpose.

5. Next, we can write our constructor, which will be as follows:

```
public static ConWHSVehicleServiceTableForm
  NewFromDataSource(FormDataSource _serviceTableDataSource)
{
    // Check first that the table that the
    // data source is bound to is supported
    if (_serviceTableDataSource.table()
```

```
                               != tableNum(ConWHSVehicleServiceTable))
              {
                  //Table %1 is not supported
                  throw error(strFmt("@SYS31187",
                      tableId2Name(_serviceTableDataSource.table())));
              }

              // no point constructing the class, before this point.
              ConWHSVehicleServiceTableForm form
                          = new ConWHSVehicleServiceTableForm();
              form.ParmServiceTableDS(_serviceTableDataSource);
              return form;
          }
```

This is a pretty straightforward constructor, but you may wonder why we construct from the data source and not the table. The reason is that the data source is passed by reference, so we can always get the current record using the `cursor()` method.

6. To simplify the class' usage, write the following method:

```
          public ConWHSVehicleServiceTable currentRecord()
          {
              return serviceTableDS.cursor()
                          as ConWHSVehicleServiceTable;
          }
```

The `cursor()` method returns the record as the global base type for all tables, which is `Common`. Although we don't need to use `AS` in this case, using the `AS` performs the cast at that point, and is a good habit when using generic types such as `Common` and `Object`.

7. Our requirement is that we control whether certain fields are editable based on the current status. The standard method to do this is to create a method called `EnableFields`. To control our three fields, write the following code:

```
          public void EnableFields()
          {
              ConWHSVehicleServiceTable serviceTable;
              boolean canEdit;

              serviceTable = this.currentRecord()
              canEdit = serviceTable.type().CanEdit()

              serviceTableDS.allowEdit(canEdit);
              serviceTableDS.allowDelete(canEdit);
```

```
// if the record can't be edited, no point
// checking each field.
    if(canEdit)
    {
        RefFieldId fieldId;
        boolean canEditField;
        FormDataObject dsField;

// this is written this way to make the code easier
// to read by making each line appear on one line
        ConWHSVehicleServiceTableType hndlr;
        hndlr = serviceTable.type();

        fieldId = fieldNum(ConWHSVehicleServiceTable,
                        VehicleId);
        canEditField = hndlr.CanEditVehicleId();
        dsField = serviceTableDS.object(fieldId);
        dsField.allowEdit(canEditField);

        fieldId = fieldNum(ConWHSVehicleServiceTable,
                        ServiceDateRequested);
        canEditField = hndlr.CanEditServiceDateRequested();
        dsField = serviceTableDS.object(fieldId);
        dsField.allowEdit(canEditField);

        fieldId = fieldNum(ConWHSVehicleServiceTable,
                        ServiceDateConfirmed);
        canEditField = hndlr.CanEditServiceDateConfirmed();
        dsField = serviceTableDS.object(fieldId);
        dsField.allowEdit(canEditField);
    }
}
```

Each preceding block would normally be written as one line, but this became unreadable as it wrapped. One line per block is preferable as it makes it easier to read and less prone to copy and paste errors. For example,

```
serviceTableDS.object(fieldNum(ConWHSVehicleServiceTabl
e, VehicleId)).allowEdit(hndlr.CanEditVehicleId());
```

8. The `active` method on the data source is triggered whenever a new record becomes active, so we should hook into this method. We will first create a method to handle this in our form handler class and write the method as follows:

```
public void HandleActivePost()
{
    this.EnableFields();
```

```
      }
```

9. Next, open the `ConWHSVehicleServiceTable` form in the designer.

10. Right-click on the **Methods** node and choose **Override** | **Init**.

11. We will need to do two things: declare an object of type `ConWHSVehicleServiceTableForm` and then construct it. We will construct the form handler after the `super()` call, because the `ConWHSVehicleServiceTable_DS` object is constructed by the call to `super()`. Write the code as follows:

```
ConWHSVehicleServiceTableForm formHandler;
public void init()
{
    super();
    formHandler =
        ConWHSVehicleServiceTableForm::NewFromDataSource(
            ConWHSVehicleServiceTable_DS);
}
```

12. Finally, to hook up the `HandleActivePost` method, right-click on the **Methods** node of the `ConWHSVehicleServiceTable` data source and choose **Override** | **active**.

13. Alter the method so that it reads as follows:

```
public int active()
{
    int ret = super();
    formHandler.HandleActivePost();
    return ret;
}
```

14. Save and close all windows, and build the package.

15. Open the D365O in your browser, which is `https://usnconeboxax1aos.cloud.onebox.dynamics.com/?cmp=usmf` on the standard development VM, at the time of publication.

16. Navigate to the service order form, creating a service order if necessary.

17. Close the form and use SQL Server Management Studio to edit `ServiceStatus` to different values in the `ConWHSVehicleServiceTable` table. Each time you open the form, check that the fields behave correctly for each change in status.

How it works...

There were a lot of new concepts in this recipe. The first was the use of the table handler class, forgetting the attribute-based constructor for now.

The table handler is useful when the logic gets very complicated and would benefit from being abstracted into a class structure.

If you compare the Insert, Update, and Delete methods to the way this was done in SalesTable and SalesTableType, you will see a key difference. In SalesTable, the call to super() was removed and the handler class calls the equivalent do method directly. Since the standard Insert, Update, and Delete methods simply call the equivalent do method anyway, this may seem fine.

There is a drawback, which detracts from the aim of making our code extensible. This is that the table events, those that live under the Events node in the table designer, do not fire unless super() is called, effectively disabling the events for insert, delete, and update. This is why the table event OnInserted on SalesTable will not fire.

The SysExtension framework is genius, but should be used with care. By using this, we have increased the overhead of writing records to the table. The practical difference may be small in this case, but should we have used this on transactional tables like InventTrans, the result could be significant.

The class is instantiated by looking at the classes that extend the base class (as specified in the call to SysExtension::getClassFromSysAttribute) for classes that have the appropriate attribute decoration.

This means that another party could extend the enum and write their own class to handle it; no over-layering is required, and we can ship updates regularly without causing our customer undue pain as they apply them.

The form was hooked up using a pattern that can be seen throughout Operations, although, the handler is sometimes constructed from the table and not the data source. This means that calls to the handler class must include the current record, which is not required in the pattern used in this recipe.

There's more...

Let's say we do not want a default value in our base class, and want to force that any class that extends the base class to implement a method we would use an interface. In our example, we could throw an error should a base class not be caught. This is fine, but it would be nice if it was caught by the compiler.

Interfaces have many uses, and some will be explored further in later chapters; however, in this case, we will need to ensure that classes that inherit from our base class implement the required methods.

This is one of the many features that interfaces provide. If we declare that a class implements an interface, it will not compile until all methods in the interface are implemented. However, there isn't a way to force a subclass to implement the interface. If the base class implements the interface, the base class must have the methods and, by inheritance, the child classes will be seen to implement the methods.

We could make the base class abstract, but this limits what we can do as we have tied them together through inheritance. Implementing an interface merely enforces that the class implements its methods, there is no inheritance.

In older versions on D365O, the standard `RunBase` abstract class used to use abstract methods, such as pack and unpack, to force the developer to implement these methods, but now Microsoft has changed this so that it uses an interface instead. If you look at the code in `RunBase`, it now implements three interfaces, of which one is `SysSaveable`, which extends `SysPackable`. This forces any class that implements `SysSaveable` to create the `pack` and `unpack` methods.

The benefits of interfaces go further. Although we can never instantiate an interface (it isn't a class, it is a contract), we can assign an instance of a class that implements it to it. This brings us back to our scenario. We want to enforce that the subclasses implement a method that isn't in the base class; if it were in the base class, there would be a default value.

Interfaces are created just like classes; just choose **Interface** from the list. In our example, the interface would be written as follows:

```
interface ConWHSVehicleServiceTableCheckable
{
    public boolean CanEdit()
    {
    }

    public boolean CanEditVehicleId()
    {
```

```
        }

        public boolean CanEditServiceDateRequested()
        {
        }

        public boolean CanEditServiceDateConfirmed()
        {
        }
    }
```

We must first remove the four methods from the base class, as we don't want a default in this scenario. Also, if the method exists in the base class, the compiler will consider that the interface methods are implemented.

Then, for each of our four `ConWHSVehicleServiceTableType` child classes, add `implements ConWHSVehicleServiceTableCheckable`. For example:

```
class ConWHSVehicleServiceTableTypeCancelled
        extends ConWHSVehicleServiceTableType
        implements ConWHSVehicleServiceTableCheckable
```

To use the interface instead, change the `ConWHSVehicleServiceForm.EnableFields` method so that the `hndlr` variable is declared and instantiated as follows:

```
ConWHSVehicleServiceTableCheckable hndlr;
hndlr = serviceTable.type() as ConWHSVehicleServiceTableCheckable;
```

This should be declared at the top, and used through the method.

The final change is to `ConWHSVehicleServiceTable.CheckCanEdit()`, which should now use the new pattern, for example as follows:

```
public boolean CheckCanEdit()
{
    if (!(this is ConWHSVehicleServiceTableCheckable))
    {
        Return true; // or throw error!
    }
    ConWHSVehicleServiceTableCheckable checkable;
    checkable = this as ConWHSVehicleServiceTableCheckable;
    if (!checkable.CanEdit())
    {
        //Service order cannot be changed.
        return checkFailed("@ConWHS:ConWHS33");
    }
    return true;
```

```
    }
```

This would result in a nasty client error should the returned class not implement the interface, which isn't desirable! We could use the `DictClass` class to check if the returned object does implement it first and give an error that will make some sense. A better solution is to use test driven development practices. With this method, we will create a test case that tests whether the methods return the expected result for each possible status, and any error would be blocked by the build server. This is covered in `Chapter 11`, *Unit Testing*.

See also...

For more information on interfaces, check out
`https://msdn.microsoft.com/en-us/library/aa892319.aspx`.

Hooking up a number sequence

The number sequence framework is used on most `Details Master` (`Main` tables) and `Details Transaction` (`Worksheet` tables) forms, for example, the sales order number is generated through a number sequence. These used to be hooked up to the form directly, or in the form handler class. This made sense previously as user interface events (new record, delete record, abandon a new record, and so on) would need to be handled. The problem with this is that if we have two forms that handle the same table, we may need to write the code twice.

The new pattern is that it is handled on the table or table handler, but called from the form or form handler class.

We will first need to create a class that defines our number sequences, and then write the code to handle them.

Getting ready

To do this, we should have a table and form complete, ideally using the handler classes for the table and form.

How to do it...

To create the number sequence definition class, follow these steps:

1. First, we will need to add an element to the `NumberSeqModule` base enum; so, locate this enum, right-click on it, and choose **Create extension**.

2. Rename the new base enum extension to `NumberSeqModule.ConWHS`.

3. Open it in the designer and add a new element. Set the **Name** property to `ConWHSVehicleManagement` and the **Label** property to `Vehicle management`.

4. Save and close the designer, and create a new class name: `ConWHSNumberSeqModule`.

5. Change the declaration so that it extends `NumberSeqApplicationModule` and overrides the following methods so that they read as follows:

```
public NumberSeqModule numberSeqModule()
{
    return NumberSeqModule::ConWHSVehicleManagement;
}
/// <summary>
/// Appends the current class to the map that links
/// modules to number sequence data type generators.
/// </summary>
[SubscribesTo(classstr(NumberSeqGlobal),delegatestr(
        NumberSeqGlobal,
        buildModulesMapDelegate))]
static void buildModulesMapSubsciber(Map
                        numberSeqModuleNamesMap)
{
    NumberSeqGlobal::addModuleToMap(
                    classnum(ConWHSNumberSeqModule),
                    numberSeqModuleNamesMap);
}
protected void loadModule()
{
}
```

 Those migrating from Dynamics AX 2012 may remember the manual job that must be run to initialize the number sequence. This is now done automatically by subscribing to `NumberSeqGlobal.buildModulesMapDelegate`.

6. To complete the `loadModule` method, we will define each number sequence from the EDT, and is done in blocks of code. The following code defines sequences for `ConWHSVehicleId` and `ConWHSVehicleServiceId`:

```
protected void loadModule()
{
    NumberSeqDatatype datatype;
    datatype = NumberSeqDatatype::construct();

    // Vehicle number
    datatype.parmDatatypeId(
            extendedtypenum(ConWHSVehicleId));
    // Unique key for the identification of vehicles.
    // The key is used when creating new vehicles
    datatype.parmReferenceHelp(
            literalstr("@ConWHS:ConWHS42"));
    datatype.parmWizardIsContinuous(false);
    datatype.parmWizardIsManual(NoYes::No);
    datatype.parmWizardIsChangeDownAllowed(NoYes::No);
    datatype.parmWizardIsChangeUpAllowed(NoYes::No);
    datatype.parmWizardHighest(999999);
    datatype.parmSortField(1);
    datatype.addParameterType(
                        NumberSeqParameterType::DataArea,
                        true, false);
    this.create(datatype);

    // Vehicle service order
    datatype.parmDatatypeId(
            extendedtypenum(ConWHSVehicleServiceId));
    // Unique key for the identification of service orders.
    // The key is used when creating new services orders
    datatype.parmReferenceHelp(
            literalstr("@ConWHS:ConWHS43"));
    datatype.parmWizardIsContinuous(false);
    datatype.parmWizardIsManual(NoYes::No);
    datatype.parmWizardIsChangeDownAllowed(NoYes::No);
    datatype.parmWizardIsChangeUpAllowed(NoYes::No);
    datatype.parmWizardHighest(999999);
    datatype.parmSortField(2);
    datatype.addParameterType(
                        NumberSeqParameterType::DataArea,
                        true, false);
    this.create(datatype);
}
```

The next part is to update the parameters form, so that we can maintain the new sequence:

1. We will now need to update the parameters form so that we can maintain them. We can save time here with some copying and pasting. Open the design for our `ConWHSVehicleParameters` form, and then the designer for the `InventParameters` form from the Application Explorer.

2. In the form design for `InventParameters`, expand **Data Sources**.

3. Right-click on the `NumberSequenceReference` data source, and choose **Copy**.

4. Change tab to our `ConWHSVehicleParameters` form designer, right-click on the **Data Sources** node, and select **Paste**.

5. We will need to refactor the code that was brought, but we will need to set up the number sequence handling code. Double-click on the `classDeclaration` node of the **Methods** node on the form.

6. Just after the first brace, enter the following lines:

```
Boolean                      runExecuteDirect;
NumberSeqReference           numberSeqReference;
NumberSeqScope               scope;
ConWHSNumberSeqAppModule     numberSeqApplicationModule;
TmpIdRef                     tmpIdRef;
container                    numberSequenceModules;
```

7. We will now need to create code to initialize the number sequence class, which is done by the following method:

```
private void numberSeqPreInit()
{
    runExecuteDirect    = false;

    numberSequenceModules =
            [NumberSeqModule::ConWHSVehicleManagement];
    numberSeqApplicationModule = new
            ConWHSNumberSeqAppModule();
    scope = NumberSeqScopeFactory::createDataAreaScope();
    NumberSeqApplicationModule::createReferencesMulti(
            numberSequenceModules, scope);
    tmpIdRef.setTmpData(
NumberSequenceReference::configurationKeyTableMulti(
            numberSequenceModules));
}
```

8. We will require a second method that performs some further initialization, but requires that the data source be set up. This must, therefore, run after the `super()` call in the `init` method. Write the post `init` initialization code as follows:

```
private void numberSeqPostInit()
{
    boolean sameAsActive =
        numberSeqApplicationModule.sameAsActive();

    numberSequenceReference_ds.object(
        fieldNum(NumberSequenceReference,
                AllowSameAs)).visible(sameAsActive);
    labelSameAs.visible(sameAsActive);
}
```

9. The preceding two methods should be placed above and below the `super()` call in the `init` method, as demonstrated in the following piece of code:

```
public void init()
{
    ConWHSVehicleParameters::Find();
    NumberSeqApplicationModule::loadAll();
    this.numberSeqPreInit();
    super();
    this.numberSeqPostInit();
}
```

10. When we copied the data source from `InventParameters`, it brought over the code as well. The `Active` method was overridden in `InventParameters` for a special case, and it is not required. Delete the `Active` method.

11. Let's cheat again and copy the tab page from `InventParameters`. Select (or open) the form designer for `InventParameters`.

 Normally, I prefer creating everything manually, but adding the number sequence elements to a form saves a lot of time and is relatively risk free from copy and paste errors or omissions.

12. Right-click on the `Tab` control and choose **Copy**.

13. Next, go back to our form's designer, right-click on the `ParameterTab` control and choose **Paste**.

14. Expand the controls, `NumberSeq` and `NumberSeqBody`. Then, delete the `ActionPane` control.

15. Within the `NumberSeq` tab page, expand the `Header` group control.

16. Change the **Text** property of the `StaticText10` control to `Set up number sequences for vehicle management documents`.

17. For consistency, and to avoid potential naming conflicts, rename the following controls:

Original control name	Correct control name
Header	NumberSeqHeader
StaticText10	NumberSeqHeaderText
GridContainer	NumberSeqQuickFilter
Grid	NumberSeqGrid

18. Finally, we don't need the tab page to be automatically declared as a global variable: select the `NumberSeq` tab page control and change the **Auto Declaration** property to `No`.

19. Save and close all designers and code editors.

20. Open the code editor for the `ConWHSVehicleParameters` table.

21. Add a new method that will return the number sequence reference, as shown in the following method:

```
public static NumberSequenceReference  NumRefServiceId()
{
    return NumberSeqReference::
        findReference(
            extendedTypeNum(ConWHSVehicleServiceId));
}
```

 It is convention to place a static method per sequence on the parameters table, and other developers will expect to find these helper functions there.

22. Build the project and look out for compilation errors and correct as required.

The final stage is to integrate the form with the number sequence framework:

1. Open the code editor for the `ConWHSVehicleServiceTableType` handler class.

2. At the top of our class, declare a variable global of type `NumberSeqFormHandler`, as shown here:

```
NumberSeqFormHandler    numberSeqFormHandler;
```

3. Next, create a method to construct an instance, if it is not alreadyin stantiated, as per the following code:

```
protected NumberSeqFormHandler numberSeqFormHandler(
    FormRun _formRun, FormDataSource _serviceTableDS)
{
    if (!numberSeqFormHandler)
    {
        RefRecId localNumSeqId;
        RefFieldId serviceIdField;

        localNumSeqId =
            ConWHSVehicleParameters::
                NumRefServiceId().NumberSequenceId;
        serviceIdField =
                fieldNum(ConWHSVehicleServiceTable,
                        ServiceId);

        numberSeqFormHandler =
            NumberSeqFormHandler::newForm(localNumSeqId,
                                        _formRun,
                                        _serviceTableDS,
                                        serviceIdField);
    }
    return numberSeqFormHandler;
}
```

4. Next, we will need to write the methods that control what happens when the various data source event methods are run. Write the methods as shown here:

```
public void formMethodClose()
{
    if (numberSeqFormHandler)
    {
        numberSeqFormHandler.formMethodClose();
    }
}

public void formMethodDataSourceCreate(
                FormRun _element,
                FormDataSource _serviceTableDS)
{
    this.numberSeqFormHandler(
            _element,
            _serviceTableDS).formMethodDataSourceCreate();
}
```

```
public void formMethodDataSourceDelete(
                    FormRun _element,
                    FormDataSource _serviceTableDS,
                    boolean _forced = false)
{
    this.numberSeqFormHandler(
                    _element,
        _serviceTableDS).formMethodDataSourceDelete(
                                            _forced);
}

public void formMethodDataSourceLinkActive(
                    FormRun _element,
                    FormDataSource _serviceTableDS)
{
    this.numberSeqFormHandler(
        _element,
        _serviceTableDS).formMethodDataSourceLinkActive();
}

public boolean formMethodDataSourceValidateWrite(
                    FormRun _element,
                    FormDataSource _serviceTableDS)
{
    boolean ret = true;

    if (!this.numberSeqFormHandler(
            _element, _serviceTableDS).
                formMethodDataSourceValidateWrite())
    {
        ret = false;
    }

    return ret;
}

public void formMethodDataSourceWrite(
                    FormRun _element,
                    FormDataSource _serviceTableDS)
{
    this.numberSeqFormHandler(
            _element,
            _serviceTableDS).formMethodDataSourceWrite();
}
```

This code does seem a lot, but it is largely the same in most implementations and, with some refactoring, it can simply be copied. The `SalesTableType` class uses this pattern.

5. The next task is to override certain methods on the `ConWHSVehicleServiceTable` table in order to call the methods we have just written.

When reading the following steps, it may seem quicker and easier to call `ConWHSVehicleServiceTable.type().formMethodDataSourceWrite()`. This would carry a significant performance overhead, as the handler would be constructed whenever a method was called.

6. Create a global variable to the form by opening the `classDeclaration` node of the form and typing the following, just after the first opening brace:

```
ConWHSVehicleServiceTableType serviceTableType;
```

7. We now need to hook up the data source event methods to our handler class. The naming scheme for the number sequence methods tells us which to use on each data source event method. The first is `formMethodClose`, so we will need to override the `Close` method at form level. Do so, and enter the following code:

```
public void close()
{
    if (!serviceTableType)
    {
        serviceTableType =
            ConWHSVehicleServiceTable.type();
    }
    serviceTableType.formMethodClose();
    super();
}
```

8. The rest override methods on the `ConWHSVehicleServiceTable` data source. To save time, override the following methods:
   - Create
   - Delete
   - LinkActive
   - ValidateWrite
   - Write

9. These methods should be written as follows:

```
public void create(boolean _append = false)
{
   super(_append);
    if (!serviceTableType)
    {
        serviceTableType =
                ConWHSVehicleServiceTable.type();
    }
    serviceTableType.formMethodDataSourceCreate(
            element, this);
}

public void delete()
{
    if (!serviceTableType)
    {
        serviceTableType =
                ConWHSVehicleServiceTable.type();
    }
    serviceTableType.formMethodDataSourceDelete(
            element, this);

    super();
}

public void linkActive()
{
    if (!serviceTableType)
    {
        serviceTableType =
                ConWHSVehicleServiceTable.type();
    }
    serviceTableType.formMethodDataSourceLinkActive(
            element, this);
    super();
}

public boolean validateWrite()
{
    boolean ret;

    ret = super();

    if (!serviceTableType)
    {
        serviceTableType =
```

```
                        ConWHSVehicleServiceTable.type();
            }
            ret = ret &&
                serviceTableType.formMethodDataSourceValidateWrite(
                    element, this);

            return ret;
        }

        public void write()
        {
            if (!serviceTableType)
            {
                serviceTableType =
                        ConWHSVehicleServiceTable.type();
            }
            serviceTableType.formMethodDataSourceWrite(
                    element, this);
            super();
        }
    }
```

10. Save and close all designers, and build the package.

11. Although we should test at each stage, this requires setting up a number sequence. The following steps are a rough guide, just so we can test the form's behavior.

12. In the web client, open the `Vehicle management` workspace, and click on parameters.

 This is to trigger the `NumberSeqApplicationModule::loadAll()` method.

13. Once open, check that the two records appear in the grid in the **Number sequences** tab.

 If they do not, we either missed adding the call to `NumberSeqApplicationModule::loadAll()` in our init method or the delegate subscription in our `ConWHSNumberSeqModule` class is incorrect.

14. Navigate to **Organizational administration | Number sequences | Number sequences**.

15. Click on **New**.

16. Enter `ConWHSServ` in the **Number sequent code** field (the prefix helps group sequence together) and `Vehicle service id` as **Name**.

17. Set **Scope** to `Company`, and enter the current company ID as **Company**.

18. Configure the **Segments** grid as shown in the following screenshot:

Segment	Value	Length
Constant	VS	2
Alphanumeric	######	6

19. Change the value for Largest to `999999` in the **General** tab.

20. The next part is the first test; expand **References** and click on **Add**.

21. Select the module from the **Area** tab; in our case, `Vehicle management`, and then `Service Id`. Click on **OK**.

22. Next, open `Vehicle management workspace` and create a new service order record to test that the various events work correctly.

How it works...

The process is done in three parts:

- Writing the class that registers our EDT in the number sequence framework
- Updating the parameter form to allow us to maintain the number sequences
- Hooking up the form so that it uses the number sequence.

The number sequence framework is not just a way to get a new number in a prescribed format. It also automatically handles what happens should the record not be saved, and what should happen if we delete a record.

Number sequence set up

Whenever we need a number sequence, we will always use the number sequence framework to declare and maintain the number sequence we need. The first part was to create a class that extends the `NumberSeqApplicationModule` class. This allows us to define the number sequences, and also set up the event that will generate the number sequence setup data.

This makes the number sequence available, and we can create the sequence using the Number Sequence form found in **Organizational administration** | **Number Sequences** | **Number Sequences**. We can create one manually and refer to the sequence defined in our class, or use the **Generate** button.

If we take a look at the `NumberSeqModule::ConWHSVehicleManagement` code, we can see that the extension is seamlessly applied to the base type, even though the extension is named `NumberSeqModule.ConWHS`. This would only work in this package, or packages, that reference it. We have not modified `NumberSeqModule`. The second point to note is that the `ConWHS` prefix we added to the element is required, as all elements inside an enum must be unique across all extensions to it.

It is the convention to be able to see and maintain the number sequences from the module to which they belong. This is why we modified our parameters form. This nicely shows the link to the number sequence reference and the number sequence code that defines how the numbers will be generated and maintained by the framework.

The scope in our case was one module, as defined by the enum; however, we can include more, should we have more complicated requirements. Looking at the implementation in the `InventParameters` form demonstrates how this would be done.

The `TmpIdRef` temporary table is used to generate the query used by the `NumberSequenceReference` data source. This was done in the `executeQuery` method.

There is a new concept demonstrated in the code for the `NumberSequenceReference` data source. The `NumberSequenceCodeId` field is actually a `RecId` relation, but is displayed as human readable. This is done by using a control of type `FormReferenceFieldGroupControl`. The data source field methods, `lookupReference` and `resolveReference` will facilitate this process.

Hooking up the number sequence

The code to tie the various form data source events to the number sequence framework was done in its most abstracted method. This would allow the service order to be extended. For example, if we added a service order type field, we could have a different sequence per type of service order without much rework to the code.

In these methods, we used the keywords `element` and `this`. On a form, the `this` keyword is the most confusing one as it changes depending on where it is used. This is because we have nested class definitions inside the main form class. So, in the context where we used it, this meant `ConWHSVehicleServiceTable_DS`. Within the root form methods, `this` means the `FormRun` object that is created when the form run, but we tend to use `element` instead, as this is always the `FormRun` instance.

There's more...

We could do the same thing to `ConWHSVehicleTable`.

We don't need a form handler class in this case; we can add the methods directly to the `ConWHSVehicleTable` form.

Declare the `NumberSeqFormHandler` class global to the form, and write the initialize method also at form level. Call the method after the `super()` call in `init`.

In each data source method we changed in the recipe, just call `numberSeqFormHandler(element, ConWHSVehicleTable_DS).<method>` directly. The `CustTable` form is a good example of this.

Creating a create dialog for details transaction forms

Most order forms use a dialog when creating a new record. This is because the fields that are needed for order creation are not the same as those displayed on the header section of the form. The dialog can be designed specifically to bring all the fields the user will want, all in view without having to hunt the various fast tabs for the field.

The complexity in the process is the interplay between the order form's data source and the dialog used to create the record. The pattern is the same for 'create forms'.

Getting ready

We should have a Details Transaction form completed, with a form and table handler.

How to do it...

To create the create dialog, follow these steps:

1. Create a new form, suffixing the details form name with `Create`; for example, `ConWHSVehicleServiceTableCreate`.
2. Drag the tables associated with the header record to the form's **Data Source** node; in our example, the `ConWHSVehicleServiceTable` table.
3. Set the properties for the `ConWHSVehicleServiceTable` data source as follows:

Property	Value
Allow Delete	No
Allow Notify	No: we want this to act as a single record dialog and disable most of the events that the data source performs for us
Auto Search	No
Insert At End	No
Insert If Empty	No
Delay Active	No

 We will need to control the behavior of the data source in this case, as it will be called from another, so we have to disable certain user options and events.

4. Override the form's `init` method and write the following piece of code:

```
// global to the form / element
ConWHSVehicleServiceTableForm serviceTableForm;
ConWHSVehicleServiceTableType serviceTableType;
/// <summary>
/// the form must be called with a form handler class
/// </summary>
public void init()
{
    if (element.args())
    {
        if (element.args().caller() is
                ConWHSVehicleServiceTableForm)
        {
            serviceTableForm = element.args().caller();
```

```
        }
    }
    if (!serviceTableForm)
    {
        //Form was incorrectly called
        throw error ("@SYS22996");
    }
    super();
    serviceTableType = ConWHSVehicleServiceTable.type();
}
```

5. Continue to override the `run` and `close` form methods with the following lines of code:

```
public void run()
{
    ConWHSVehicleServiceTable.clear();
    ConWHSVehicleServiceTable_DS.create();
    super();
}

public void close()
{
    if(serviceTableType)
    {
        serviceTableType.formMethodClose();
    }
    super();
}
```

6. We will now need to adjust some of the `ConWHSVehicleserviceTable` data source's methods; start this by overriding the `research` method and writing the following piece of code:

```
public void research(boolean _retainPosition = false)
{
    //super(_retainPosition) Disable the refresh feature.
}

public void reread()
{
    // Allow the DS to reread only if saved
    if (ConWHSVehicleServiceTable.RecId)
    {
        super();
    }
}
```

```
void write()
{
    // this ensures that the form close if
    // the number sequence can't be used
    // and passes a null record back
    try
    {
        serviceTableType.formMethodDataSourceWrite(
                        element, this);
        super();
    }
    catch (Exception::Error)
    {
        ConWHSVehicleServiceTable.RecId = 0;
        serviceTableForm.ParmServiceTableCreated(
                        ConWHSVehicleServiceTable);
        element.close();
        throw Exception::Error;
    }

    this.reread();
    this.refresh();
    // update the handler form with the new record.
    serviceTableForm.ParmServiceTableCreated(
                        ConWHSVehicleServiceTable);
}

void create(boolean append = false)
{
    // only allow create if the current record
    // hasn't been saved
    if (!ConWHSVehicleServiceTable.ServiceId)
    {
        super(append);
        serviceTableType.formMethodDataSourceCreate(
                        element, this);
    }
}
```

7. Apply the `Dialog - basic` pattern to the **Design** node.
8. Complete the Design properties, but set the **Caption** property to `New vehicle service order`.
9. Complete the form layout according to the pattern. Use the following as a guide:
   - Within the **Dialog Commit Content** pattern element, use the `Fields and Field Groups` pattern, and add fields and field groups as desired.

- The **OK** and **Cancel** buttons in the pattern are `Command Buttons`, and the pattern will hide the **Command** property. Make the **OK** button the default button.

10. Next, open the `ConWHSVehicleServiceTableForm` class and add the following methods:

```
public str CreateFormName()
{
    return formStr(ConWHSVehicleServiceTableCreate);
}

public boolean  create()
{
    Args        args = new Args();
    FormRun     createFormRun;

    ConWHSVehicleServiceTable    currentRecord;
    currentRecord    = this.currentRecord();

    args.name(this.CreateFormName());
    args.caller(this);

    createFormRun = classfactory.formRunClass(args);
    createFormRun.init();
    createFormRun.run();
    if (!createFormRun.closed())
    {
        createFormRun.wait();
    }
    if (createFormRun.closedOk())
    {
        return true;
    }
    else
    {
        serviceTableCreated = currentRecord;
        return false;
    }
}
```

11. Open the `ConWHSVehicleServiceTable` form, open the code for the `ConWHSVehicleServiceTable.active` method, and change it so it reads as follows:

```
public void create(boolean _append = false)
{
```

```
ConWHSVehicleServiceTable newServiceTable;
if(formHandler.create())
{
    newServiceTable =
            formHandler.ParmServiceTableCreated();

    if (newServiceTable)
    {
        super(_append);
        ConWHSVehicleServiceTable.data(
                            newServiceTable);
        this.setCurrent();
    }
}
}
```

12. Now we should save all, build, and test. You should test the New button on the Vehicle service form, and also the New button on the workspace.

How it works...

When the user clicks **New** (or the form is opened with a menu item that has **Open Mode** set to Yes), the form triggers a task that calls the current data source's Create method. In our case, we must let the data source do this; however, at this point, we will open the create dialog using the create method we wrote on the form handler.

The create method is a standard way to call any form from code. Never use the form name as a string literal without using an intrinsic function; in this case, formStr.

This calls the create dialog that is set up so the normal form events no longer fire. We will initialize the form from the form handler class in order to pass back the new record.

Once control returns back to our details form, we will replace the data of the record with the record created by the create dialog; this was done in the data([Common]) method.

The key activities can be seen in this diagram:

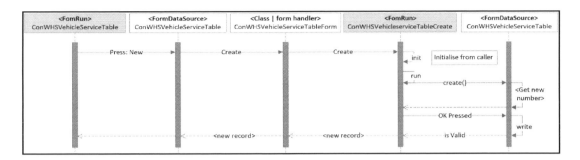

Creating a SysOperation process

This framework provides a simple method to allow us to write routines that can be synchronous or asynchronous with no further effort to allow this to happen.

The complexity in creating a routine that is run in a batch process is how to store the various parameters that the routine may require. This was done in the previous version using the RunBaseBatch framework. This older framework stored this data in a loosely typed blob, and required special handling should the developer add or change the parameters. It had other problems, including the fact that the data and process were tightly coupled.

The SysOperation framework provides a new, and simpler way to create processes. It decouples the data (or parameters) from the process by using a data contract. The data contract is a class that is the parameter for the entry point to the class that performs the process. The framework adds further help in automatically creating a dialog from the data contract, which will use the EDTs in the contract to provide the label, and even drop-down lists based on the table reference on the EDT.

To use the framework, we will need the following three classes:

- **Controller**: This is a class that extends SysOperationServiceController, which controls both the UI and instantiation of the processing class
- **Data contract**: This is a class that contains the properties required by the process class
- **Processing class**: This is the class that actually does the work

We can use this to create any process, and the pattern below can be reused for your own needs. In this recipe we will create a process that the user can use to change the vehicle's group.

How to do it...

The first part of this is to create the data contract, which is done by following these steps:

1. Create a new class named `ConWHSVehicleGroupChangeContract`.

2. Complete the declaration as follows:

```
[DataContract]
class ConWHSVehicleGroupChangeContract
        extends SysOperationDataContractBase
{
    ConWHSVehicleId       vehicleId;
    ConWHSVehicleGroupId vehicleGroupId;
}
```

3. Then add the data member property methods, as shown here:

```
[DataMember]
public ConWHSVehicleId vehicleID(ConWHSVehicleId
                                    _vehicleId = vehicleID)
{
    vehicleID = _vehicleID;
    return vehicleID;
}
[DataMember]
public ConWHSVehicleGroupId vehicleGroupId(
                ConWHSVehicleGroupId
                    _vehicleGroupId = vehicleGroupId)
{
    vehicleGroupId = _vehicleGroupId;
    return vehicleGroupId;
}
```

Now, to create the class that performs the update, let's follow these steps:

1. Create a new class named `ConWHSVehicleGroupChange`.

2. Within the class, declare the data contract as a global variable to the class, as follows:

```
public ConWHSVehicleGroupChangeContract contract;
```

This allows other objects to set this property directly, which needs to be thought through carefully. It is safe in this case as we call the `Run` method with the contract, and call `Validate` within the `Run` method. This allows a caller to set the contract property and call `Validate` before `Run` is called.

3. This class will have the following methods as a minimum:
   - `public Run(<data contract>)`
   - `public boolean Validate()`
   - `public <class> Construct()`

4. Create these methods as follows:

```
public boolean Validate() {
    If (contract.VehicleId() == "")
    {
        //Vehicle Id must be specified
        return checkFailed("@ConWHS:ConWHS45");
    }
    If (!ConWHSVehicleTable::Exist(contract.VehicleId()))
    {
        //Vehicle %1 does not exist
        return checkFailed(strFmt("@ConWHS:ConWHS46",
                    contract.VehicleId()));
    }
    If (contract.VehicleGroupId() == "")
    {
        //Vehicle group is required
        return checkFailed("@ConWHS:ConWHS47");
    }
    If (!ConWHSVehicleGroup::Exist(
                contract.VehicleGroupId()))
    {
        //Vehicle group %1 does not exist
        return checkFailed(strFmt("@ConWHS:ConWHS48",
                    contract.VehicleGroupId()));
    }
    return true;
}
public void Run(ConWHSVehicleGroupChangeContract)
{
    if(!this.Validate())
    {
        return;
    }
    ttsBegin;
    this.UpdateVehicleGroup();
    ttsCommit;
}
private void UpdateVehicleGroup()
{
    ConWHSVehicleTable vehicle =
                ConWHSVehicleTable::Find(
```

```
                                contract.VehicleID(), true);

        if(vehicle.RecId != 0)
        {
            vehicle.VehicleGroupId = contract.VehicleGroupId();
            vehicle.update();
        }
    }
}
```

The next part of the process is to create the controller class, which is done as follows:

1. Create a new class called `ConWHSVehicleGroupChangeController`.
2. Modify `classDeclaration` so that it extends `SysOperationServiceController`.
3. Next, override the `Caption` method and change this to return `Vehicle group change` as a label. This sets the caption, if it is added to a batch queue.
4. Do the same for the `parmDialogCaption` method; this sets the title of the dialog that the framework creates from the data contract.
5. Finally, we will need an entry point, which is a `main` method. The method should be created as per the following lines of code:

```
public static void main(Args _args)
{
    ConWHSVehicleGroupChangeController  controller;

    controller = new ConWHSVehicleGroupChangeController(
                classStr(ConWHSVehicleGroupChange),
                methodStr(ConWHSVehicleGroupChange,
                        Run),
                SysOperationExecutionMode::Synchronous);
    controller.startOperation();
}
```

6. Save the changes and create **Action Menu Item** in our project.
7. Name the menu item as `ConWHSVehicleGroupChangeController` and set the **Object Type** property to **Class** and the **Object** property to `ConWHSVehicleGroupChangeController`.
8. Add this to the `PeriodicTask` submenu of the `ConWHSVehicleManagement` menu and build the project.

How it works...

We will get a dialog with a field created automatically from the contract. We can even submit it to the batch queue. Pretty cool, and very little additional effort!

This witchcraft does deserve an explanation.

As our class extends `SysOperationServiceController`, we get a lot of functionality, the first being that it can construct a dialog from the data contract. However, how did it know?

When the `new` method executed, the framework looked at the `Run` method and determined the contract from the method's input parameter.

The call to `startOperation` caused the system to build the UI and handle the code execution based on what the user does. The dialog is constructed using the EDTs specified in the data member methods. Since we constructed the EDTs correctly with reference to the main table, it can also provide a simple lookup for us.

This explains why the new method requires the class and method names, but the third parameter is an execution mode. This comes into its own if we execute the controller programmatically. **Synchronous** means it will run in line with the current process, unless the user is elected to Run in the background. If this was chosen, the execution method would have changed to `ScheduledBatch`.

 The `classStr` and `methodStr` intrinsic functions, as explained in the previous chapters, are used to check whether the element the functions refer to exists at compile time.

If you run this process twice, you will see the previous options are remembered and act as defaults. This is because the contract is serialized and deserialized to the user's usage data.

There's more...

There is another method to write the `Main` method in the controller class. This is to specify the class and method in the menu item's **Parameter** property, for instance, `ConWHSVehicleGroupChange.Run`. We can then use the `initializeFromArgs` method to build the controller. This is in common use, but since this property is free text, the compiler will not pick up that this value is invalid.

Executing code using the batch framework

To force the process through the batch framework, we will use the execution modes: `ReliableAsynchronous` and `ScheduledBatch`.

Both of these methods submit jobs to the batch server for execution, where the `ReliableAsynchronous` method auto-deletes the jobs after execution.

The jobs do not execute immediately, but within a minute of submission; the batch server polls for waiting jobs every minute. We should use this method to perform asynchronous or scheduled jobs that require heavy processing.

Programmatically speaking, we wouldn't want to use the `ScheduledBatch` mode. This would be set based on the user choosing to run as a background task.

To submit the task as `ReliableAsynchronous`, simply change the code that constructs the controller to use this execution mode. On execution, you may notice that the information message indicates that nothing was done, but if you wait for about a minute and check the vehicle record, you will see that it has succeeded. You can also see the batch history for this.

Calling a process from a form

The example in this recipe simply demonstrates the framework, but the example is not particularly useful. To do so, it would be better to call the process from the vehicle form and default the parameters to the current vehicles.

To do this, we will need to fetch the constructed contract and update it with the record set by the caller from the `Args` object.

The following code does this:

```
public static void main(Args _args)
{
    ConWHSVehicleGroupChangeController   controller;
    ConWHSVehicleTable   vehicle;

    switch (_args.dataset())
    {
        case tableNum(ConWHSVehicleTable):
            vehicle = _args.record();
            break;
    }
    if(vehicle.RecId == 0)
    {
        //Active buffer required.
```

```
        throw error ("@SYS25821");
    }
    controller = new ConWHSVehicleGroupChangeController(
            classStr(ConWHSVehicleGroupChange),
            methodStr(ConWHSVehicleGroupChange,
                    Run),
            SysOperationExecutionMode::Synchronous);

    ConWHSVehicleGroupChangeContract contract;
    contract = controller.getDataContractObject('_contract');
    if(!contract)
    {
        //Function %1 was called with an invalid value
        throw error (
            strFmt("@SYS23264",
                classStr(ConWHSVehicleGroupChangeController)));
    }
    contract.VehicleGroupId(vehicle.VehicleGroupId);
    contract.VehicleId(vehicle.VehicleId);
    controller.startOperation();
    if(FormDataUtil::isFormDataSource(vehicle))
    {
        //This will call the table's data source's research
        // method to refresh the data from the table.
        // The true parameter will keep the current record
        FormDataUtil::getFormDataSource(vehicle).research(true);
    }
}
```

We will then need to add the action menu item to our form. On the main `FormActionPane` control, add a new Action Pane Tab, and set the **Caption** property to `Vehicles`. Create a button group with the **Text** property set to `@SYS9342`.

Finally, drag the action menu item to the button group and set the following properties:

Property	Value
Data Source	`ConWHSVehicleTable`: This sets `args.Record()`
Needs Record	`Yes`: This disables the menu item if there is no current record
Save Record	`Yes`: This is default, but we could end up with an error due to optimistic concurrency
Multi Select	`No`: If multiple records are selected, disable the button

Build and test the new feature with at least two vehicles to prove that the values are not defaulting from your user's usage data.

Using the data contract to make changes to the dialog

Let's take a step back to the point where we were calling the `main` method of `ConWHSVehicleGroupChangeController` directly.

The system very cleverly constructs the user interface; it does this simply by adding the data contract's data member directly to the dialog. There are some simple changes we can make to the data contract to control how they are displayed.

We can make these changes by altering the decoration at the top of each data member. The following examples are useful for this:

`SysOperationLabel("..."),`	This sets the label displayed on the dialog
`SysOperationHelpText("...");`	This sets the help text for the resulting control
`SysOperationDisplayOrder ("...")`	This causes the control to be placed first in the resulting dialog

The completed code for the data member methods is as follows:

```
[DataMember,
 SysOperationControlVisibility(false)]
public ConWHSVehicleId VehicleId(
        ConWHSVehicleId _vehicleId = vehicleId)
{
    vehicleId = _vehicleId;
    return vehicleId;
}

//New vehicle group
//Please select a new vehicle group for the vehicle
[DataMember,
 SysOperationLabel(literalStr("@ConWHS:ConWHS50")),
 SysOperationHelpText(literalStr("@ConWHS:ConWHS51")),
 SysOperationDisplayOrder('1')]
public ConWHSVehicleGroupId VehicleGroupId(
        ConWHSVehicleGroupId _vehicleGroupId = vehicleGroupId)
{
    vehicleGroupId = _vehicleGroupId;
    return vehicleGroupId;
}
```

Build and test the new form and feel free to test the other `SysOperation` attributes. We don't need the `Attribute` suffix in Operations.

Adding an interface to the SysOperation framework

We can do a lot by just decorating the contract data methods but, sometimes, we need more control. This recipe steps through adding more control to the user interface created by the `SysOperation` framework.

Getting ready

We just need an existing SysOperation process class that we wish to add a customized interface to.

If you are following on from the previous recipe, remove the `SysOperationControlVisibility` attribute from the `VehicleId` data method.

How to do it...

To add the user interface, please follow these steps:

1. Create a class named `ConWHSVehicleGroupChangeUIBuilder`. Add `extendsSysOperationAutomaticUIBuilder` to the class declaration.
2. We need two dialog fields that we will later bind to the data contract; the completed `classDeclaration` should look like this:

```
class ConWHSVehicleGroupChangeUIBuilder
    extends SysOperationAutomaticUIBuilder
{
    DialogField vehicleIdField;
    DialogField vehGroupIdField;
}
```

3. We will now need to bind the contract's data member methods to the dialog fields. This is done in the `postBuild` method. Override the `postBuild` method with the following piece of code:

```
public void postBuild()
{
    ConWHSVehicleGroupChangeContract contract;
    super();
    contract = this.dataContractObject();

    vehicleIdField = this.bindInfo().getDialogField(
            contract,
            methodStr(ConWHSVehicleGroupChangeContract,
                    VehicleId));
    vehGroupIdField = this.bindInfo().getDialogField(
            contract,
            methodStr(ConWHSVehicleGroupChangeContract,
                    VehicleGroupId));

}
```

4. In order to handle dialog field events, we will need to create suitable methods and register them as an override. Create a method called `validateVehicleGroup`, as shown here:

```
public boolean validateVehicleGroupId(FormStringControl
    _control)
{
    ConWHSVehicleGroupChangeContract localContract;
    ConWHSVehicleGroupChange localValChange;

    localContract = new
        ConWHSVehicleGroupChangeContract();
    localContract.vehicleId(vehicleIdField.value());
    localContract.vehicleGroupId(_control.valueStr());

    localValChange = ConWHSVehicleGroupChange::Construct();
    localValChange.contract = localContract;
    return localValChange.validate();
}
```

The method declaration has to match the method we will register as an override. We can achieve this by overriding the required method on a form control of the right type. The first parameter will always be the form control object that triggered the event.

5. Now that we have a validate method, we will need to hook it to the dialog field's event. In the `postBuild` method overriden earlier, add the following lines at the end of the method:

```
vehGroupIdField.registerOverrideMethod(
    methodStr(FormStringControl, validate),
    methodStr(ConWHSVehicleGroupChangeUIBuilder,
        validateVehicleGroupId),
    this);
```

Nearly done! However, we haven't handled hiding the vehicle ID field if it was called from a vehicle record. We can't determine this from within the UI builder class; only the controller's `main` method knows this. This means we will need a mechanism to tell the UI builder whether or not to hide the field. Since we attach the UI builder to the data contract, we will add a hidden field to the data contract, as follows:

1. First, change the decoration in `classDeclaration` of `ConWHSVehicleGroupChangecontract` so that it is associated with the UI Builder:

```
[DataContract, SysOperationContractProcessing(
        classStr(ConWHSVehicleGroupChangeUIBuilder))]
```

2. Then add a variable declaration to `classDeclaration`, as follows:

```
NoYesId hideVehicleId;
```

3. Add a data member method for the variable with the `visibility` attribute:

```
[DataMemberAttribute,
  SysOperationControlVisibilityAttribute(false)]
public NoYesId HideVehicleId(
    NoYesId _hideVehicleId = hideVehicleId)
{
    hideVehicleId = _hideVehicleId;
    return hideVehicleId;
}
```

4. Finally, we will need to modify our controller's `main` method to handle the case where it was called from a vehicle record, which is done like this:

```
public static void main(Args _args)
{
    ConWHSVehicleGroupChangeController  controller;
    ConWHSVehicleTable  vehicle;
    switch (_args.dataset())
```

```
        {
            case tableNum(ConWHSVehicleTable):
                vehicle = _args.record();
                break;
        }
        controller = new ConWHSVehicleGroupChangeController(
                    classStr(ConWHSVehicleGroupChange),
                    methodStr(ConWHSVehicleGroupChange,
                                Run),
            SysOperationExecutionMode::Synchronous);

        ConWHSVehicleGroupChangeContract contract =
                    controller.getDataContractObject(
                        '_contract');
        if(!contract)
        {
            //Function %1 was called with an invalid value
            throw error (
                strFmt("@SYS23264",
                classStr(ConWHSVehicleGroupChangeController)));
        }
        controller.initParmDefault();
        controller.loadFromSysLastValue();
        controller.parmShowDialog(true);
        contract.HideVehicleId(false);

        if(vehicle.RecId != 0)
        {
            contract.VehicleGroupId(vehicle.VehicleGroupId);
            contract.VehicleId(vehicle.VehicleId);
            contract.hideVehicleId(true);
        }

        controller.saveLast();
        controller.startOperation();
        //vehicle.IsDataSource() is deprecated
        if(FormDataUtil::isFormDataSource(vehicle))
        {
            FormDataUtil::getFormDataSource(vehicle).
                                        research(true);

        }
    }
```

5. Save all and build the project to test how this works.

How it works...

By using this method, we have added a coupling to the process class structure by means of the binding to the UI builder. In order to avoid this, we would use inheritance to define a data contract base class and extend it for the purposes of this binding.

The process may seem a little complicated at first but, when we break this down, it will become clearer what is actually happening.

The first task was to declare to the `DialogField` variables that we want added to the resulting dialog, and then to bind them to the data contract data methods. However, in order for this to work, we had to bind the UI builder class to the data contract. We did this by adding the `SysOperationContractProcessing` attribute to the data contract.

Once this is done, the `DialogField` variables are now bound to the data contract methods. We then wrote a method to validate the vehicle group control, and bound this to the control's validate event using the control's `registerOverrideMethod` method.

Once this is all done, the dialog created by the framework can be validated interactively, allowing the user to correct any errors without having to start again.

5
Business Intelligence

In this chapter, we will cover the following recipes:

- Creating aggregate dimensions
- Creating aggregate measurements
- Creating aggregate data entities
- Creating and using key performance indicators

Introduction

Business intelligence (often referred to as BI or analytics) has evolved a great deal in this release; many elements of BI that were devolved to external applications are now first class citizens of the development environment. We will now define dimensions and measurements in an Operations project that are built and released as any other Operations project. Our role in this is to provide the basis which the business intelligence designer will use to develop powerful business intelligence solutions.

When developing a BI solution, it is usual to create a new project that references the packages it analyzes. This allows the solutions to be developed at the same time, and also allows the analytics and other projects to be deployed independently. Of course, if the data structures change in a way that breaks the analytics solution, the build server will usually highlight this.

When planning this type of work, the analytics should be designed along with the main solution design and not as an afterthought, even though we will start analytics later in the project lifecycle. This results in the data structures being correctly designed with analytics and reporting in mind; when we come to develop the analytics element of the project, we should be able to do so without changes to the underlying tables. Changes to underlying tables could be considered like adding a basement garage to your house.

The recipes in this chapter are based on creating an analytics project for customer invoice analysis.

Creating aggregate dimensions

Aggregate dimensions are used to define attributes that splice the data they are associated with. The dimension is therefore based on a table or view and will have one or more attributes, which are the ways we will allow the data to be spliced. Defining the data in this way allows exceptionally fast data analysis. This is because the data is expanded into a data warehouse database automatically by Operations.

In some cases, you may want to create a view to simplify the process, in which case, use the view as the Table property.

Getting ready

Before we start, it is best to create a new model for a new package and add references as required. These are usually, `Application Platform`, `Application Foundation`, `Application Suite`, and any other whose elements we intend to use. When delivering an implementation project, it is usually best to create one package for analytics.

How to do it...

Dimensions should be based on views in order to denormalize the data. This is to let the users see name and description fields, and not the identity columns, so the first part is to create or extend a view to allow this data to be easily accessed.

To create the view, follow these steps:

1. Create a new view called `ConWHSVehicleTableExpanded`.
2. Add the `ConWHSVehicleTable` table as the root data source, and `ConWHSVehicleGroup` as a child data source, as shown in the following screenshot:

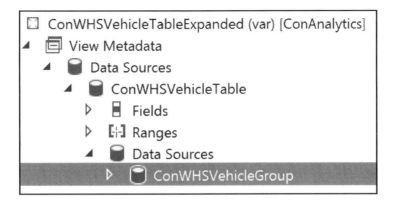

3. Either set the **Use Relations** property on the ConWHSVehicleGroup data source, or add a relation manually.
4. Add all non-system fields from the ConWHSVehicleTable table, and the Description field from ConWHSVehicleGroup. Rename this field to VehicleGroupDescription and set the **Label** property to Vehicle Group.
5. Save and close the view.

The following steps create the dimension attribute based on the view:

1. In the project, add a new item, and in the **Add New Item** dialog, select **Analytics** from the left-hand list and **Aggregate Dimension** from the right.
2. Name the new item as ConWHSVehicles. This has to be unique amongst other aggregate dimensions.
3. Set the **Table** property to ConWHSVehicleTableExpanded, as this is the table that has the data we need.

 The system has determined that the main data source of the view has a primary key and has used this to correctly create the attribute used as a unique key; do not delete this key. All attributes that are company-specific should include the DataAreaId field.

4. Right-click on the @ **Attributes** node and choose **New Dimension Attribute**.
5. Change **Name** and the **Name Field** properties to VehicleGroupDescription.
6. Right-click on the attribute and choose **New Dimension Field Reference**.
7. Specify VehicleGroupDescription as the **Dimension Field** property, and then add DataAreaId.

Adding a field reference will automatically set the attribute's **Name** property, which is why we add the fields in this order.

8. Repeat this for the `VehicleType` and `Description` fields.
9. Right-click on the **Hierarchies** node and choose **New Dimension Attribute Hierarchy**.
10. Right-click on the new attribute hierarchy and choose **New Dimension Hierarchy Level**. Add a level for **Source Attribute**`VehicleType` first, and then `VehicleGroup`.
11. The result should look like the following screenshot:

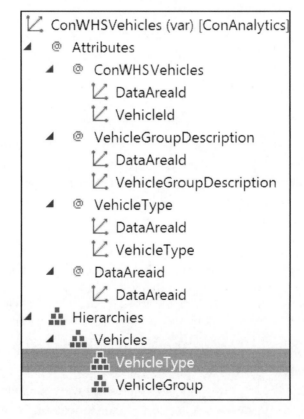

12. Save and close the designer.

How it works...

This is used as a definition when we create the aggregate measures. The view was a necessary step in order to simplify access to the data in a way that users can relate. We will then define attributes. Although we add the aggregate dimension to the aggregate measure, the user will use the attributes to splice the data.

We based the attribute on the vehicle table, so we can easily relate this to the service table, which is what we will be analyzing. The hierarchy is not mandatory, and it is used when we want to predefine the analytic hierarchies at this time.

See also

For more information on Analytics in Operations, please visit *Analytics* (`https://ax.help.dynamics.com/en/wiki/analytics/`)

Creating aggregate measures

These can be thought of as cubes from prior releases of Operations and form that basis to which we analyze our data. They contain the aggregate data that the dimensions splice or pivot on.

Getting ready

You may find that the drop-downs used in properties may not work in this recipe; to resolve this, simply build the project before you start.

How to do it...

First, we will need to create a view that flattens the service data into one view. To do this, follow these steps:

1. Create a new view called `ConWHSVehicleServiceExpanded`.
2. Add the `ConWHSVehicleSErviceTable` table as the root data source and `ConWHSVehicleServiceLine` as a child data source, as shown in the following screenshot:

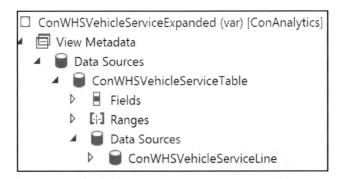

3. Either set **Use Relations** property on the `ConWHSVehicleServiceLine` data source, or add a relation manually.
4. Add all non-system fields from the `ConWHSVehicleServiceTable` table, and the `ItemId` field from `ConWHSVehicleServiceLine`.
5. Save and close the view.

We can now create the aggregate measure, which is done by following these steps:

1. In the project, add a new item, and in the **Add New Item** dialog, select **Analytics** from the left-hand list and **Aggregate Measurement** from the right.
2. Name the new item as `ConWHSVehicleServiceMeasure`.

 You may notice that many existing aggregate measures are suffixed with `Cube`; this is the legacy naming convention from AX 2012.

3. The designer will open with a default measure group node named `MeasureGroup1`. Rename this to `ServiceInformation`.
4. Set the **Table** property to `ConWHSVehicleServiceExpanded`.
5. We will add three measures, a count of service records, a count of items used, and a count of vehicles. Right-click on the **Measures** node and choose **New Measure**; add them using the following settings:

Name	Default Aggregate	Field
ServiceRecords	Count	ServiceId
Items	Count	ItemId
Vehicles	Count	VehicleId

 To add sum aggregates for value or quantity fields, set the **Default Aggregate** property to Sum.

6. Let's add the aggregate dimensions first by expanding the **Dimensions** node and noticing that it has already created two dimensions: Company and Date_.

 The underscore is to avoid problems should this be deployed to **SQL Server Analysis Services (SSAS)**. If you save without this underscore, you will get a warning. This also occurs for other Transact-SQL keywords, such as Description.

7. Rename the Date_ dimension and the sub-node to ServiceDate, as shown in the following screenshot:

```
▲  ↙ ServiceDate
    ▲  ☐ ServiceDate
        ☐ BIDateDimensionValue.Date == ConWHSVehicleServiceExpanded.
```

8. It will have guessed the relation for the Company dimension automatically; however, it has no idea how to relate the Date_ dimension to the view. Select the relation node (the final node under the ServiceDate dimension) and set the **Related Field** property to ServiceDateRequested.

9. The completed ServiceDate and Company dimensions should look like the following screenshot:

```
▲  ↙ Company
    ▲  ☐ Company
        ☐ BICompanyView.id == ConWHSVehicleServiceExpanded.DataAreaId
▲  ↙ ServiceDate
    ▲  ☐ ServiceDate
        ☐ BIDateDimensionValue.Date == ConWHSVehicleServiceExpanded.ServiceDateRequested
```

10. Let's add our `ConWHSVehicles` aggregate dimension: drag the `ConWHSVehicles` aggregate dimension from the project to the **Dimensions** node.

11. In this case, if you expand the new dimension, you will see that that the `VehicleId` relation is set for us; if this is not set, we must specify it.

12. Let's add a standard dimension to our aggregate measure. From **Application Explorer**, locate the `ReleasedProducts` aggregate dimension from **Analytics | Perspectives | Aggregate Dimensions**.

13. Drag `ReleasedProducts` to the **Dimensions** node.

14. This time, the relation is not set. To do this, set the **Dimension Attribute** property to `ReleasedProducts`.

 This was selected as this is the key attribute and has `ItemId` as the key attribute. Convention guides us to know that the attribute with the same name as the aggregate dimension is the key attribute. Of course, we can simply open the aggregate dimension in the designer to check.

15. Select the new relation and the **Related Field** property to `ItemId`. The current state of our design should be as in the following screenshot:

⬡ ConWHSVehicleServiceMeasure (var) [ConAnalytics]
- ◢ [ıl] ConWHSVehicleServiceExpanded
  - ◢ @ Attributes
  - ◢ ⬡ Measures
    - ⬡ ServiceRecords
    - ⬡ Items
    - ⬡ Vehicles
  - ◢ ⟋ Dimensions
    - ▷ ⟋ Company
    - ◢ ⟋ ServiceDate
      - ◢ ⬚ ServiceDate
        - ⬚ BIDateDimensionValue.Date == ConWHSVehicleServiceExpanded.ServiceDateRequested
    - ◢ ⟋ ConWHSVehicles
      - ◢ ⬚ ConWHSVehicleTableExpanded
        - ⬚ ConWHSVehicleTableExpanded.VehicleId == ConWHSVehicleServiceExpanded.VehicleId
    - ◢ ⟋ ReleasedProducts
      - ◢ ⬚ InventTableExpanded
        - ⬚ InventTableExpanded.ItemId == ConWHSVehicleServiceExpanded.ItemId

16. Finally, let's add a custom attribute to the aggregate measure. This is not normally done, because they can't be reused elsewhere. Right-click on the @ **Attributes** node and select **New Dimension Attribute**.

17. Complete as before, the result should be as per the following screenshot:

18. Save and close the designer.

19. Build the project and perform database synchronization.

Next, we will configure the entity refresh batch job.

1. In order for the data to be deployed and automatically refreshed, navigate to **System administration** and choose **Setup | Entity Store**.

2. Select the entities that should be refreshed and click on **Refresh**.

3. In the **Configure refresh** dialog, expand **Run in the background**, click on **Recurrence**, and configure as per the following screenshot:

Only make this as frequent as it needs to be. As this will run for the selected entities, we can configure entities so that they are refreshed at different rates.

4. Press **OK** on the **Define recurrence** dialog, and **OK** on the **Configure refresh** dialog.

How it works...

The aggregate measure defines the values we wish to display and the dimensions by which we will filter and splice the data. It may seem odd that we don't have measures such as `VehiclesServicedThisYear`, but this isn't a function of a measure. This is accomplished by a combination of the `ServiceDate` dimension and the `Vehicles` measure.

The entity refresh creates and maintains the data in the data warehouse database. This is `AxDW` on development environments, and for the cloud deployed sandbox, you will get this from LCS.

If you open the SQL Server Management Studio, the tables are created as follows:

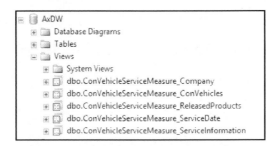

You can query this data to diagnose why measures or **key performance indicators (KPIs)** may not work as expected.

Creating aggregate data entities

Aggregate data entities allow us to use aggregate measures in the same way we would use a table. They can also be used to expose the aggregate data through OData. This example will be used to create a chart form part in the next recipe.

Getting ready

We will need an aggregate measure for this, so we are following on from the previous two recipes.

How to do it...

To create the aggregate data entity, follow these steps:

1. Create new item by choosing **Analytics** from the left pane of the **Add New Item** dialog and **Aggregated Data Entity** from the right. Name the entity `ConWHSVehicleServiceDataEntity`.
2. Drag the `ConVehicleServiceMeasure` aggregate measure to the **DataSource** node.
3. Expand the **Measures** node and drag all three measures to the **Fields** node.
4. We can also add dimensions as fields; in our case, we will need the `ServiceDate` dimension. Drag `ServiceDate` to the **Fields** node.
5. To make this more useful as an aggregate data entity, we will choose a specific attribute of this dimension. Set the **Attribute** property to `Month`.
6. This aggregate data entity should be grouped by vehicle; to add the Vehicle ID to the field list, right-click on the **Fields** node and select **New Mapped Field**.
7. Set the properties of this, as shown here, and set them in the order listed as follows:

Property	Value
Name	Vehicle
Measure Group	`ServiceInformation`: this is what we renamed from `Measure1` when we created the aggregate measure.
Dimension	ConWHSVehicles
Attribute	ConWHSVehicles
Extended Data Type	`ConWHSVehicleId`: this should be set automatically

8. We will now need to build the project, and then synchronize the database.

How it works...

Aggregate data entities are similar to the other entities, in that, they can be seen as tables, used to export data to Excel, and therefore, can be used for analytics outside of **PowerBI**. They are actually stored as views.

We can also use them as data sources in chart controls, giving more easily digestible information to the user without navigating away.

Creating and using key performance indicators

Key performance indicators, in Operations provide a simple way to create metrics that can be viewed within Operations. In our case, we shall create a KPI that targets a number of service orders in a month.

Getting ready

First, we should have created an aggregate measure before we start this.

How to do it...

Follow these steps to create the KPI:

1. Create a new item; select **Analytics** from the left-hand list and **Key Performance Indicator** from the right.
2. Set the **Name** field to `ConWHSVehicleServiceThisMonth` and press **Add**.
3. Drag the `ConWHSVehicleServiceMeasure` aggregate measure from the project onto the KPI. This sets the **Measurement** property for us.
4. Complete the remaining properties, as follows:

Property	Value
Label	Service orders
Bad Threshold	20
Good Threshold	1

Scoring Pattern	LessIsBetter
Menu Item Name	Must leave this blank

5. On the **Value** node, set the properties as follows:

Property	Value
Measure Group	ServiceInformation
Measure	ServiceRecords

 We are basing our KPI on the number of service orders in a month.

6. Expand the **Value** node, and add a new range to the **Ranges** node and configure the properties, as shown here:

Property	Value
Dimension	ServiceDate
Attribute	Month
Name	MonthRange

 The default **Period** is Current, and the KPI will know that we mean the current period based on the **Attribute** property.

7. We can now add trends. Under the **Trend** node, create a new trend and set the properties as shown here:

Property	Value
Dimension	ServiceDate
Attribute	Week
Name	WeeklyTrend
Item Count	10, this means 10 weeks in this case

Label	Weekly trend

8. Now, we should create the top trend, which shows the top n contributory factors to the value. Complete the new trend as follows:

Property	Value
Trend Type	TopTrend
Dimension	ConWHSVehicles
Attribute	VehicleGroupDescription
Name	TopTrend
Label	Vehicle groups
Item Count	5, this means the top 5 vehicle groups

9. Finally, let's add a bottom trend, which is done as follows:

Property	Value
Trend Type	BottomTrend
Dimension	ConWHSVehicles
Attribute	VehicleGroupDescription
Name	BottomTrend
Label	Vehicle groups
Item Count	5, this means the bottom 5 vehicle groups

 We will choose a different measure for this, but we can use the same measure for both.

10. You can create multiple trends of each type, and they will appear as options to the user. Try and create a top trend for vehicle types.
11. Save and close the designer.

To test our KPI we should create a tile for the KPI so we can add it to a workspace. This is done by the following steps:

1. Create a new tile called `ConWHSVehicleServiceThisMonthTile`.
2. Drag the `ConWHSVehicleServiceThisMonth` KPI onto the tile in the designer. This sets the **Type** property to `KPI` and the **KPI** property to `ConWHSVehicleServiceThisMonth`.
3. Set **Label** to `Vehicle service orders` and the **Size** property to `Wide`.
4. Save and close the designer.

Add the tile to the vehicle management workspace form:

1. We will need to add this to a workspace. Locate the `ConWHSVehicleWorkspace` form in Application Explorer.
2. Right-click on the form and choose **Create extension**.
3. Change the suffix so that it is named `ConWHSVehicleWorkspace.ConAnalytics`.
4. Open the form in the designer.
5. Right-click on the `PanoramaSectionTiles` tab page and choose **New | Tile Button**.
6. Set the **Name** and **Tile** properties to `ConWHSVehicleServiceThisMonthTile`.

Build the project and synchronize the database:

1. Right-click on the project and choose **Properties**.
2. Change **Synchronize Database on Build** to `True`.
3. Press **OK**.
4. Build the project.

To test the KPI, follow these steps:

1. Open the Operations client; in our case, we can just open the following URL:

   ```
   https://usnconeboxax1aos.cloud.onebox.dynamics.com/?cmp=usmf
   &mi=ConWHSVehicleWorkspace
   ```

2. If you receive an error that the KPI does not exist, rebuild the project with the **Synchronize Database on Build** project property set to `True`.
3. The KPI will display with no data; to set this up, navigate to **System administration | Setup | Data cache | Data cache parameters**.
4. Select the **Cache refresh** tab page.
5. If you have a batch group set up for system jobs, enter this in the **Batch group** field; otherwise, leave it blank.

6. Click on **Initialize batch job**.

7. Open **System administration** I **Inquiries** I **Batch jobs**.

8. The batch job, `Data cache refresh batch`, will be in the list and will remain executing. This may seem unusual for batch jobs, as they normally have a recurrence; however, this job runs continuously.

9. If the batch job is not executing, ensure that the `Microsoft Dynamics 365 for Operations Batch Management Service` windows service is running.

10. Wait around a minute for the data to process and test the workspace again.

Testing the workspace:

1. First, you should create some test data so we can test if our KPI works correctly. We will probably need around 30 orders for multiple vehicle types and groups.

2. The KPI tile contains a concise summary of the KPI and will resemble the following screenshot:

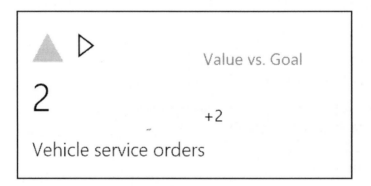

3. If you click on the tile, you are taken to the KPI view.

4. In this view, the user can change the defaults we supplied in the KPI, change the trend views, and apply different filters to those supplied. The view should look like the following screenshot:

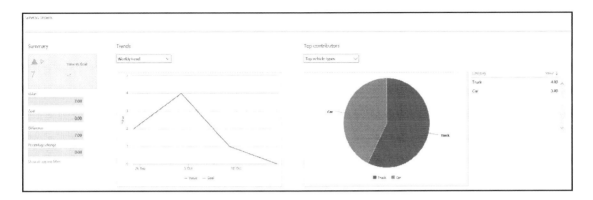

How it works...

The simple KPI definition is a powerful tool. The KPI definition has enough information to define both the tile and the KPI workspace.

There's more...

Power BI is a business intelligence tool used to design and view BI reports. A good resource to learn about Power BI is available for the following link:

Guided Learning for Power BI (`https://powerbi.microsoft.com/en-us/guided-learning/?WT.mc_id=PBIService_GettingStarted`)

In order to leverage Power BI, a few more steps are required.

The basic steps are as follows:

1. Ensure that you have set up your O365 accounts with access to Power BI Free or Power BI Pro. To sign up for a free account, use this link:

   `https://powerbi.microsoft.com/en-us/documentation/powerbi-admin-free-with-custom-azure-directory/`

2. Register the Power BI app and get a Client ID and Application Key. The details of this are listed here:

```
https://powerbi.microsoft.com/en-us/documentation/powerbi-develope
r-register-a-web-app/
```

3. Open Operations and navigate to **System administration** | **Setup** | **Power BI** and complete the form with the Client ID from the previous step; an example set up is shown in the following table:

Field	Value
Azure AD authority URL	`https://login.windows.net` (default)
Azure AD Power BI resource URI	`https://analysis.windows.net/powerbi/api`(default)
Azure AD tenant	`contoso.com` - the tenant you signed up with.
Client ID	From the previous step
Application key	From the previous step
Redirect URL	`https://<production url>/oauth`
Power BI API Address	`https://api.powerbi.com/beta/myorg`

Also see the following link:

```
https://ax.help.dynamics.com/en/wiki/configuring-powerbi-integration/
```

In order to author and distribute Power BI reports, use the following link:

```
https://blogs.msdn.microsoft.com/dynamicsaxbi/2016/06/23/authoring-and-distribu
ting-power-bi-reports-with-dynamics-ax7/
```

When following this for a cloud solution, where you want to see recent data from the sandbox environment, do it on the sandbox server. You can connect using the AxDW database defined in LCS, but suffixed with `database.windows.net`. Connect using the `Database` tab, as the AxDW account won't have access to the server.

6
Security

In this chapter, we will cover the following recipes:

- Creating privileges
- Creating duties
- Creating security roles
- Creating policies

Introduction

When designing the security model, there are three methods depending on the solution. For ISV solutions, the security should be designed into the main package and shipped together. This also goes for partner solutions for new customer implementations when the package is a discreet package of functionality. Sometimes, customers need roles customized for their own needs, and these roles may encompass privileges for both new and existing functionalities. In this case, a new package should be developed. Having a separate package also aids work planning efficiency.

Should the end user customer develop their own security model, this should always be in a new package; although, the same functionality can be achieved within the application.

The security model in Operations is broken down into the following structure:

- Roles
- Duties
- Privileges
- Policies

The primary structure of the security model includes Process cycles, Roles, Duties, and Privileges. We will explore these first before taking a look at Policies and Code Permissions.

Entry points define the access level granted to methods of entry to Operations functionality, such as menu items and services.

Permissions define access to tables and fields, server methods (such as a service call where the code won't run under the user's security context), and form controls (buttons, fields, or other controls placed on a form).

As a part of the functional requirements definition, the business processes are analyzed, along with the roles that perform them. The business processes will then be mapped to the Operations system processes. This is used for many purposes, including gap fit level, training plans, testing plans, and so on. This method of analyzing roles and processes also fits nicely into the Operations security model, allowing the security model to be designed based on this.

The security model that we design and implement should always be simple to use, following the pattern of the standard roles provided by Microsoft. An important design principle is to think of the user's roles, and not to think of specific users, which should result in the following outcomes:

- Reduced number of roles
- Less complicated assignment of users to roles
- Roles are easier to maintain, with reduced risk of errors, such as the unintended assignment of a privilege to a user

Creating privileges

Privileges are normally created for each menu item (display, output, or action) for an access level. Every menu item should be in a privilege, but you can add more than one menu item to a privilege if they must never be assigned different permissions, such as menu items that point to the same form. This is the most granular level, and will be grouped into duties and roles later.

Since the privilege assigns the access level, we will usually have two--to provide view only, and to maintain (full) access rights.

Getting ready

We will just need an Operations project open in Visual Studio.

How to do it...

To create a privilege to provide view access to the vehicle form, follow these steps:

1. Choose to add a new item to the project.
2. In the **Add New Item** dialog, select **Security** from the left-hand list and **Security Privilege** from the right.
3. Enter ConWHSVehicleTableView in the **Name** field and click on **Add**.
4. Complete the **Description** property; this should describe to the security administrator what this privilege grants access to.
5. Complete the **Label** property by giving it a short description to the security administrator, such as View vehicle records.

> It can be a good idea to include a text or even a prefix in the text to uniquely identify which module this security element relates. The security administrator will only be able to easily see the **Label** and **Description** properties, and it could be easy to confuse the security element with another.

6. In the designer, drag the ConWHSVehicleTable menu item onto the **Entry Points** node.
7. Change the entry point's **Access Level** property to Read.
8. To create the privilege to maintain the vehicle table, create a new privilege named ConWHSVehicleTableMaintain.
9. Complete the **Description** property.
10. Complete the **Label** property. For example, Maintain vehicle records.
11. In the designer, drag the ConWHSVehicleTable menu item onto the **Entry Points** node.
12. Change the entry point's **Access Level** property to Delete.
13. Should the form have any associated data entities, such as those that allow us to edit the form's data in Excel, they should also be added to the privilege under the **Data Entity Permissions** node with the appropriate access level.

How it works...

The privileges are simply a way to grant permissions to an entry point, which can be services, to a duty, role, or even directly to a user. Typically, we only add entry points to a privilege, such as menu items. In order to grant access to the user, the system applies the access level to form controls and data sources. When we set the **Needed Permission** property on form controls, it can have the effect of hiding the control if the privilege doesn't grant the needed permission.

Since we can't extend security privileges, we would always create a new privilege. This is not a real restriction, and helps enforce good practice; we can't get more granular than a privilege, in terms of assigning permissions to a user. We should never over-layer (customize) an existing security privilege, as there is no need as duties and roles are extensible.

There's more...

On the vehicle form, we have a button that allows us to change the vehicle group, and this should be hidden for the view privilege. When adding controls to forms, where the system can't determine the needed permission, we must set it on the control whilst designing the form. In our case, the button was created with a **Needed Permission** property of Update. So, the button will be hidden when the privileges granted to the user are less than Update.

In some cases, we may wish to elevate the permission level above that of the privilege's access level. This is a very special case, and is done by following these steps:

1. Expand the **Entry Points** node and the ConWHSVehicleTable entry point.
2. Right-click on the **Controls** node and choose **New Control**.
3. In the **Name** property, type the name of the control, such as ConWHSVehicleGroupChangeController.
4. Select the appropriate **Grant** property and to grant access, make it Update.

We can also use the **Form Control Permissions** node to grant this type of permission to forms not associated with the menu item.

Impact on licensing

Operations is licensed based on named users. Based on your organization's requirements, a mix of **client access license** (**CAL**) types can be bought.

The user's CAL type is determined by the entry points (effectively, the menu items) to which they have read access or higher. For each menu item, we have two properties that control which license type will be required:

- `ViewUserLicense`: This is when a user is given `Read` access to this menu item
- `MaintainUserLicense`: This is when a user is given `Update` or higher access to this menu item

The CAL type is determined by the highest user license type to which the user is assigned. We are not forced to enter values in these menu item properties, but it would be a breach of the license agreement to create a menu item to open a standard form if we don't match the user license type of the original menu item. Microsoft reserves the right, at their expense, to inspect the system.

Security administrators should plan a cyclic approach to security. Check with the **Named User License Counts** report and adapt the security setup to ensure that you are complying with the license.

Checking and maintaining license compliance is the license holder's responsibility.

See also

- *Security and data entities*
  (`https://docs.microsoft.com/en-us/dynamics365/operations/dev-itpro/data-entities/security-data-entities`)

Creating duties

A duty is a collection of one or more privileges. The paradigm is that we are creating a list of duties that the role will perform, and, therefore, add the required privilege in order for the role to be able to perform that duty.

It is common to have only one privilege in a duty, but more can be added, for example, the set up forms may be added to one duty.

Duty names are suffixed with a verb to denote the action the duty will allow the role to perform; common suffixes are Maintain, Inquire, and Approve. In order to determine the correct suffix, look at the standard duties and suffix your duties using the same naming convention.

How to do it...

To create a duty, follow these steps:

1. Choose to add a new item to the project.
2. In the **Add New Item** dialog, select **Security** from the left-hand list and **Security Duty** from the right.
3. Enter `ConWHSVehicleTableInquire` in the **Name** field and click on **Add**.
4. Complete the **Description** property; this should describe to the security administrator what this duty does, such as "Responds to inquiries in to vehicle records".
5. Complete the **Label** property by giving a short description for the security administrator, such as `Inquire into vehicle records`.
6. In the designer, drag the `ConWHSVehicleTableView` security privilege onto the **Privileges** node.
7. Repeat this for all duties required, for example a `ConWHSVehicleTableMaintain` duty that will have the `ConWHSVehicleTableMaintain` privilege.

How it works...

You can consider that a duty is a collection of security privileges, which it is; however, when designing the security model, we would do this the other way around--we design the role with the required duties, and then add the required security privilege to support the duty.

There's more...

When extending the standard application, we often create new forms and therefore new menu items. The security privilege may therefore be required for an existing duty. In this case we would create an extension of the required duty. To do this, we would right click on that duty, and choose **Create extension**, remembering to change the .extension suffix to one the relates to the model we a developing: application elements belong to a model, and models belong to a package. We can then just drag the privilege from the project onto the duty. This same process would be followed should we wish to add a new duty and an standard role - or an existing role in a different package.

Creating security roles

A role is a collection of duties and privileges. The role is what we associate with a user, which can be done automatically based on the employee's information, such as their position in the company. The security roles should be thought of in terms of the personas that first appeared with Dynamics AX 2012. The change is intended to move the thinking away from creating groups of functionality to design the roles based on how the organization is structured. For example, a Sales manager would be in a Sales manager role, which will have duties assigned. The duties have privileges, which in turn give access to the sales manager in order to perform that role.

In our case, we could consider that they have three roles: vehicle management supervisor, vehicle service supervisor, and vehicle service entry clerk. When defining the roles, we do so by defining the duties that each role will have. The naming convention is similar to other objects, and suffixed with the type of role. These types include Supervisor, Manager, Clerk, or others should these not fit the required role; for example, `ConWHSVehicleManager` would have the `Maintain` duties for vehicle master data.

We can add privileges directly to a role, but we should be strict and only add duties directly to a role. This assists in maintenance, and, additionally, it is a best practice check to have all privileges in one or more duties, and all duties must be in one or more roles.

We can also add roles as a sub-role. This may help in rare cases, but, again, try to avoid this. It makes maintenance a little more restrictive for the security manager. They may want to grant or restrict access to the sub-role without changing the rights of the parent role.

How to do it...

To create a role, follow these steps:

1. Choose to add a new item to the project.
2. In the **Add New Item** dialog, select **Security** from the left-hand list and **Security Role** from the right.
3. Enter `ConWHSVehicleManager` in the **Name** field and click on **Add**.
4. Complete the **Description** property; this should describe to the security administrator what this duty does, such as `Managers vehicle master data`.
5. Complete the **Label** property by giving a short description to the security administrator, such as `Responsible for the maintenance of vehicle records and associated set up data`.
6. In the designer, drag the duties that provide full rights to the vehicle and set up menu items onto the **Duties** node.
7. Repeat this for all roles required.

How it works...

Technically, this is straightforward. The complicated part is designing the security model with the customer in order to have a common view of security from a human resource perspective. When security roles are synchronized with the organizational hierarchy, security becomes more of a human resource management process than an IT administrator role.

See also...

- *Role-based security*
  (`https://docs.microsoft.com/en-us/dynamics365/operations/dev-itpro/sysadmin/role-based-security`)

Creating policies

The term "Security policies" is a slight misnomer. It is also known under a more accurate term of **Extensible Data Security** (**XDS**). It is an evolution of record level security that was deprecated from AX 2012: you could still do this, but it wasn't a recommended approach.

In this scenario, we will create a policy that only allows access to vehicles of type truck. In this scenario, we have a team that only has access to trucks when creating service orders.

How to do it...

To create a role, follow these steps:

1. Choose to add a new item to the project.
2. In the **Add New Item** dialog, select **Data Model** from the left-hand list and **Query** from the right.
3. Enter `ConWHSVehicleTruckPolicy` in the **Name** field and click on **Add**.
4. In our new query, drag the `ConWHSVehicleTable` table to the **Data Sources** node.
5. Add the `VehicleType` field to the **Fields** list by right-clicking on the **Fields** node and choosing **New | Field**.
6. Drag the field onto the **Ranges** node.
7. On the new `VehicleType` range, change the **Value** property to `Truck`.

 When deployed, this will be updated for us. We can also use the enum's value as the type is not extensible.

8. Save and close the query designer.
9. Add a new item to the project.
10. In the **Add New Item** dialog, select **Security** from the left-hand list and **Security Policy** from the right.
11. Enter `ConWHSVehicleTruckPolicy` in the **Name** field and click on **Add**.
12. Set **Label** to `Vehicle management clerk vehicle table access policy`.

13. Set **Help Text** to `Restricts access to the vehicle table so that only trucks can be selected.`

14. Set **Primary Table** to `ConWHSVehicleTable`. This tells Operations the name of primary table in the **Query** property.

15. Enter `ConWHSVehicleTruckPolicy` into the **Query** property.

16. Leave **Use Not Exist Join** as `No`. Otherwise, this would have the effect of making the policy allow inactive vehicles only.

17. Set **Constrained Table** to `Yes`.

18. Leave **Operation** as `Select`; we are intending this policy to come into effect when selecting records.

19. Using the *Creating security roles* recipe, create a role for a Truck service entry clerk called `ConWHSVehicleTruckServiceClerk`.

20. Set **Context Type** to `RoleName` and enter `ConWHSVehicleTruckServiceClerk` in the **Role Name** property.

21. Finally, set the **Enabled** property to `Yes`.

How it works...

When the user in the policy's role opens a form, or when a drop-down is displayed, the system will create a query that combines the form's data source with the policy's query definition as an `Exists` or `Not Exists` join. The query cannot be changed by the user, and is enforced at kernel level.

Here's a word of caution: since the data policy is defined using a query, it could add significant server load, especially, when the query is not written efficiently. In order to use policies, there should be a clear business case, and it may be more appropriate to have a secondary list page instead. The policies should be based on business process rules, where access must be restricted for security purposes. See the link in *See also* for more details.

So, creating a policy that is based on data the user enters, such as vehicles for a particular vehicle group, indicates that it isn't a policy but a filter on the vehicles list page. Policies are normally based on rules that are unaffected by user setup, such as an enum.

This could very easily have an impact on performance, so the ranges and joins we create in the query must be written correctly and covered by appropriate indexes.

There's more...

We can also constrain related tables and views; for example, restraining access to vehicle service records that are not linked to vehicles of type `Truck`.

We can do this in two ways--tables that have a relation defined, and those that don't, which includes views.

To add a constrained table, follow these steps:

1. Right-click on the **Constrained Tables** node and choose **New | Constrained Table**.
2. Set the **Constrained** property to `Yes`.

 Constrained tables can be nested, and we can add intermediary tables to eventually get to the table we want to constrain. We may not want these intermediary tables to be constrained, and would therefore leave this value to be `No`.

3. Set the **Name** property to `ConWHSVehicleServiceTable`.
4. Select `ConWHSVehicleTable` in the **Table Relation** property.

To add a view, or a table without a relation, use the Constrain Expression option instead. In this case, we have a **Value** property, where we enter the relation. For example, `ConWHSVehicleTable.VehicleId == ConWHSVehicleServiceTable.VehicleId`. The value is not validated, so we must ensure that it is correct.

See also...

- *Best Practices, Tips and Tricks for Implementing XDS (Extensible Data Security) policies*
(https://blogs.msdn.microsoft.com/daxserver/2013/06/26/best-practices-tips-and-tricks-for-implementing-xds-extensible-data-security-policies/)
- *Security architecture*
(https://docs.microsoft.com/en-us/dynamics365/operations/dev-itpro/sysadmin/security-architecture)
- *Security Policies Properties for AX 2012*
(https://msdn.microsoft.com/en-us/library/gg731857.aspx)

This is still relevant in Dynamics 365 for Operations

7
Leveraging Extensibility

In this chapter, we will cover the following recipes:

- Extending standard tables without customization footprint
- Creating data event handler methods
- How to customize a document layout without an over-layer
- Extending standard forms without customization footprint
- Using a form event handler to replace a lookup
- Creating event handler methods
- Creating your own query functions

Introduction

The focus on this chapter is how to extend the standard software without an over-layer. To those that come from Dynamics AX 2012 or prior, it may not seem a big issue: over-layering was the only choice, and when compared to other products in the space, it was one of its key features. When we over-layer, the system copies the code into the package's layer and the developer makes changes to this copy. It is all seamless and has worked well since Axapta 1.5.

The problem is when we need to service the application, such as deploying a hotfix, we will need to check for conflicts and potentially update our code. Also, if we have an ISV solution that over-layers a package, we will need an update from the ISV if the hotfix modifies an over-layered element.

The other downside of over-layer is that we can't have two ISV solutions that over-layer the same element. This has always been a problem, and it can only be solved by manually merging in a higher layer.

The solution Microsoft has for this is called extensibility. This is where we store the changes we want to make in a delta change format in a separate object. This means that two ISVs and the customer could all add fields to the `SalesLine` table, and not version-lock the customer. All of these fields are merged by the system, and the table will have all fields in all packages added to the table in SQL. There is no longer a need to have separate tables with the additional fields and code in order to avoid over-layering a table.

Extending standard tables without customization footprint

Table extensions provide a way to add fields to a table without over-layering. This means that we don't need to perform a code merge when the base package is changed.

In this recipe, we will add a field to the `SalesConfirmHeaderTmp` table, which we will use in the *How to customize a document layout without an over-layer* recipe.

It is common to have the main development work in one package, and reports in a higher package, as this can help with deploying updates. When deciding which package this table extension should be done in, we need to consider the scope of its usage should be. If we create the additional fields in a reporting package, which references a main development package, the main development package will not be able to use this field.

Sometimes a report drives the requirement for additional fields. So, it can seem natural to add the new fields to a table extension in the reporting package. This means that we will need a table and form extension in the reporting package, which may seem fine until a piece of code in the main development package needs the field. The references in packages only goes in one direction, the main development package cannot see the additional fields in the reporting package - even though they physically exist in the base table.

In the above type of scenario, the fields should be added to a new project in the main development package. Look back to `Chapter 1`, *Starting a New Project*, for the discussion on packages.

In the example in this recipe, the field is specific to a reporting package, because the field is added to a temporary table that is only used for the report generation.

Getting ready

Create a new project in a new model to report, for example, `ConReports`, as a new package, which is an extension package.

How to do it...

To add a field to a table as an extension, follow these steps:

1. Locate the `SalesConfirmHeaderTmp` table in the Application Explorer.
2. Right-click on it and choose **Create extension**.
3. Remembering that all element names must be globally unique, rename the new extension from `SalesConfirmHeaderTmp.extension` to `SalesConfirmHeaderTmp.ConReports`.
4. Open the table extension in the designer.
5. Locate the EDT name in the Application Explorer.
6. Drag the `Name` EDT to the **Fields** node.
7. Rename the field to `ConSalesPoolName`.
8. Set the **Label** property to `@SYS84547` (`Sales pool`).
9. Save and close the designer.

How it works...

This recipe is closely linked to the next two recipes, and some explanation is required as to how we knew which tables to modify. To keep this information in one place, this explanation is in the *There's more...* section of the *How to customize a document layout without an over-layer* recipe.

This creates an entity that only stores the changes to the element being extended. This is true of all extensions. There is no copying from layer to layer; it is a reference and a list of changes.

The actual source of the table extension is shown in the following piece of code:

```
<?xml version="1.0" encoding="utf-8"?>
<AxTableExtension xmlns:i="http://www.w3.org/2001/XMLSchema-instance">
  <Name>SalesConfirmHeaderTmp.ConReports</Name>
  <FieldGroupExtensions />
  <FieldGroups />
```

```
    <FieldModifications />
    <Fields>
      <AxTableField xmlns=""
        i:type="AxTableFieldString">
        <Name>ConSalesPoolName</Name>
        <ExtendedDataType>Name</ExtendedDataType>
        <Label>@SYS84547</Label>
      </AxTableField>
    </Fields>
    <Indexes />
    <Mappings />
    <PropertyModifications />
    <Relations />
  </AxTableExtension>
```

When the project is built and the database synchronization is done, the physical table `SalesConfirmHeaderTmp` will have the base fields plus the fields in all of its extensions. This is why the field needs to be prefixed.

There's more...

You can also extend the field groups. This allows us to add fields to a field group that is used in forms to keep the presentation consistent and reduce the number of changes and code maintenance effort.

We can also add indexes and relations.

The indexes are created within the physical table in SQL, so these must also be prefixed to ensure that we don't cause any collisions (duplicate name).

Creating data-event handler methods

The data-event handlers handle the delegates exposed on every table. These delegates are listed under the **Events** node.

These events do not fire if the associated method (for example, `insert`) is overridden on the table and `super()` is not called.

How the event handler methods are organized is up to the developer; they just need to be placed logically so that others will find them easily.

In our case, the event handler is used purely for a report and populating a field on insert that is used in a report. So, we will place these methods in a helper class.

Getting ready

This recipe continues from the previous recipe.

How to do it...

To create a data event handler, follow these steps:

1. Create a new `ConReportManager` class.
2. Open the table design for the table in question; in our case, double-click on the `SalesConfirmHeaderTmp.ConReports` table extension.
3. Expand **Events** and locate **onInserting**.

 The `onInserted` event is too late as we want to fill in a field before the record is written; if we subscribed to `onInserted`, the data will not be saved.

4. Right-click on the event and choose **Copy event handler method**. This will create a code snippet, and place it in the paste buffer.
5. Open the `ConReportManager` class, and paste in the code generated by step 4 into the class body, as shown here:

```
class ConReportManager
{
    /// <summary>
    ///
    /// </summary>
    /// <param name="sender"></param>
    /// <param name="e"></param>
    [DataEventHandler(tableStr(SalesConfirmHeaderTmp),
     DataEventType::Inserting)]
    public static void SalesConfirmHeaderTmp_onInserting(
      Common sender, DataEventArgs e)
    {
    }
```

```
}
```

Look at the event declaration: it references the table, not the extension. This is important, as the extension is not a table, and the system correctly changes the subscription to the correct table.

6. Next, we will need to write the code, and the obvious code to write may seem to be as follows:

```
SalesConfirmHeaderTmp header = sender;
SalesTable        salesTable;

select SalesPoolId
   from salesTable
   where SalesTable.SalesId == header.SalesId;

header.ConSalesPoolName = SalesPool::find(
   SalesTable.SalesPoolId).Name;
```

This would be wrong, as we assume that the sales order record will never be deleted - and once invoiced, they can be deleted. What we should do is add `SalesPoolId` to the `CustConfirmJour` table, which is the permanent record of that confirmation.

7. Create an extension of `CustConfirmJour`, called `CustConfirmJour.ConReports`.
8. Drag the `SalesPoolId` EDT from the Application Explorer, and rename it to `ConSalesPoolId`.
9. Right-click on the **onInserting** event and choose **Copy event handler method**.
10. Paste the method into the body of our `ConReportManager` class.
11. Adjust the method so that it reads as follows:

```
/// <summary>
/// Handles the inserting event of <c>CustConfirmJour</c>
/// </summary>
/// <param name="sender"></param>
/// <param name="e"></param>
[DataEventHandler(tableStr(CustConfirmJour),
 DataEventType::Inserting)]
public static void CustConfirmJour_onInserting(
                    Common sender, DataEventArgs e)
{
    CustConfirmJour jour = sender;
    jour.ConSalesPoolId = jour.salesTable().SalesPoolId;
```

}

The record is passed by reference, and we must not call `insert` or `update`.

12. Finally, adjust our `SalesConfirmHeaderTmp` handler so it reads as follows:

```
/// <summary>
/// Handles inserting event <c>SalesConfirmHeaderTmp</c>
/// </summary>
/// <param name="sender">The calling record</param>
/// <param name="e"></param>
[DataEventHandler(tableStr(SalesConfirmHeaderTmp),
 DataEventType::Inserting)]
public static void SalesConfirmHeaderTmp_onInserting(
   Common sender, DataEventArgs e)
{
    alesConfirmHeaderTmp header = sender;
    CustConfirmJour jour;
    select ConSalesPoolId
        from jour
        where jour.RecId == header.JournalRecId;
    header.ConSalesPoolName =
        SalesPool::find(jour.ConSalesPoolId).Name;
}
```

13. Save and close the designer.
14. To test this, perform a full build including database sync and create a sales confirmation. Then, check that the `SalesPoolId` field was populated in the `CustConfirmJour` table.

How it works...

The event handlers we wrote in this recipe are bound when the package is built--no changes are made to the base packages and we can ship the package as a deployable package to a different system and it should all work fine.

The subscribers are not called in any order, and this cannot be relied upon. So, the code must be written in a way that doesn't make this assumption. When considering transaction durability, the events are called within the transaction of the caller--and throwing an exception will cause the whole transaction to be aborted.

There's more...

Adding fields as an extension is relatively straightforward, but we also need to handle events such as modifiedField and validateField.

If these are overridden on the table, we could use a Pre or Post-event handler. However, these are not always overridden, and these types of event handlers should always be the last choice; these are discussed later in this chapter.

To handle these events, we would subscribe to the appropriate data event. There are two methods for each: a present-continuous (ing) method and a past tense (ed) method.

The ing methods are called before the event fires, and the ed method fires after the event. They only fire on super(); so, if the developer doesn't call super() in the method, the event will not fire. This is the case on SalesLine, SalesTable, PurchLine and PurchTable, for example.

Locate the table InventTable in the Application Explorer, right click on it and choose **Open designer**. Expand the **Events** node, and right click on the onValidatedField event (which is actually a delegate). Let's use the **Copy event handler method** option which will place the following code in the paste buffer:

```
/// <summary>
///
/// </summary>
/// <param name="sender"></param>
/// <param name="e"></param>
[DataEventHandler(tableStr(InventTable),
 DataEventType::ValidatedField)]
public static void InventTable_onValidatedField(
    Common sender, DataEventArgs e)
{
}
```

This helps, but the DataEventArgs object doesn't contain anything about the field being validated, or a method by which we return false should it not be valid.

You can then change the code using the following pattern:

```
/// <summary>
/// Validates the fields on the <c>InventTable</c> table
/// </summary>
/// <param name="sender"></param>
/// <param name="e"></param>
[DataEventHandler(tableStr(InventTable),
 DataEventType::ValidatedField)]
```

```
public static void InventTable_onValidatedField(
                            Common sender, DataEventArgs e)
{
    ValidateFieldEventArgs fieldArgs = e;
    Boolean                 ok;
    switch(fieldArgs.parmFieldId())
    {
        case fieldNum(InventTable, ProdPoolId):
            //if(<condition>)
            //{
            //    ok = checkFailed("message");
            //}
            break;
    }
    if(!ok)
    {
        fieldArgs.parmValidateResult(false);
    }
}
```

We chose to use the onValidateField event delegate because we would never handle field validation, or modify events on tables that we don't enter data into. As discussed in previous chapters, these events are triggered from the form control, passed through to the data source, and finally the table.

Should we add a field to an extension of InventTable, the code in the event handler would be the same; that is the tableStr, methodStr, and fieldNum functions would all use InventTable and not the name of the extension. The event handler is simply triggered when the event happens, the code we write will be able to see all fields added to the current package and fields in all packages to which the current package references.

The other specialized classes under DataEventArgs that are useful are as follows:

Class	Usage
ValidateFieldEventArgs	onValidatedField onValidatingField
ValidateEventArgs	onValidateWrite onValidatingWrite onValidateDelete onValidateingDelete
ModifyFieldEventArgs	onModifiedField onModifyingField

How to customize a document layout without an over-layer

The example here is to add an extension field to a print-managed standard document without over-layering the report. We will use the sales order confirmation report to add the sales order pool's name to the report.

There are two main types of reports: listing reports and documents. The documents, such as the sales order confirmation document, use temporary tables to make the layout easier to write. Any report can use this technique, but it is more common on document layouts and complicated listing reports.

It is often good practice to have a separate model for reports. Reports can use elements that we have written across packages, for example, we may have an extension package and an ISV package that has elements we wish to report on, but we don't want to link our package as a dependency on the ISV package.

We won't cover the actual report design in this recipe, as report design is beyond the scope of this book; but we will cover all other areas.

We have already added the fields and event handlers in the prior two recipes; we just need to add the field to the report.

How to do it...

To add a field to the report, follow these steps:

1. Locate the `SalesConfirm` report in the Application Explorer.
2. Right-click on the report and choose **Duplicate in project**.
3. Rename the report to `ConSalesConfirm`.
4. Open the report in the designer and expand the **Datasets** and **SalesConformHeaderDS** nodes. Then, look for the new extension field in the **Fields** node. If this does not appear, right-click on each data set and choose **Restore**.
5. You can now proceed to design the report as per your requirements.

The next stage is integrating the report so that our new report is used instead of the standard report. To do this, follow these steps:

1. We will need to add an event handler to a delegate exposed by Microsoft on the `PrintMgmtDocType` class called `getDefaultREportFormatDelegate`. The following code does this, the commented out sections are there for reference should you wish to extend other documents:

```
/// <summary>
/// Allows the SSRS Report used for the Print
/// management based reports to be overridden
/// </summary>
/// <param name = "_docType">The PrintMgmtDocumentType
/// </param>
/// <param name = "_result">The EventHandlerResult</param>
[SubscribesTo(classstr(PrintMgmtDocType),
 delegatestr(PrintMgmtDocType,
 getDefaultReportFormatDelegate))]
public static void DefaultReportFormat(
                        PrintMgmtDocumentType _docType,
                        EventHandlerResult _result)
{
    switch (_docType)
    {
        case PrintMgmtDocumentType::SalesOrderConfirmation:
            _result.result(
                ssrsReportStr(ConSalesConfirm, Report));
            break;
        case PrintMgmtDocumentType::WHSPickListShippingLoad:
        case
PrintMgmtDocumentType::WHSPickListShippingShipment:
        case PrintMgmtDocumentType::WHSPickListShippingWave:
            //_result.result(
            //   ssrsReportStr(ConPickListShipping,
            //                  Report));
            break;
        case PrintMgmtDocumentType::WHSPickListProd:
            //_result.result(
            //   ssrsReportStr(ConPickListProduction,
            //                  Report));
            break;
        case PrintMgmtDocumentType::SalesOrderPackingSlip:
            //_result.result(
            //   ssrsReportStr(ConSalesPackingSlip,
            //                  Report));
            break;
        case PrintMgmtDocumentType::SalesOrderInvoice:
            //_result.result(
            //   ssrsReportStr(ConSalesInvoice, Report));
            break;
```

```
                case PrintMgmtDocumentType::SalesFreeTextInvoice:
                    //_result.result(
                    //  ssrsReportStr(ConFreeTextInvoice, Report));
                    break;
                case PrintMgmtDocumentType::CustAccountStatement:
                    //_result.result(
                    //  ssrsReportStr(ConCustAccountStatement,
                    //                Report));
                    break;
                case PrintMgmtDocumentType::PurchaseOrderRequisition:
                    //_result.result(
                    //  ssrsReportStr(ConPurchPurchaseOrder,
                    //                Report));
                    break;
                case PrintMgmtDocumentType::PurchaseOrderReceiptsList:
                    //_result.result(
                    //  ssrsReportStr(ConPurchReceiptsList,
                    //                Report));
                    break;
                case PrintMgmtDocumentType::CustCollectionLetter:
                    //_result.result(
                    //  ssrsReportStr(ConCustCollectionJour,
                    //                Report));
                    break;
            }
        }
```

2. Save and close the designers and build the project. You will need to deploy the reports once this is done in order to test it. To do this, right-click on the report and choose **Deploy reports**.

How it works...

Even though the data set in the report is the base table, it shows our extension fields. It will also show all extension fields for the packages that the reports package references. The process of report design is straightforward from that point onwards.

The integration has been well thought out by Microsoft and has, therefore, exposed a delegate that they handle. In the method that calls this delegate, the code determines if it has been handled and will use the result arguments for the report name.

There more...

Some knowledge of the database was required in order to know which tables we had to add extension fields to, and just reading the code is not only daunting, but also impractical. This example was chosen specifically as it isn't easy to find. This recipe is much easier when the field is to be added to a form. We can see the menu item in the URL in the client, and from there, find the form and the table.

The temporary tables used were found simply by opening the `SalesConfirm` report and looking at the data sources it uses. We knew which report it was, based on consistent naming conventions.

Sales documents start with `Sales`, and are following by the document type, which is as follows:

- SalesQuotation
- SalesConfirm
- SalesPackingSlip
- SalesInvoice

Purchasing documents start with `Purch`, and are also suffixed with the document type:

- PurchPurchaseOrder
- PurchReceiptsList
- PurchPackingSlip
- PurchInvoice

These documents are created through the `FormLetter` framework. The pattern is that each document has a header and lines table that forms the permanent data, allowing the reports to be reproduced exactly as they were when first printed, even if the order has been changed or deleted. These are referenced as journals. The tables follow a similar convention, as shown in the following table:

Document	Journal header table	Journal line table
SalesQuotation	CustQuotationJour	CustQuotationTrans
SalesConfirm	CustConfirmJour	CustConfirmTrans
SalesPackingSlip	CustPackingSlipJour	CustPackingSlipTrans
SalesInvoice	CustInvoiceJour	CustInvoiceTrans

PurchPurchaseOrder	VendPurchOrderJour	None
PurchReceiptsList	VendReceiptsListJour	VendReceiptsListTrans
PurchPackingSlip	VendPackingSlipJour	VendPackingSlipTrans
PurchInvoice	VendInvoiceJour	VendInvoiceTrans

When we used the **Copy event handler method** option on the event, this merely created a valid method declaration for use. It does not modify the source table or add any reference. The code can therefore be added manually; it was just to save time. The reference is created when the project is built.

Creating event handler methods

We have already created an event handler in the previous recipe.

So far, we have created an event handler for data events using the `DataEventHandler` decoration and a delegate event handler using the `SubscribesTo` decoration. We can also add handlers directly to any public method.

There are two types: a pre-event and a post-event handler. One example of where we may need to do this is the `SalesTable.insert()` method. This doesn't call `super()`, so we can't use a data event handler.

The actual insert occurs within the `SalesTableType` class in the `insert()` method. If you want access to the sales table record, you need to add the handler to the table as the record being inserted is a private variable to the class.

Event handlers like this are used to integrate specific solutions, so the handler will be in a class in the specific package.

Getting ready

We will just need a Dynamics 365 for Operations project and a class that requires the event handler open in the designer.

How to do it...

To create a pre-event or post-event handler, follow these steps:

1. Open the designer for the table or class that we want to add a handler for, such as the `SalesTable` table.

2. Locate the method we wish to handle and right-click on it: select **Copy event handler method | Pre-event handler** (or **Post-event handler** as required). This creates a method declaration into the paste buffer.

3. Paste the method declaration into the target class for a pre-event handler on `SalesTable.Insert()`, which will be as follows:

```
/// <summary>
///
/// </summary>
/// <param name="args"></param>
[PreHandlerFor(tableStr(SalesTable),
  tableMethodStr(SalesTable, insert))]
public static void SalesTable_Pre_insert(
    XppPrePostArgs args)
{
}
```

4. What we do at this point depends on the requirements; the common methods in `args` are as follows:

Method	Use
`boolean existsArg(str)`	Does the handled method have the parameter
`AnyType getArThig(str)`	This returns the method's parameter value using the parameter's name. It is returned as an `AnyType` object. For example, if we are handling `SalesTine.insert(Boolean _skipMethod = false),` we can get the value of `_skipMethod` using `args.getArg('_skipMethod')`. There is no validation; we will use `existsArg` to check first. This is not an intrinsic function, and we can't cause a compilation error to highlight any runtime errors.
`AnyType getArgNum(int)`	This gets the handled method's parameter by using its position from the left.
`AnyType getThis()`	This gets the instance of the object, in our case, the current `SalesTable` record. There is no compiler validation on the type, so we must check this manually. Again, we can't use intrinsic functions to force a compilation error.

`AnyType getReturnValue`	This is only useful on post-event handlers and gets the value the method has returned. We would usually use this in conjunction with the `setReturnValue` method.
`setReturnValue(AnyType)`	This is only useful on post-event handlers and lets us override the value the method returns.
`setArg(str, AnyType)`	This allows us to set the method's parameter named in this method.
`setArgNum(int, AnyType)`	This allows us to set the method's parameter by its position from the left.

5. Once done, save and close the designer.

How it works...

Pre-event and post-event handlers work in the same way as the other event handlers, but these carry a risk of regression. The events we handle through this technique are not delegates, and the developer did not specifically write the method to be handled in this way: otherwise they would have written a delegate. The reason we are restricted to public methods is because these are considered as a public API, and will not be changed or deprecated without a proper procedure. Protected methods can be changed without warning, and we could, therefore, find that our code no longer works.

Private methods are private for a reason: you can't guarantee the internal class state, or how these will be called.

This also reinforces that we need to be careful when assigning public, protected, or private to a method. Always make your methods as private as possible, as this not only ensures that your code can't be called erroneously, but it also makes it easier for other developers to use your code correctly.

Extending standard forms without customization footprint

Adjusting the layout of a form, as an extension, has been made very easy for us. This is covered in the first part of the recipe. We will also cover a new technique to work with form code.

Getting ready

We just need a Dynamics 365 for Operations project open.

How to do it...

To write a form extension for the sales order form, `SalesTable`, follow these steps:

1. Locate the desired form in the Application Explorer, right click on it and choose **Create extension**. This will add a new form extension to our project.
2. Locate the new form extension in our project, and rename it so it will remain globally unique, for example, `SalesTable.Con`.
3. Open the form extension in the designer.
4. We can now drag any field or field group, including extension fields that are available to the current package, to the design.
5. We can also choose to change properties of the controls on the form's design. The rule here is that, if it lets you change, it will work.

> Remember that whilst doing this, all changes should be at the lowest level possible as this ensures consistency and minimizes maintenance effort.

This covers the design, but not the code. We can right-click on most methods and use Copy event-handler method to create a pre-event or post-event handler. This may suffice in some cases, but we can go further. In the November update, we can now create extension classes that act as an extension to the form's code.

The following example explains one of the many benefits that may not immediately be obvious.

To create an extension class for a form's code, follow these steps:

1. Create a new class that must end in _Extension; so, for a `SalesTable` extension, use `ConSalesTable_Extension`.

> For this to work, we only need to have the `ExtensionOf` decoration and ensure that the name ends in _Extension.

2. The class declaration should read as follows:

```
[ExtensionOf(formStr(SalesTable))]
final class ConSalesTable_Extension
```

3. In this example, we will determine the caller record by handling the initialized event and use the stored record that is scoped to the form when we close the form. The code for this is as follows:

```
[ExtensionOf(formStr(SalesTable))]
final class ConSalesTable_Extension
{
    Private CustTable conCustTable;
    [FormEventHandler(formstr(SalesTable),
     FormEventType::Initialized)]
    public void initializedFormHandler(xFormRun formRun,
                                       FormEventArgs e)
    {
        Args args = formRun.args();
        switch(args.dataset())
        {
            case tableNum(CustTable):
                conCustTable = args.record();
                break;
        }
    }
    [FormEventHandler(formstr(SalesTable),
     FormEventType::Closing)]
    public void initializedFormHandler(xFormRun formRun,
                                       FormEventArgs e)
    {
        if(conCustTable.RecId != 0)
        {
            if(FormDataUtil::isFormDataSource(
                conCustTable))
            {
                FormDataUtil::getFormDataSource(
                    conCustTable).research(true);
            }
        }
    }
}
```

We do not normally prefix variables in our own code, but in the preceding case we prefixed CustTable with Con. The extension class is like a decoration, and the variables we create must be unique in the scope of the form instance.

If you want to write a method to override a form-control event, just as a modified event of `ItemId`, we will perform the following steps:

1. Add the following lines to the `initializedFormHandler` method created earlier:

    ```
    FormDataObject itemIdDataObject;
    itemIdDataObject = this.SalesLine_DS.object(
        fieldNum(SalesLine, ItemId), 1);

    itemIdDataObject.registerOverrideMethod(
        methodStr(FormDataObject, modified),
        methodStr(ConSalesTable_Extension,
                  modifiedItemIdHandler), this);
    ```

2. Then add the override handler, as follows:

    ```
    /// <summary>
    /// Handles the modified event of the
    /// ItemId data source field
    /// </summary>
    /// <param name = "itemIdFieldObject"></param>
    public void modifiedItemIdHandler(
                    FormDataObject itemIdFieldObject)
    {
        // write what should happen here
    }
    ```

 `FormDataObject` has the settings for the data source field, such as `AllowEdit`. It also has a `dataSource()` method to fetch the `FormDataSource` object. This would be needed if the method didn't already have access to the form's data sources, which it does, as they are declared public.

3. This is it. We should experiment and get used to this paradigm before using it for real.

How it works...

The form extension works like any other extension; they are delta changes that are applied when the package is deployed.

The new concept here is the extension class. The term extension is used specifically to avoid confusion with the `extends` keyword. Extension classes are automatically instantiated in place of the standard class and allow them to be augmented. There is no access to private methods, but we can add state variables and access them along with the form's public variables and methods. Critically, we do have full access to the data sources on the form. The event handlers can be created as instance methods, which grants them access to the extension class's variables and methods, but also the public variables and methods in the class we created the extension for.

The class must be created as final, because it is only instantiated in the current package. There can be extension classes in other packages, which we cannot access, and should not want to. The whole point is for us to know that in this package, that form's class will be instantiated as this class.

There's more...

There are many more types of extensions that we can perform, but all follow the same theme. Ensure that the name we give is named correctly and is unique (and certainly doesn't have the suffix of `.extension`).

You can tell which objects can have extension due to the Application Explorer having a node form then; for example, **Menu Items** is followed by the **Menu Item Extensions** node. Or simply, if you can select **Create extension**, you can!

Developing in this way requires a slight paradigm shift in order to make it seem natural. It seems that those new to writing this way are thinking from a customization (over-layer) viewpoint and the solution seems to be more of a brute force workaround than a real solution.

For example, when writing an event handler, the event only has access to the public variables and methods of the caller. We can, however, use reflection to gain access to the caller's private variables and methods. If we are doing this, it usually means we are thinking about the solution in the wrong way. The tooling in Visual Studio is improved with each release, and the ability to make changes via extension has increased significantly each time.

Reflection is a large topic, and discouraged by many, as it will make our code vulnerable to regression as Microsoft release updates. For more information on this topic, please see the following link:

```
https://msdn.microsoft.com/en-us/library/f7ykdhsy(v=vs.110).aspx.
```

Although the purpose of this book is to provide recipes to extend Dynamics 365 for Operations through the means of extension, it is important to keep in mind the reason for avoiding over-layering: maintainability and serviceability. If we make a hacky change to avoid an over-layer, (like reflection and in some cases pre-event or post-event handlers), we can actually make the code less maintainable. Worse than that, the system may compile and pass your test scripts and still fail when deployed to production as we have made an assumption about the internal state of a class. The point I am trying to make is to keep in mind the reasons we avoid over-layering standard code, which isn't just to avoid it. It is to realize the many benefits in terms of ease of deployment, and maintainability of code as updates are released.

Using a form event handler to replace a lookup

This is a common requirement of an event handler, and deserves its own recipe. Prior to Update 3 in November 2016, these event handlers had to be placed in a utility class; we can now have a class that acts as an extension to the form's code-behind.

This was covered in the previous recipe, and if you are using this technique, the event handler should be written there without the `static` keyword.

Getting ready

Ideally, we should have a form extension class written for this; otherwise, we just need a Dynamics 365 for Operations project open.

How to do it...

To add a custom lookup to a control on a standard form, please follow these steps

1. Create a new class that could be a generic sales order utility class, or ideally a form extension class (see previous recipe for this).

The naming is key so that we can easily find it. There is no obvious link that we have done this, so naming and documentation is critical.

2. The first example is to make the sales order create dialog using a lookup form. As standard (in the November release), the lookup only contains the account number and account. This example binds the custom lookup to the customer account's lookup event, as follows:

```
/// <summary>
/// Override the customer lookup on the sales order create
/// dialog in order to use a lookup with the address
/// </summary>
/// <param name="sender">calling control</param>
/// <param name="e">form events</param>
[FormControlEventHandler(formControlStr(SalesCreateOrder,
    SalesTable_CustAccount),
    FormControlEventType::Lookup)]
  public static void SalesTable_CustAccount_OnLookup(
    FormControl sender,
    FormControlEventArgs e)
{
    FormStringControl    custAccountCtrl = sender;
    CustTable            selectedCustomer;
    FormRun              formRun;
    Form                 custTableLookupForm;

    custTableLookupForm = new
                      Form(formStr(CustTableLookup));
    FormControlCancelableSuperEventArgs eventArgs = e;
    Args formArgs = new Args();
    formArgs = new Args();
    formArgs.name(formStr(CustTableLookup));
    formArgs.caller(sender.formRun());

    selectedCustomer =
                CustTable::find(custAccountCtrl.text());
    if (selectedCustomer.RecId != 0)
    {
        formArgs.lookupRecord(selectedCustomer);
    }
    formRun = FormAutoLookupFactory::buildLookupFromCustomForm(
            custAccountCtrl,
            custTableLookupForm,
            AbsoluteFieldBinding::construct(
                fieldStr(CustTable, AccountNum),
```

```
                        tableStr(CustTable)),
                    formArgs);
            custAccountCtrl.performFormLookup(formRun);
            eventArgs.CancelSuperCall();
    }
```

If you wish to create your own lookup, it is also fine. Just create a new form using `Lookup` `- basic pattern`. Let's use an example where we are writing a custom product lookup:

1. We need to bind the select control (the `ID` column, such as the `Item Id` field in our example).
2. Add the data source as usual (or write a view and use that) and complete the design pattern. When adding fields to the grid, change the `Auto Declaration` property of the `ID` column to `Yes`. The control will probably be called `Grid_ItemId` by default, which is fine.
3. Override the `init` method so we can tell the form that the `Grid_ItemId` control will contain the data that we want to return. This is done with the following code:

```
void init()
{
    DictField               dictField;
    FormStringControl       callerControl;

    if (!element.args())
    {
        throw error(strfmt("@SYS22862", element.name()));
    }

    super();

    element.selectMode(Grid_ItemId);
}
```

4. Next, we should handle the filtering of the control based on the calling control, which is done with the following code:

```
public void run()
{
    FormStringControl   callerControl;
    boolean             filterLookup    = false;

    callerControl = SysTableLookup::getCallerStringControl(
                                element.args());

    filterLookup = SysTableLookup::filterLookupPreRun(
                                callerControl,
```

```
                                        Grid_ItemId,
                                        InventTable_DS);

            super();

            SysTableLookup::filterLookupPostRun(filterLookup,
                                        callerControl.text(),
                                        Grid_ItemId,
                                        InventTable_DS);
        }
```

 InventTable_DS is the default data source name if we added the InventTable table. Replace this as required with the data source name of the actual table used.

5. We should now create a menu item, and add it to an appropriate security privilege.

Lookups in Operations don't always use a form and, in fact, they are usually automatic based on the autoLookup field group. We can write such a lookup programmatically:

1. Create a class, ConGeneralHandlers, for example, and add the following method:

```
/// <summary>
///     Performs a lookup on the <c>InventTable</c> table.
/// </summary>
/// <param name="_lookupCtrl">
///     The <c>FormStringControl</c> control that the
///     lookup will be attached to.
/// </param>
/// <param name="_itemId">
///     The item that is used to filter the lookup.
/// </param>
public static void lookupItemId(
    FormStringControl    _lookupCtrl,
    ItemId               _itemId)
{
    SysTableLookup          sysTableLookup
    Query                   query = new Query();
    QueryBuildRange         queryBuildRange;
    QueryBuildDataSource    queryBuildDataSource;
    sysTableLookup = SysTableLookup::newParameters(
                        tableNum(InventTable),
                        _lookupCtrl)
    queryBuildDataSource = query.addDataSource(
```

```
                                       tableNum(InventTable));

        if (_itemId)
        {
            queryBuildRange = queryBuildDataSource.addRange(
                            fieldNum(InventTable, ItemId));
            queryBuildRange.value(queryValue(_itemId));
        }

        sysTableLookup.addSelectionField(
                            fieldNum(InventTable, ItemId));
        sysTableLookup.addLookupMethod(
                            tableMethodStr(InventTable,
                                                itemName));
        sysTableLookup.addLookupMethod(
                            tableMethodStr(InventTable,
                                                modelGroupId));
        sysTableLookup.addLookupMethod(
                            tableMethodStr(InventTable,
                                                itemGroupId));
        sysTableLookup.addLookupField(
                            fieldNum(InventTable,
                                                ItemType));

        sysTableLookup.parmQuery(query);
        sysTableLookup.performFormLookup();
    }
```

2. We may need to replace the super call on the lookup method on the field within a data source; this is done by right-clicking on the **Methods** node for the data source field in question and choosing **Override** | **Lookup**. Remove the super() call so you don't get two lookups!

3. To use it as before in an event handler is done as follows:

```
/// <summary>
/// Override the item lookup on the sales order form
/// </summary>
/// <param name="sender">ItemId caller control</param>
/// <param name="e">args so we can cancel super</param>
[FormControlEventHandler(formControlStr(SalesTable,
                                            SalesLine_ItemId),
 FormControlEventType::Lookup)]
public static void SalesLine_ItemId_OnLookup(
                        FormControl sender,
                        FormControlEventArgs e)
{
    FormStringControl                     itemIdCtrl;
```

```
FormControlCancelableSuperEventArgs eventArgs;

eventArgs = e;
itemIdCtrl = sender;

ConGeneralhandlers::lookupItemId(
                    itemIdCtrl,
                    itemIdCtrl.text());
eventArgs.CancelSuperCall();
}
```

4. These techniques can be used as desired to adjust or replace the lookups in Dynamics 365 for Operations without any customization to the standard code.

How it works...

The first part is to use a custom form. The binding to the lookup event is done using a specific event handler for this purpose. These events have one very important feature, apart from allowing us to bind to a form control event; in that, they pass the arguments object as a FormControlEventArgs object.

We can then cast this as a FormControlCancelableSuperEventArgs object. When we call the CancelSuperCall() method, it tells the calling control not to call its super. In the case of a lookup event, we would otherwise end up with two lookups: our new lookup and then the standard lookup.

Apart from gathering information, the other key part is that we construct the FormRun object using a factory, which creates FormRun so that it behaves as a lookup and not just a form.

The second part was to create our own lookup, which was largely repeating what we have already learnt. Just follow the pattern. However, the pattern does need a little help, so it understands how to behave itself. This is why we have to override the init and run methods. Even so, this is a lot less effort than in prior releases.

The third part was to create a lookup programmatically. This is often preferable for simple lookups, and we could also add child data sources and filters to the query. This was done in two methods, as it is common to use lookups like this in our own code. So the lookup method could be used as the lookup method on a data source field.

Creating your own query functions

Query functions are used in user queries. One of the issues they can solve is when submitting batch routines, where a query range would be based on the current date.

One such function is `currentDate()`. This is used in a query range as `(currentDate())`. The system sees the round brackets and knows to look for a query function. Whenever the query is executed, the system will use the current system date.

In prior editions of AX, we would add public static methods to the `SysQueryRangeUtil` class. This would mean an over-layer and, consequently, Microsoft has provided a way to add new query functions without over-layering.

How to do it...

To create a query function, follow these steps:

1. Create a new class in the project and name it `ConQueryRangeFunctions`.
2. To add a query function to the class, in this case, to get the current worker record ID, write the following lines of code:

```
[QueryRangeFunction]
public static str CurrentWorkerNum()
{
    RefRecId currentWorkerRecId =
            HcmWorkerLookup::currentWorker();
    HcmWorker worker;

    if(currentWorkerRecId == 0)
    {
        // if we return and empty string, it will match all
        // records. So return a string that will both cause
        // the no records to be found in the query range,
        // but also to give the user a clue as to what
        // happened. You should create this as a label,
        // without spaces, us the following as an example.
        return '#NotFound#';
    }
    select PersonnelNumber
        from worker
        where worker.RecId == currentWorkerRecId;

    return worker.PersonnelNumber;
}
```

You may notice that it tries to add Attribute to the end, if you use intelli-type, and that some of the methods in `SysQueryRangeUtil` also end in Attribute. This is the old convention and is no longer required.

3. The second part of the trick is how to use it. Build the project and open `https://usnconeboxax1aos.cloud.onebox.dynamics.com/?cmp=USMF&mi =HcmWorkerListPage` in your browser.

4. Select the **OPTIONS** action pane tab, as shown in the following screenshot:

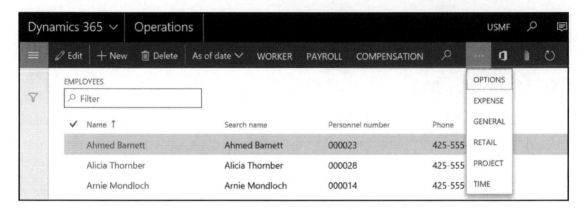

5. Click on **Advanced Filter/Sort** and add a range for `Personnel number`, as shown in the following screenshot:

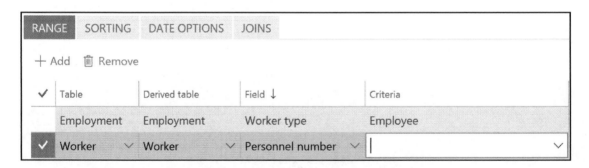

6. Type the following line of code into the **Criteria** column and press **OK**:

```
(ConQueryRangeFunctions::CurrentWorkerNum())
```

7. You should see, when using the `Contoso` demo data in the `USMF` company, that only the user `Julia Funderburk` is shown.

8. If you click on the heading for **Personnel number**, our query function code is also listed as a **matches** criterion. As these functions are usually used when submitting routines or printing reports, the advanced filter dialog is more commonly used.

How it works...

When the package is built, the `QueryRangeFunction` attribute directs the compiler to make them available for use in query dialogs. The syntax in the brackets is not X++, it is interpreted at runtime and just looks similar. The round bracket instructs the compiler to expect a field or function name, and any function not in the base `SysQueryRangeUtil` class requires the `(<class name>::<function name>())` format.

The error checking is limited and the errors aren't helpful. For example, if we forget one of the colons, we will get an error suggesting that a right parenthesis is wrong. There is also no help to the user as to how to use them from within the user interface; so, we must provide documentation with these functions.

Apart from that, we get a very powerful way to provide the users with some very powerful functions that they can use to simplify and automate their processes.

8
Data Management, OData, and Office

In this chapter, we will cover the following recipes:

- Creating data entities
- Extending standard data entities
- Importing data through data import/export
- Reading, writing, and updating data through OData

Introduction

Microsoft Dynamics 365 for Operations is a cloud solution, and even when it is available on-premise, the obvious high availability/disaster recovery solution would be to switch to Microsoft Azure. So, even when our solution is designed to be on-premise, we shouldn't write our integrations to access local area network resources.

All integrations should have a service endpoint that will be accessed by Dynamics 365 for Operations.

To facilitate writing integrations that are agnostic of the local network resources, Microsoft has evolved the **Data Import/Export Framework** (**DIXF**) in this release, to help resolve many of the integrations issues we will often face. It also opens up a much more integrated way in which we can communicate with Microsoft Office.

In this chapter we will cover the usage and extensibility options for data entities, and also how to interact programmatically with our data entities through OData.

Creating a data entity

In this task, we will create a data entity for our vehicle table, which we will extend in order to demonstrate how data entities can be used. We will also use this to allow us to maintain vehicle data through the Office add-in and make it a public OData entity.

Getting ready

We will just need to have a Dynamics 365 for Operations project open, and a table for which we want to create a data entity.

How to do it...

To create the data entity, follow these steps:

1. In the project, add a new item. Within the **Add New Item** dialog, select **Data Model** from the left-hand list, and then **Data Entity** from the right.
2. Enter ConWHSVehicleTableEntity as **Name** and press **Add**.
3. We will then get a **Data Entity Wizard** dialog and select ConWHSVehicleTable in the **Primary datasource** drop-down list.

 As you scroll down, the drop-down list can resize, causing an item to be selected by mistake, it is therefore easier to use the *Page Up* and *Page Down* keys to locate the table.

The **Entity** category is not correct by default; use the following table to select the correct category:

Table group	Entity category
Main, Group	Master
Worksheet (all types)	Document
Transaction (all types)	Transaction
Parameter	Parameter
Reference	Reference

4. The dialog made a guess that `Con` was a prefix and stripped this from the **Public entity name** and **Public collection name** fields; the prefix should be put back to avoid the chance of naming collision.

> The defaults will create a public interface for access by other applications, such as Microsoft Office, a staging table for use with the Data Import/Export Framework, and security privileges in order to control who has access to this entity.

5. Click on **Next**.

> On this page, we can add related data sources and virtual fields. In our case, this is not required, and we will cover this option in the *There's more...* section.

6. If we check **Convert labels to field names**, it will use the field's labels for the field names. This is not usually desirable; the label may need the context of field group in order for us to know which field it relates to. Do not check this checkbox.

A grid is created based on the table's definition, which will be used as the settings used to generate the data entity. These settings are usually correct; in our case, the grid is as follows:

	Field name	Data entity field	Data type	EDT type name	Mandatory	Label id	Label	Help Text id	Help text
✓	VehicleId	VehicleId	String	ConWHSVehicleId	✓	@ConWHS:ConWHS21	Vehicle Id	@ConWHS:ConWHS20	The unique id of the vehicle table
✓	Description	Description	String	Description	☐	@SYS7576	Description		
✓	VehicleGroupId	VehicleGroupId	String	ConWHSVehicleGroupId	✓	@ConWHS:ConWHS3	Vehicle group	@ConWHS:ConWHS4	The vehicle group id
✓	VehRegNum	VehRegNum	String	ConWHSVehRegNum	☐	@ConWHS:ConWHS25	Registration	@ConWHS:ConWHS24	The vehicle registration number
✓	AcquiredDate	AcquiredDate	Date	ConWHSAcquiredDate	☐	@ConWHS:ConWHS12	Date acquired	@ConWHS:ConWHS13	The date the vehicle was acquired
✓	VehicleType	VehicleType	Enum		☐	@ConWHS:ConWHS1	Vehicle type	@ConWHS:ConWHS2	The type of vehicle
☐	DataAreaId	DataAreaId	String	DataAreaId	☐	Company	Company	ID for an area of data	ID for an area of data

> We can make additional fields mandatory; however, if we decide to uncheck a mandatory field, we will get an error unless it is specified in code before the actual record is inserted or updated. This can be useful when the mandatory field is inferred from another field in the data entity.

7. Click on **Finish**.

The wizard has created the following objects for us:

Element	Description
ConWHSVehicleTableEntity	This is the data entity
ConWHSVehicleTableStaging	This is a table used to stage data when importing via the Data Import/Export Framework
ConWHSVehicleTableEntityMaintain	This is a security privilege to allow us full access to the data entity
ConWHSVehicleTableEntityView	This is a security privilege to allow view-only access to the data entity

8. Build the project and synchronize it with the database.
9. Open the main form for the data entity; in our case, the `Vehicles` form, which can be accessed directly using the following URL:

```
https://usnconeboxax1aos.cloud.onebox.dynamics.com/?cmp=usmf
&mi=ConWHSVehicleTable
```

10. On the top right of the screen, the Office icon has a new option, **OPEN IN EXCEL**, as shown in the following screenshot:

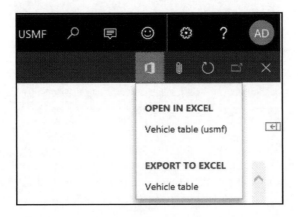

11. If you hover the mouse over the **Vehicle table (usmf)** link, you will see that it is our entity, as shown in the following screenshot:

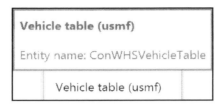

12. This is the public entity name we specified in the wizard, and we can change it by changing the **Public Entity Name** property on the data entity.

13. Click on the **Vehicle table (usmf)** link, and then click **Download** in the **Open in Excel** dialog.

14. Once Microsoft Excel opens, you may get the following warning:

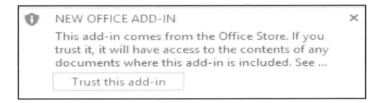

15. Click on **Trust this add-in**.

16. Next, click on **Sign in**, and sign in using the same account you used for logging into Dynamics 365 for Operations.

   Once signed in, it will populate a sheet with the data from the `ConWHSVehicleTable` table, but only add the mandatory fields. To test the entity, we should add a few fields.

17. In the add-in, click on **Design** and then click on the edit icon next to the
    ConWHSVehicleTable table, as shown in the following screenshot:

18. In the next page, select all of the fields in the **Available fields** list and press the
    Add button that is just above the **Selected fields** list.
19. Click on **Update**, and then click **Yes** to the warning.
20. Click on **Done**, which takes us out of the design experience, and then press
    Refresh to fetch the new data.
21. Our sheet should now have the data from the vehicle table, as shown in the
    following screenshot:

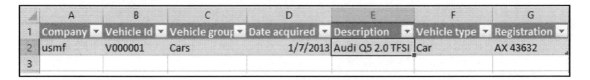

	A	B	C	D	E	F	G
1	Company	Vehicle Id	Vehicle group	Date acquired	Description	Vehicle type	Registration
2	usmf	V000001	Cars	1/7/2013	Audi Q5 2.0 TFSI	Car	AX 43632
3							

The headings are labels in your user's language, and the enumerated
types are also translated.

22. Edit one or more of the fields using the add-in to select the values when they
    have a drop-down list or date picker. Do not change the **Vehicle Id** value, but
    you can test this yourself in a different test to see what happens.
23. Click on **New** in the add-in in order to add a new vehicle, and complete the sheet
    as required. Once done, the result should be similar to the following screenshot:

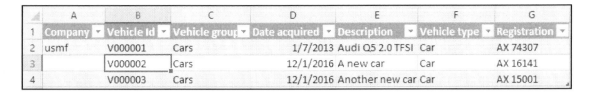

	A	B	C	D	E	F	G
1	Company ▾	Vehicle Id ▾	Vehicle group ▾	Date acquired ▾	Description ▾	Vehicle type ▾	Registration ▾
2	usmf	V000001	Cars	1/7/2013	Audi Q5 2.0 TFSI	Car	AX 74307
3		V000002	Cars	12/1/2016	A new car	Car	AX 16141
4		V000003	Cars	12/1/2016	Another new car	Car	AX 15001

The **Company** column was left blank, and we should actually remove this column from the sheet. If you remember that the link had the company within the link's name, this connection is bound using that company ID.

24. Once done, click on **Publish**; the entity will be refreshed with the company ID that was actually used when the records are created.
25. Finally, refresh the **Vehicles** form in Dynamics 365 for operations, and you will see the records within the vehicles list page.
26. Close the Excel worksheet.
27. Ideally, we would want to control which fields are available, so open the `ConWHSVehicleTableEntity` data entity in the designer.

The properties are very similar to those of a table, and the nodes in the design share those of both queries and tables. In fact, this is created in the SQL server database as a view and, if we synchronized the database, we could view the data in SQL Server Management Studio.

28. Add the fields you would like to see by default to the **AutoReport** field group.
29. You may also have noticed that the `VehicleGroupId` field did not have a drop-down list in Excel, and the foreign key relation does not help in this case. We will need a custom lookup, as shown in the following piece of code:

```
/// <summary>
/// A custom lookup for vehicle group ids
/// </summary>
/// <param name = "_fields">
/// This is the fields' meta data provided by the
/// office add-in
/// </param>
/// <returns>
/// A serialized list of vehicle group ids
/// </returns>
[SysODataAction(
    'ConWHSVehicleTableEntityVehicleGroupLookup',
    false),
```

```
    SysODataCollectionAttribute('_fields', Types::String),
    SysODataFieldLookup(fieldStr(ConWHSVehicleTableEntity,
                              VehicleGroupId))]
public static str LookupVehicleGroupId(Array _fields)
{
    RefFieldName vehicleGroupIdFld;
    vehicleGroupIdFld = fieldStr(ConWHSVehicleTableEntity,
                                 VehicleGroupId);

    // Build a field and value map from the _fields Array
    Map fieldMap;
    fieldMap = OfficeAppCustomLookupHelper::getFieldMap(
            tableStr(ConWHSVehicleTableEntity), _fields);

    // Determine the company that the office add-in is
    // connected to, otherwise it will return data from DAT
    DataAreaId dataAreaId = curExt();
    RefFieldName dataAreaIdFld;
    dataAreaIdFld = fieldStr(ConWHSVehicleTableEntity,
                              DataAreaId);
    if (fieldMap.exists(dataAreaIdFld))
    {
        dataAreaId = fieldMap.lookup(dataAreaIdFld);
    }

    // Construct the result object, and add our ID
    // field to the list as the first element in the array
    OfficeAppCustomLookupListResult result;
    result = new OfficeAppCustomLookupListResult();
    result.determinationFields().value(1,
                                     vehicleGroupIdFld);
    // declare the resultString here (latest) as it needs
    // to be in scope for when it is set, and returned to
    // the caller
    str resultString;

    // Check that the key field is in the supplied metadata
    if (OfficeAppCustomLookupHelper::fieldsBound(
        result.determinationFields(), fieldMap))
    {
        int counter = 1;
        // change to the company the office add-in
        // is connected to
        changecompany(dataAreaId)
        {
            ConWHSVehicleGroup vehicleGroups;
            // Add the vehicle group ids to the value array
            while select VehicleGroupId
```

```
                    from vehicleGroups
                    order by VehicleGroupId
         {
                    result.items().value(counter,
                              vehicleGroups.VehicleGroupId);
                    counter++;
         }
    }
    resultString = result.serialize();
}
return resultString;
}
```

30. Rebuild the project and test the add-in again; you will get the fields that you added to the field group along with the drop-down list on the **Vehicle group** column.

How it works...

When we created the entity with a public interface, it actually creates a service that office communicates with. The Excel file we downloaded was just to allow connection to the data entity using OData. We aren't reading records directly, the records are read from Dynamics 365 for Operations and are written back when we publish the changes.

The authentication goes through our Microsoft Office 365 account, and when hosted in Azure, the add-in takes care of the complexities of this integration for us. It is secure (and it also honors XDS data policies), yet available everywhere.

Until we got to writing the lookup, the process was remarkably easy, if we take into account the result we achieve with such little effort. It, therefore, stood out that we had to write quite a complicated method for the lookup.

The method does look a little daunting; however, when broken down, it becomes easier to understand.

The first key part of the method is the `SysODataFieldLookup` decoration, which is how it knows for which field the lookup is bound.

As we are using a static version of the pattern, the `_fields` parameter provides both metadata and the value of each field in the dataset. This is converted into the `fieldMap` map for ease of use.

We will need this in order to work out which company we are working in, so we will return data from that company. This differs from other static methods; in that, it is called with a company context. This is done by looking up the value of the `dataAreaId` field as follows:

```
dataAreaIdFld = fieldStr(ConWHSVehicleTableEntity, DataAreaId);
if(fieldMap.exists(dataAreaIdFld))
{
    dataAreaId = fieldMap.lookup(dataAreaIdFld);
}
```

 We have to check if it exists before we look it up; if not, it will throw an error if the key doesn't exist in the map.

Before adding the values to the array, we should check that the `VehicleGroupId` field is bound (is in the `_fields` array). We used `OfficeAppCustomLookupHelper::fieldsBound()` for this. In our case, it is semantically equivalent to checking that the field exists in the `fieldMap` map.

The actual lookup data is constructed by the following line of code:

```
result.items().value(counter, vehicleGroups.VehicleGroupId);
```

The `result.items()` function is an array or string values.

To return the data, it has to be serialized to a string, which was done by the following line of code:

```
resultString = result.serialize();
```

There's more...

There are a few special methods that are used when writing a data entity, which are as follows:

Method	Description
`updateEntityDataSource`	This is called when updating an existing record
`deleteEntityDataSource`	This is called when deleting a record
`insertEntityDataSource`	This is called when inserting a new record
`initializeEntityDataSource`	This is called when a record is initialized.

These methods are used so that we can update related records that are not directly affected by the tables in the entity. A good example is when a table is related to `DirPartyTable`. We can't simply delete the related party record in this case when the parent is deleted, as it may be used in other roles.

The following are sample methods for a fictitious `ConWHSHaulierTableEntity`, which has a main data source, `ConWHSHaulierTable`, and a child data source, `DirPartyBaseEntity`.

In this method we will check if the entity is the `DirPartyBaseEntity` data source, and if it is, it executes logic to handle the `DirPartyTable` and `LogisticsPostalAddress` tables. These tables are part of complicated structures, and the helper ensures that they are inserted correctly:

```
public boolean insertEntityDataSource(
        DataEntityRuntimeContext _entityCtx,
        DataEntityDataSourceRuntimeContext _dataSourceCtx)
{
    boolean ret;

    switch (_dataSourceCtx.name())
    {
        case dataEntityDataSourceStr(ConWHSHaulierTableEntity,
                                DirPartyBaseEntity):
            DirPartyBaseEntityHelper partyHelper;
            partyHelper = new DirPartyBaseEntityHelper();
            partyHelper.preInsertEntityDataSource(_entityCtx,
                                        _dataSourceCtx,
                dataEntityDataSourceStr(
                        ConWHSHaulierTableEntity,
                        LogisticsPostalAddressBaseEntity));

            ret = super(_entityCtx, _dataSourceCtx);

            if (ret)
            {
                partyHelper.postInsertEntityDataSource(_entityCtx,
                                _dataSourceCtx,
                    dataEntityDataSourceStr(
                            ConWHSHaulierTableEntity,
                            LogisticsPostalAddressBaseEntity));
            }
            break;
        default:
            ret = super(_entityCtx, _dataSourceCtx);
    }
```

```
        return ret;
    }
```

The following code handles the deletion logic and will correctly handle the update to the global address book (`DirPartyTable`), removing the links correctly for us:

```
public boolean deleteEntityDataSource(
                DataEntityRuntimeContext _entityCtx,
                DataEntityDataSourceRuntimeContext _dataSourceCtx)
{
    boolean ret;

    switch (_dataSourceCtx.name())
    {
        case dataEntityDataSourceStr(ConWHSHaulierTableEntity,
                                     DirPartyBaseEntity)):
            DirPartyBaseEntityHelper partyHelper;
            partyHelper = new DirPartyBaseEntityHelper();
            partyHelper.deleteEntityDataSource(_dataSourceCtx);
            break;
        default:
            ret = super(_entityCtx, _dataSourceCtx);
    }
    return ret;
}
```

The final method in this set is the code to handle what happens when records are updated, this is identical to the `insertEntityDataSource` method except that the method is called `updateEntityDataSource`.

The following method is called when the record is initialized; the code in this method is used correctly to initialize the global address book data structures:

```
public void initializeEntityDataSource(DataEntityRuntimeContext _entityCtx,
DataEntityDataSourceRuntimeContext _dataSourceCtx)
{
    super(_entityCtx, _dataSourceCtx);

    if (_dataSourceCtx.name() ==
            dataEntityDataSourceStr(ConWHSHaulierTableEntity,
                                    DirPartyBaseEntity))
    {
        // Takes care of maintaining the reference to existing
        // parties if this record provides a party number. This is
        // because, even though we may be inserting the customer
        // record, the party may already exist.
        DirPartyBaseEntity::
                initializeDirPartyBaseEntityDataSource(
```

```
                    _entityCtx,
                    _dataSourceCtx);
        }
    }
```

You can see examples of how these are used in many of the standard entities; a good example is `CustCustomerEntity`.

See also

The following links provide some guidance on related features and background to data entities and OData:

- *Add templates to Open lines in Excel menu*
  (`https://ax.help.dynamics.com/en/wiki/add-templates-to-open-lines-in-excel-menu/`)
- *Open lines in Excel from journals and documents*
  (`https://ax.help.dynamics.com/en/wiki/open-lines-in-excel-from-journals-and-documents/`)
- *Create Open in Excel experiences*
  (`https://ax.help.dynamics.com/en/wiki/off101-office-integration-enable-users-to-edit-data-in-excel/`)

 The preceding link shows how to create a lookup using a pattern that differs from how it is used within standard software and in this recipe. I chose to use the pattern from the standard software instead of the version in this guide.

- *Office integration troubleshooting*
  (`https://ax.help.dynamics.com/en/wiki/office-integration-troubleshooting/`)
- *Security and data entities*
  (`https://ax.help.dynamics.com/en/wiki/security-and-data-entities/`)

Extending standard data entities

Extensibility is becoming more and more pervasive in the development paradigm of Dynamics 365 for Operations, and it is important to be able to have extensible data entities; otherwise, we would have to write new ones to be able to use a field we added to a table as an extension.

In this example, we will create an extension for the Released product creation entity, named `EcoResReleasedProductCreationEntity`.

Getting ready

Part of this recipe is to add an extension field so we can import data into it, so the first part is to create an extension for the `InventTable` table with a new field. This is optional, but is included in order to demonstrate how this is done.

To follow this optional step, create a table extension for the `InventTable` table and add a new field of type `Name` called `ConWHSAdditionalName`. Also, add this to a form extension so we can see the results.

How to do it...

To create a data entity extension, follow these steps:

1. In the Application Explorer, expand **Data Model** and then **Data Entities**. Right-click on `EcoResReleasedProductCreationEntity` and select **Create extension**.
2. Rename the suffix from `.Extension` to `.ConWHS`, or your package name.

> After examining the **Data Sources** node, we can see that it is not based directly on `InventTable`, but on a data entity. We will, therefore, need to create an extension for this before we can add the field.

3. Locate `EcoResReleaseProductEntity`, create an extension, and rename it appropriately.
4. Expand the **Data Sources** nodes and then **InventTable**, and then locate the extension field (`ConWHSAdditionalName`). Right-click on the field and choose **Copy**.

5. Collapse the **Data Sources** node and right-click on the entity's root **Fields** node. Right-click on the **Fields** node and select **Paste**.

> Alternatively, you can right-click on the **Fields** node, choose **New** | **Mapped Field**, and complete the property sheet.

6. Save and close the data entity.

7. Open the `EcoResReleasedProductCreationEntity.ConWHS` data extension in the designer and expand the **Data Sources** and **EcoResReleasedProductEntity** nodes.

8. Locate the `ConWHSAdditionalName` field and use copy and paste to add it to the data entity's **Fields** node.

9. Since this will be used within the Data Import/Export Framework, we will need to add the field to the staging table. This cannot be done automatically as we are working with an extension--the system can't add fields to the standard table as that would result in an over-layer.

10. Locate the `EcoResReleasedProductCreationStaging` table and create an extension; name it appropriately.

11. Add the `ConWHSAdditionalName` field as we did on `InventTable`; you can use copy and paste to do this.

> We can work out which table is the staging table by looking at the **Data Management Staging** property of the original data entity, which is `EcoResReleasedProductCreationStaging` in this case.

12. For completeness, add the `ConWHSAdditionalName` field to the staging table for the `EcoResReleasedProductCreationEntity` data entity.

13. Save all and build the project.

> You will need to add a reference to `Dimensions` to your package in order for the build to succeed.

14. Finally, synchronize the project with the database.

How it works...

The data entity extension works in a similar way to any other extension--it stores a delta change in an XML definition file that is merged with the base entity when the project is built. Should we look at the entity within the client, which we do in the next recipe, we will see that the fields exist as if they were part of the entity.

As it was a mapped field, we don't need to write any special code in order to persist this through the staging table to the target table. Since this data entity is not public, it can't be used with the Office add-in or through OData; it is intended to be used within the Data Import/Export Framework.

There's more...

The extent by which application objects (such as forms, tables and data entities) are extensible will evolve with each release. Currently, we can add data sources, ranges, relations, field groups, and table maps to data entities. We cannot add new methods or change existing ones, as this would result in no practical difference to an over-layer (except it could be worse, as no tooling would exist for conflict management). Instead, we would subscribe to the many event delegates.

Importing data through Data Import/Export Framework

This recipe is usually a system administration function, but is needed in order to test our data entities. It also gives us more insight into understanding how our data entities work.

Getting ready

This recipe follows on from the previous one, where we are testing a data entity extension.

How to do it...

To import and export data using the Data Import/Export Framework, follow these steps:

1. Open Dynamics 365 for Operations in Internet Explorer; use the following link on a Development virtual machine:

```
https://usnconeboxax1aos.cloud.onebox.dynamics.com/?cmp=USMF
```

2. The first step, after making any change to the data entities, is to refresh the entity list. Open the **Data management** workspace, select **Framework parameters**, and click on **Refresh entity list** in the **Entity settings** tab page. This happens asynchronously, and you will get a message when it is complete; you may need to click in and out of forms for the message to appear.

3. Next, we will need to check that the fields exist and are mapped correctly on the **Data management** workspace; click on **Data entities**.

4. Type in `Released products` into the filter control and select **Entity: "Released products"** from the drop-down list.

5. Click on **Target fields** and check that the field exists in the list. If not, you need to rebuild the project and synchronize the project to the database. A full build using **Dynamics 365 | Build models** may be required if this persists.

6. Then, click on **Modify target mapping**. The grid may be empty, and if we haven't specified any specific mapping previously, we can use the **Generate mapping** button to create the default field mapping for us.

7. If we have specified specific mapping in this previously, clicking on **Generate mapping** will delete it. You can click on **New** and complete the line, or use the **MAPPING VISUALIZATION** tab page. In this form, drag the field from the right-hand list to the corresponding field on the left.

8. Now the mapping is done, let's export some data. On the **Data management** workspace, click on **Export**.

> It may seem odd to export a data entity that is used to create data, but the following steps are used to create an import template used later in the recipe.

9. Complete the form, as shown in the following table:

Field	Value
Name	ReleasedProductCreationExport
Target data format	EXCEL
Entity name	Released product creation
Skip staging	Yes
Default refresh type	Full push only

Select fields	All fields

10. Once complete, click on **Add entity**.
11. This creates a new tile. With this selected, click on **Export** from the top-button ribbon.

 The message suggests that you refresh the page; it means that the refresh icon on the top-right of the form, not the browser refresh button.

12. After some time, it will report that it succeeded. Click on **Download package** and say **Yes** to the message that follows.
13. This downloads a ZIP file, which we can use as an import template.
14. Copy the spreadsheet and, in the copy, remove all rows except the first two; as we will use the first product as a template to save having to look up valid values: we are only testing that it works for now.
15. Change the **ItemNumber** and **ProductNumber** columns to X1000 (an item number that has not yet been used).
16. Fill in the **ConWHSAdditionalName** column with something useful.
17. Save to the Documents folder and close the spreadsheet.
18. Go back to the Dynamics 365 for Operations client, and navigate back to the **Data management** workspace. Click on **Import**.
19. Complete the fields as follows:

Field	Value
Name	ReleasedProductCreationImport
Source data format	EXCEL
Entity name	Released product creation

20. Click on **Import**.
21. Check the mapping by clicking on **View map** on the newly created tile, and note that the mapping is done for us.
22. Locate the spreadsheet created earlier and press **Open**.
23. Click on **Upload**.

24. This can take a while on a development VM, so just be patient and click the form refresh button every so often. Eventually, you will get a tile as shown in the following screenshot:

25. Click on **View staging data** and check that the **Additional name** field is completed. If not, the mapping was probably not completed correctly.
26. After a short time later, the tile will change to show that the records are now in the target. Check this by opening the release products form; check that all fields were populated correctly.

How it works...

There is a lot to the Data Import/Export Framework, some of which we will cover further in the next recipe. In this case, we will create a simple export to create a template that we then used to import some test data. The mapping worked based on name matching, and this is usually the best method, especially for loading test data.

See also

- *Data entities and packages framework* (https://ax.help.dynamics.com/en/wiki/using-data-entities-and-data-packages/)
- *Data entities home page* (https://ax.help.dynamics.com/en/wiki/data-entities-home-page/)

Reading, writing, and updating data through OData

In this example, we will create a sample OData console application in order to demonstrate how to connect and communicate through OData.

In order to start, you will need to create an application within your organization's Azure ID. You will need the application ID--an official guide as to how to do this is available at `https://ax.help.dynamics.com/en/wiki/dynamics-ax-7-services-technical-concepts-guide/`

Getting ready

The following doesn't have to be done in the Dynamics 365 for Operations development virtual machine. However, it will need to have access to the URL.

How to do it...

To import and export data using the Data Import/Export Framework, follow these steps:

1. Create a new project but, this time, choose Visual C# from the `Templates` node and then Console Application from the right. Name the project `ConODataTest` and place it in the `project` folder that we set up for source control. Ensure that the name space is also `ConODataTest`.

2. We will now need to install some NuGet packages. Within Visual Studio, navigate to **Tools** | **Nuget Package Manager** | **Package Manager Console**.

   > *"NuGet is the package manager for the Microsoft development platform including .NET. The NuGet client tools provide the ability to produce and consume packages. The NuGet Gallery is the central package repository used by all package authors and consumers."* - (`https://www.nuget.org/`)

3. In the Package Manager console, type the following commands:
   - `Install-Package Microsoft.Bcl.Build`
   - `Install-Package Microsoft.Bcl`
   - `Install-Package Microsoft.Net.Http`
   - `Install-Package Microsoft.OData.Core -Version 6.15.0`

- Install-Package Simple.OData.Client -Version 4.24.0.1
- Install-Package Microsoft.Data.OData
- Install-Package Microsoft.OData.Client
- Install-Package Microsoft.IdentityModel.Clients.ActiveDirectory

Simple.OData.Client is added as an alternative and is not used in this example. This is why the specific 6.15.0 version of Microsoft.OData.Core was used. If Simple.OData.Client is not being used, the version need not be specified.

4. Restart Visual Studio, otherwise, the build will fail without any message as to why.
5. Next, we will need an add-in for Visual Studio in order to read the metadata and generate types for us. Navigate to **Tools | Extensions and Updates**.
6. Click on **Online** on the left and type OData Client Code in the **Search Visual Studio Gallery** text box.
7. Select **OData v4 Client Code Generator** from the list and click on **Download**.
8. Once installed, you will be asked to restart Visual Studio.
9. Once restarted, choose to add a new item to the project. Select **OData Client** from the list. Name it OdataClient.tt and click on **Add**.

A tt file is a transformation file, and its purpose will become more apparent as we progress.

10. Toward the top of this file, you will see the following line:

```
public const string MetadataDocumentUri = "";
```

11. Change it so that it reads as follows:

```
public const string MetadataDocumentUri =
"https://usnconeboxax1aos.cloud.onebox.dynamics.com/data/$metad
ata";
```

12. Check that you have access to https://usnconeboxax1aos.cloud.onebox.dynamics.com/ in the browser and that you can log in. Minimize (do not close) the browser and go back to

Visual Studio.

13. With the `ODataClient.tt` file open in the code window, click on **Save** or press *Ctrl + S*. You will receive a security warning, click on **OK** to proceed. This will take a few minutes to proceed, as it is a generated client and type code for all public entities.

> Once complete, you will see a new `ODataClient.cs` file nested under the `ODataClient.tt` file with many methods. The file is around 40 MB, so opening it will take a while and is best avoided.
> Should you find that Visual Studio starts to perform slowly, ensure that you have closed `ODataClient.tt` and `ODataCilent.cs` and then restart Visual Studio.

14. We can now start writing the code for our test; add a new class to the project named `ODataTest`.

15. Add the following using statements to the top of the file:

```
using System;
using System.Threading.Tasks;
using Microsoft.IdentityModel.Clients.ActiveDirectory;
using Microsoft.OData.Client;
using ConODataTest.Microsoft.Dynamics.DataEntities;
```

16. To simplify the process, create the follow data contract classes in order to aid passing parameters. Add them just below the using statements, and above the `ODataTest` class definition:

```
class ODataUserContract
{
    public string userName;
    public string password;
    public string domain;
}
class ODataApplicationContract
{
    public string applicationId;
    public string resource;
    public string result;
}
public class ODataRequestContract
{
    public string company;
}
```

We would usually use get/set methods here, but I used public variables to save space for this test.

17. In the class body, declare the following class variables:

```
class ODataTest
{
    public const string OAuthHeader = "Authorization";
    public ODataUserContract userContract;
    public ODataApplicationContract appContract;
    public ODataRequestContract request;

    string authenticationHeader;
    public string response;
```

The OAuthHeader and authenticationHeader variables are key to the process of authentication with Dynamics 365 for Operations.

18. The code to authenticate with Azure AD is as follows:

```
private AuthenticationResult GetAuthorization()
{
    UriBuilder uri = new
UriBuilder("https://login.windows.net/" + userContract.domain);

    AuthenticationContext authenticationContext
        = new AuthenticationContext(uri.ToString());
    UserPasswordCredential credential = new
        UserPasswordCredential(
        userContract.userName, userContract.password);

    Task<AuthenticationResult> task =
authenticationContext.AcquireTokenAsync(
        appContract.resource,
            appContract.applicationId, credential);

    task.Wait();
    AuthenticationResult
        authenticationResult = task.Result;
    return authenticationResult;
}
```

19. Now, create a public method that will be called in order to log on:

```
public Boolean Authenticate()
{
    AuthenticationResult authenticationResult;
    try
    {
        authenticationResult = GetAuthorization();
        //this gets the authorization token, this
        // must be set on the Http header for all requests
        authenticationHeader =
            authenticationResult.CreateAuthorizationHeader();
    }
    catch (Exception e)
    {
        response = "Authentication failed: " + e.Message;
        return false;
    }
    response = "OK";
    return true;
}
```

20. Each method that makes a call to Operations must set up a resources instance, which has an event handler in order to set the authentication key. This method should be written as follows:

```
private Resources MakeResources()
{
    string entityRootPath = appContract.resource + "/data";
    Uri oDataUri = new Uri(entityRootPath,
                            UriKind.Absolute);
    var resources = new Resources(oDataUri);
    resources.SendingRequest2 += new
        EventHandler<SendingRequest2EventArgs>(
            delegate (object sender,
                        SendingRequest2EventArgs e)
    {
        // This event handler is needed to set
        // the authentication code we got when
        // we logged on.
        e.RequestMessage.SetHeader(OAuthHeader,
            authenticationHeader);
    });
    return resources;
}
```

21. The next three methods are to demonstrate reading, updating, and creating records through OData:

```
public System.Collections.ArrayList GetVehicleNameList()
{
    System.Collections.ArrayList vehicleNames;
    vehicleNames = new System.Collections.ArrayList();

    var resources = this.MakeResources();
    resources.ConWHSVehicleTables.AddQueryOption(
        "DataAreaId", request.company);
    foreach (var vehicle in resources.ConWHSVehicleTables)
    {
        vehicleNames.Add(vehicle.Description);
    }
    return vehicleNames;
}
public Boolean UpdateVehicleNames()
{
    var resources = this.MakeResources();
    resources.ConWHSVehicleTables.AddQueryOption(
        "DataAreaId", request.company);
    foreach (var vehicle in resources.ConWHSVehicleTables)
    {
        vehicle.Description = vehicle.VehicleId
            + " : OData did it";
        resources.UpdateObject(vehicle);
    }
    try
    {
        resources.SaveChanges();
    }
    catch (Exception e)
    {
        response = e.InnerException.Message;
        return false;
    }
    return true;
}
public Boolean CreateNewVehicle(
    ConWHSVehicleTable _newVehicle)
{
    var resources = this.MakeResources();
    _newVehicle.DataAreaId = request.company;
    resources.AddToConWHSVehicleTables(_newVehicle);
    try
    {
        resources.SaveChanges();
    }
    catch (Exception e)
    {
```

```
            response = e.InnerException.Message;
            return false;
        }
        return true;
    }
```

22. Finally, we can write our main method. Open the `Program.cs` file and ensure that we have the following using statements at the top:

```
using System;
using ConODataTest.Microsoft.Dynamics.DataEntities;
```

23. Write the main method as follows (use the application ID you generated from your Azure AD application):

```
static void Main(string[] args)
{
    ODataApplicationContract appContract;
    appContract = new ODataApplicationContract();
    appContract.resource =
"https://usnconeboxax1aos.cloud.onebox.dynamics.com";
    appContract.applicationId = "<your application Id>";

    ODataUserContract userContract = new
        ODataUserContract();
    Console.WriteLine("Use the O365 account that you use to log
in to Dynamics 365 for Operations");
    Console.Write("O365 Username: ");
    userContract.userName = Console.ReadLine();
    Console.Write("O365 Password: ");
    userContract.password = Console.ReadLine();
    Console.WriteLine("This is your tenant, such as
yourdomain.com or <yourtenant>.onmicrosoft.com");
    Console.Write("O365 Domain: ");
    userContract.domain = Console.ReadLine();
    ODataTest test = new ConODataTest.ODataTest();
    test.userContract = userContract;
    test.appContract = appContract;
    if (!test.Authenticate())
    {
        Console.WriteLine(test.response);
    }
    test.request = new ConODataTest.ODataRequestContract();
    test.request.company = "USMF";
    System.Collections.ArrayList vehicleNames =
test.GetVehicleNameList();
    foreach (var vehicleName in vehicleNames)
    {
```

```
                Console.WriteLine(vehicleName);
        }

        Console.WriteLine("Changing vehicle descriptions");
        test.UpdateVehicleNames();

        ConWHSVehicleTable vehicle = new ConWHSVehicleTable();

        Console.WriteLine("Create a new Vehicle");
        Console.Write("Vehicle Id: ");
        vehicle.VehicleId = Console.ReadLine();
        Console.Write("Vehicle group: ");
        vehicle.VehicleGroupId = Console.ReadLine();
        Console.Write("Description: ");
        vehicle.Description = Console.ReadLine();
        test.CreateNewVehicle(vehicle);
        Console.WriteLine("Press enter to continue.");
        Console.ReadLine();
    }
```

24. To see what is going on, add some breakpoints and use the debugger and run it (press *F5*); don't step into code that would open `ODataClient.cs`; this can take a long time to open.

How it works...

To describe this, it is best to step through the key parts of the code.

The first part was clicking on save on the `ODataClient.tt` file. This created the class by reading the URL we entered in the `metadataDocumentURI` variable. When the file is saved, it triggers the generation of code using metadata from Dynamics 365 for Operations. If you click on **Save**, and then cancel the security warning, the `ODataClient.cs` file will be emptied.

Within the code we wrote, the first key part is the authentication, which works by authenticating with Azure AD and fetching an authentication, which is used with each submission request. The authorization code was determined in the `GetAuthorization` method.

The log on URI is always `https://login.windows.net/` plus your domain. If your O365 account was `julia@contoso.com`, the URI would be `https://login.windows.net/conto so.com`.

We can't send a username and password directly; we have to create a credential using the following code (from the `ActiveDirectory` namespace):

```
UserPasswordCredential credential = new
    UserPasswordCredential(
        userContract.userName, userContract.password);
```

The authentication is performed by the following code:

```
Task<AuthenticationResult> task = authenticationContext.AcquireTokenAsync(
    appContract.resource,
    appContract.applicationId, credential);

task.Wait();
AuthenticationResult authenticationResult = task.Result;
```

This differs from the current Microsoft sample code, as we now have to use an asynchronous call; using a task, the `task.wait()` line essentially makes the code execute synchronously. This is OK for sample code, but it is more useful to use an asynchronous call when writing a production application as we can create a more user-responsive application.

The `Authenticate` method calls the `GetAuthorization` method and does two things. First, we have a `try catch` statement to return a nicer message to the user upon failure (we will populate the `response` public variable and return false); secondly, this is where the `authenticationHeader` variable is set. This, we will need for the requests we make.

Within the `Program` class, in the `Main` method, we will construct `ODataUserContract` and complete the variables for `username`, `password`, and `domain` using the `Console.ReadLine()` method. We will construct the `ODataTest` class and call `Authenticate()`.

Once authenticated, we can work with the data. The three test methods, `GetVehicleNameList`, `UpdateVehicleNames`, and `CreateNewVehicle`, all have a similar pattern.

Each method makes a call to `MakeResources`, which is done by the following lines of code:

```
string entityRootPath = appContract.resource + "/data";
Uri oDataUri = new Uri(entityRootPath,
                       UriKind.Absolute);
var resources = new Resources(oDataUri);
resources.SendingRequest2 += new
    EventHandler<SendingRequest2EventArgs>(
       delegate (object sender,
         SendingRequest2EventArgs e)
{
    e.RequestMessage.SetHeader(OAuthHeader,
        authenticationHeader);
});
```

The `entityRootPath` variable is the Dynamics 365 for Operations URL plus `data`; on the development virtual machine, this is `https://usnconeboxax1aos.cloud.onebox.dynamics.com/data`. We can specify HTTP headers on the request, so we have to add an event handler. This, essentially, set the `Authorization` header property, which is what `OAuthHeader` constants equates to.

Each of the methods can then do what they need to; all requests are to use the `resources` object and, when each request is made, the event handler will be called to set the authorization header property.

The following line sets the company; however, if we omit this, it will use the user's default company, which may be desirable in some cases:

```
resources.ConWHSVehicleTables.AddQueryOption(
    "DataAreaId",
    request.company);
```

The first example was to read `ConWHSVehicleTableEntity` into a list, which was done using the following code:

```
//System.Collections.ArrayList vehicleNames;
foreach (var vehicle in resources.ConWHSVehicleTables)
{
    vehicleNames.Add(vehicle.Description);
}
```

The request to the server is done when it reaches `resources.ConWHSVehicleTables`, which is when the data is actually read. The `vehicleNames.Add(...)` function simply adds our chosen field to a list. You may wonder why the resource's object knows to call the collection `ConWHSVehicleTables` and the singleton `ConWHSVehicleTable`. This is determined from the `PublicCollectionName` and `PublicEntityName` properties we specified when we created the `ConWHSVehicleTableEntity` data entity.

The next example was how to update data and was done by writing the following piece of code:

```
foreach (var vehicle in resources.ConWHSVehicleTables)
{
    vehicle.Description = vehicle.VehicleId +
                            " : OData did it";
    resources.UpdateObject(vehicle);
}
try
{
    resources.SaveChanges();
}
catch (Exception e)
{
    response = e.InnerException.Message;
    return false;
}
return true;
```

The `resoures.UpdateObject(object)` method records that we have made a change, but does not write this back. The changes are actually saved by the `resources.SaveChanges()` method. This will call Dynamics 365 for Operation's validation logic for the record and, if this fails, it will throw an exception. The `e.InnerException.Messages` is actually JSON, and you can traverse this by giving the message back to the users.

The next example is to create a new vehicle. This is very simple code. We will just create an instance of the `ConWHSVehicelTable` class, populate it with the required values (`VehicleId`, `DataAreaId`, `VehicleGroupId`, and so on), and call the appropriate `AddTo` method. In this case, it is `AddToConWHSVehicleTables(ConWHSVehicleTable)`.

There is a lot we can do with OData, and the best way to learn is to use this example.

See also

The following link contains simple examples for OData, Soap, and JSON. You may wish to change the code to match the patterns in this recipe as you use them:

- *Microsoft / Dynamics-AX-Integration*
  (`https://github.com/Microsoft/Dynamics-AX-Integration/tree/master/ServiceSamples`)
- *Data management and integration through data entities*
  (`https://ax.help.dynamics.com/en/wiki/data-management-and-integration-through-data-entity/`)
- *OData* (`https://ax.help.dynamics.com/en/wiki/odata-in-dynamics-ax-7/`)
- *NuGet* (`http://www.nuget.org/`)

9

Consuming and Exposing Services

In this chapter, we will cover the following recipes:

- Creating a service
- Consuming a Dynamics 365 for Operations SOAP service
- Consuming a Dynamics 365 for Operations JSON service
- Consuming an external service within Dynamics 365 for Operations

Introduction

This chapter focuses on how to create services in Dynamics 365 for Operations, and how to consume them in external applications. This does not include OData services, which was covered in the previous chapter.

The method in which services are created hasn't changed significantly from Dynamics AX 2012 (the prior release to Dynamics 365 for Operations). The key difference is that web methods don't need to be marked as an entry point.

The consumption of Dynamics 365 for Operations' services has changed considerably. This means that any current integration from external apps will need changes to the method of authentication and how the input contracts are created. Having said so, the changes should be akin to a refactoring exercise for custom services accessed through SOAP.

The **Application Integration Framework** (**AIF**) has been removed in this release, so document services are not available; this is replaced by OData. Custom services are still available, but no longer require the AIF. They are accessed using the path defined by the levels Service Group, Service, and Operation, and we will see this later in this chapter.

Completely new to this release is JSON, and it is the preferred method of interaction with the API. JSON may be new to most X++ developers, but there is a lot of technical guidance available online on how to use it.

Finally, we will consume an external service from within Dynamics 365 for Operations.

Creating a service

There are three parts to creating a new service:

- Create a class that contains the business logic
- Create a service that has operations that reference operations to the class's methods
- Create a service group

The service group is a collection of one or more services, and acts as the service reference should we consume it within Visual Studio. We will see how this translates to a URI in the next recipe.

In this example, we will have two service operations: one to get a list of vehicles, and one to update a vehicle's group. The XML documentation has been omitted to save space.

Getting ready

We will just need a Dynamics 365 for Operations visual studio project open.

How to do it...

To create the service, follow these steps:

1. First, create a new class that will hold our service methods and name this class `ConWHSVehicleServices`.

2. The first service will be to update the `Vehicle` service group, for which we have a contract and processing class already created (`ConWHSVehicleGroupChangeContract`, `ConWHSVehicleGroupChange`), to write this method; write a method as follows:

```
public void ChangeVehicleGroup(
        ConWHSVehicleGroupChangeContract _contract)
{
    ConWHSVehicleGroupChange changeGroup =
            new ConWHSVehicleGroupChange();
    changeGroup.Run(_contract);
}
```

 This will work, but the consumer will not thank us for the lack of error handling. We could either return a Boolean on success or write a return contract. A return contract is the most useful way to return the result status.

3. To allow a meaningful reply, we will create a data contract class. Create a new class called `ConWHSMessageContract`, and complete it as follows:

```
[DataContract]
class ConWHSMessageContract
{
    boolean success;
    str      message;
    [DataMember]
    public boolean Success(boolean _success = success)
    {
        success = _success;
        return success;
    }
    [DataMember]
    public str Message(str _message = message)
    {
        message = _message;
        return message;
    }
}
```

4. Now update the method so that it reads as follows:

```
public ConWHSMessageContract changeVehicleGroup(
        ConWHSVehicleGroupChangeContract _contract)
{
    ConWHSMessageContract message =
            new ConWHSMessageContract();
    ConWHSVehicleGroupChange changeGroup =
            new ConWHSVehicleGroupChange();

    try
    {
        updateGroup.contract = _contract;
        if(updateGroup.Validate())
        {
            updateGroup.Run(_contract);
            message.Success(true);
        }
        else
        {
            message.Success(false);
            // Could not update vehicle %1 to vehicle
            // group %2
            message.Message(strFmt("@ConWHS:ConWHS53",
                            _contract.VehicleId(),
                            _contract.VehicleGroupId()));
        }
    }
    catch
    {
        message.Success(false);
        //Could not update vehicle %1 to vehicle group %2
        message.Message(strFmt("@ConWHS:ConWHS53",
                            _contract.VehicleId(),
                            _contract.VehicleGroupId()));

    }
    return message;
}
```

5. Next, let's try and get a little adventurous and return a list of vehicles. In this method, we will return a list of contracts, each representing a vehicle record. We will first need a contract to store vehicle data; create one as follows:

```
[DataContract]
class ConWHSVehicleTableContract
{
```

```
ConWHSVehicleId      vehicleId;
Description          description;
ConWHSVehRegNum      vehRegNum;
ConWHSAcquiredDate   acquiredDate;
ConWHSVehicleType    vehicleType;
ConWHSVehicleGroupId vehicleGroupId;

[DataMember]
public ConWHSVehicleGroupId VehicleGroupId(
     ConWHSVehicleGroupId _vehicleGroupId =
                          vehicleGroupId)
{
    vehicleGroupId = _vehicleGroupId;
    return vehicleGroupId;
}
[DataMember]
public ConWHSAcquiredDate AcquiredDate(
    ConWHSAcquiredDate _acquiredDate = acquiredDate)
{
    acquiredDate = _acquiredDate;
    return acquiredDate;
}
[DataMember]
public ConWHSVehicleId vehicleId(
    ConWHSVehicleId _vehicleId = vehicleId)
{
    vehicleId = _vehicleId;
    return vehicleId;
}
[DataMember]
public ConWHSVehicleType VehicleType(
    ConWHSVehicleType _vehicleType = vehicleType)
{
    vehicleType = _vehicleType;
    return vehicleType;
}
[DataMember]
public ConWHSVehRegNum VehRegNum(
    ConWHSVehRegNum _vehRegNum = vehRegNum)
{
    vehRegNum = _vehRegNum;
    return vehRegNum;
}
[DataMember]
public Description Description(
    Description _description = description)
{
    description = _description;
```

```
                return description;
            }
        }
```

 We could simply use the table as the contract, but using a data contract class allows us greater control over the data passed between Dynamics 365 for Operations and the external application that is using the service.

6. Close the code window for the contract class and open the code window for the ConWHSVehicleServices class.

7. We cannot return an array of classes in Operations in the same way that C# can; instead, we construct a List and tell the compiler the type that the list contains. This is done by the AifCollectionType attribute added to the start of the method. Complete the method, as shown in the following piece of code:

```
[AifCollectionType('return',
                   Types::Class,
                   classStr(ConWHSVehicleTableContract))]
public List GetVehicles()
{
    List vehicleList;
    ConWHSVehicleTable    vehicles;
    ConWHSVehicleTableContract contract;

    vehicleList = new List(Types::Class);

    while select vehicles
    {
        contract = new ConWHSVehicleTableContract();
        contract.vehicleId(vehicles.VehicleId);
        contract.vehicleGroupId(vehicles.VehicleGroupId);
        contract.vehicleType(vehicles.VehicleType);
        contract.vehRegNum(vehicles.VehRegNum);
        contract.acquiredDate(vehicles.AcquiredDate);
        vehicleList.addEnd(contract);
    }
    return vehicleList;
}
```

8. We will now have our two methods that will become service methods. To create the service, add a new item to the project by choosing **Services** from the left-hand list and **Service** from the right. **Name** the service `ConWHSVehicleServices` and click on **Add**.

9. Select the root **ConWHSVehicleServices** node and set the **Class** property to `ConWHSVehicleServices` (the class we wrote).

10. Enter a description for the service, such as `Provides services for vehicles`.

11. The **External Name** property should be specified as a simpler form of the service name. As it will be within a service group, we don't need the prefix. `VehicleServices` is appropriate for this property.

12. Enter a namespace in the **Namespace** property, such as `http://schemas.contoso.com/ConWHS`. The URL does not have to exist, as it is used as a name space for the service.

13. Right-click on the **Service Operations** node and select **New Service Operation**.

14. Select one of the two methods in the **Method** property and make the **Name** property the same as the **Method** property.

15. Repeat this for the next service method.

16. Save and close the service designer window.

17. Create a new item in our project; this time, **Service Group** from the **Services** list. Name it `ConWHSServices`.

18. Create a label for `Contoso vehicle management services` and enter the ID in the **Description** property.

19. Locate the `ConWHSVehicleServices` service in the project or Application Explorer and drag it onto the **ConWHSServices** node in the designer; this adds the service to the service group.

20. Remove the `ConWHS` prefix from the **Name** property as this is superfluous.

21. Save and close all designers and build the project.

How it works...

The first new concept was how Dynamics 365 for Operations handles collections. In C#, we would return a typed collection or an array (`MyClass[]`), and we could use the `foreach` command to iterate through it.

 This is not supported in X++, so we have to return a `List` instead. Since we actually want to return a typed collection to the caller, we will use the `AifCollectionType` attribute to tell the compiler how to do this.

The next part was to create a service and service group, which simply instructs the system to generate public services exposing the methods we added to the service.

We will see how this is used in the next recipe.

Consuming a Dynamics 365 for Operations SOAP service

In this recipe, we will create a new C# project to consume the service created in the previous recipe.

Before we start, we should understand the Azure AD authentication concepts explained in the *Reading, writing, and updating data through OData* recipe, in Chapter 8, *Data Management, Odata, and Office*. Many of the concepts in the following recipes extended the concepts we covered in this chapter.

In this example, we will create a SOAP service reference.

Getting ready

We are continuing the *Creating a service* recipe, which must be completed and built before we continue.

How to do it...

To consume a Dynamics 365 for Operations service using SOAP, follow these steps:

1. Create a new project; this time, choose **Visual C#** from the **Templates** node and then **Console Application** from the right. Name the project `ConServiceTest` and place it in the project folders that we set up for source control. Ensure that the namespace is also `ConServiceTest`.

2. We will now need to install some NuGet packages. Within Visual Studio, navigate to **Tools** | **Nuget Package Manager** | **Package Manager Console**.

3. In the Package Manager console, type the following command:

```
Install-Package Microsoft.IdentityModel.Clients.ActiveDirectory
```

4. Right-click on the **References** node in the project and choose **Add Service Reference**.

5. Enter `https://usnconeboxax1aos.cloud.onebox.dynamics.com/soap/services/ConWHSServices` in the **Address** field and click on **Go**.

 This is the Operations URL with `/soap/services/` added, followed by the service group name.

6. Expand the **ConWHSServices** node and select **VehicleService**.

7. Change the **Namespace** field to `ConWHS` and click on **OK**.

8. Create a new class called `Authenticate`.

 We will reuse this class, so this simplifies the process and allows us to reuse the code throughout the project.

9. We will need two classes: the contract class so we can pass data to the `Authenticate` class, and the `Authenticate` class itself.

 The concepts are the same as described in the *Reading, writing, and updating data through OData* recipe of `Chapter 8`, *Data Management, Odata, and Office*; they are just separated in order to make the code reusable.

10. Write the following piece of code:

```
class AuthenticationContract
{
    public string UserName { get; set; }
    public string Password { get; set; }
    public string Domain { get; set; }
    public string ApplicationId { get; set; }
    public string Resource { get; set; }
    public string Response { get; set; }
}
```

This time, we will use property methods instead, as this method allows more flexibility. For example, if we omit the set; argument, the property is read-only:

```
public class Authenticate
{
    public const string OAuthHeader = "Authorization";
    string bearerkey;
    public AuthenticationContract Authentication
        { get; set; }
    public string BearerKey
    {
        get { return bearerkey; }
    }
    public Boolean GetAuthenticationHeader()
    {
        AuthenticationResult result;
        try
        {
            result = GetAuthorization();
            // This gets the authorization token, this
            // must be set on the Http header for all
            // requests
            bearerkey =
                result.CreateAuthorizationHeader();
        }
        catch (Exception e)
        {
            if (e.InnerException != null)
            {
                Authentication.Response =
                    "Authentication failed: " +
                    e.InnerException.Message;
            }
            else
            {
```

```
                    Authentication.Response =
                        "Authentication failed: " +
                        e.Message;
                }
            return false;
        }
        Authentication.Response = "OK";
        return true;
    }
    public UserPasswordCredential GetCredential()
    {
        string uri = this.GetSecurityURI();
        UserPasswordCredential credential;

        credential =
            new UserPasswordCredential(
                Authentication.UserName,
                Authentication.Password);
        return credential;
    }
    public string GetSecurityURI()
    {
        UriBuilder uri;
        uri = new UriBuilder(
            "https://login.windows.net/" +
            Authentication.Domain);
        return uri.ToString();
    }
    private AuthenticationResult GetAuthorization()
    {
        UserPasswordCredential credential;
        credential = GetCredential();

        AuthenticationContext context
        = new AuthenticationContext(GetSecurityURI());

        Task<AuthenticationResult> task =
            context.AcquireTokenAsync(
                Authentication.Resource.TrimEnd('/'),
                Authentication.ApplicationId,
                credential);

        task.Wait();
        return task.Result;
    }
}
```

11. You can close the code editor for this class.

12. Create a new class called `SOAPUtil`.

 The code in this class was 'inspired' by a sample utility provided by this URL:
`https://github.com/Microsoft/Dynamics-AX-Integration/blob/mas`
`ter/ServiceSamples/SoapUtility/SoapHelper.cs`.

13. Set the using declarations to the following lines of code:

```
using System;
using System.Linq;
using System.ServiceModel;
using System.ServiceModel.Channels;
```

14. To simplify the usage, we will need a utility class. This should be written as follows:

```
public class SoapUtil
{
    public const string OAuthHeader = "Authorization";

    public static string GetServiceURI(
        string _service,
        string _d365OURI)
    {
        string serviceName = _service.Split('.').Last();
        if (serviceName == "")
        {
            serviceName = _service;
        }

        return _d365OURI.TrimEnd('/') + "/soap/services/"
                                     + serviceName;
    }
    public static EndpointAddress GetEndpointAddress(
        string _uri)
    {
        EndpointAddress address;
        address = new EndpointAddress(_uri);
        return address;
    }
    public static Binding GetBinding(
        EndpointAddress _address)
    {
        BasicHttpBinding binding;
        binding = new BasicHttpBinding(
            BasicHttpSecurityMode.Transport);
```

```
// Set binding timeout and other configuration
// settings
binding.ReaderQuotas.MaxStringContentLength =
    int.MaxValue;
binding.ReaderQuotas.MaxArrayLength = int.MaxValue;
binding.ReaderQuotas.MaxNameTableCharCount =
    int.MaxValue;

binding.ReceiveTimeout = TimeSpan.MaxValue;
binding.SendTimeout = TimeSpan.MaxValue;
binding.MaxReceivedMessageSize = int.MaxValue;

var httpsBindingElement =
    binding.CreateBindingElements().
    OfType<HttpsBindingElement>().FirstOrDefault();
if (httpsBindingElement != null)
{
    // Largest possible is 100000, otherwise throws
    // an exception
    httpsBindingElement.MaxPendingAccepts = 10000;
}

var httpBindingElement =
    binding.CreateBindingElements().
    OfType<HttpBindingElement>().FirstOrDefault();
if (httpBindingElement != null)
{
    httpBindingElement.MaxPendingAccepts = 10000;
}
return binding;
    }
}
```

 The `GetBinding` method is the key one here. We will authenticate through what is called a bearer key, which is implemented by setting the Authorization header variable; so, we will write a binding manually so that the binding in `App.Config` does not interfere.

15. Close the code editor and create a new class called `UpdateVehicleGroup`.

16. Set the `using` statements as follows:

```
using System.ServiceModel.Channels;
using System.ServiceModel;
```

17. Write the following method:

```
public ConWHS.ConWHSMessageContract UpdateSOAP(
```

```
                AuthenticationContract _authContract,
                ConWHS.ConWHSVehicleGroupChangeContract _change)
    {
                Authenticate auth = new Authenticate();
                auth.Authentication = _authContract;
                ConWHS.ConWHSMessageContract message;
                // If we fail to get the authorization bearer
                // key, stop and return the error through
                // the message contract
                if (!auth.GetAuthenticationHeader())
                {
                    message = new ConWHS.ConWHSMessageContract();
                    message.Success = false;
                    message.Message = auth.Authentication.Response;
                    return message;
                }
                string bearerKey = auth.BearerKey;

                string endPoint;
                endPoint = SoapUtil.GetServiceURI(
                    "ConWHSServices",
                    _authContract.Resource);

                EndpointAddress address;
                address= SoapUtil.GetEndpointAddress(endPoint);

                Binding binding = SoapUtil.GetBinding(address);

                ConWHS.VehicleServiceClient client;
                client = new ConWHS.VehicleServiceClient(
                                binding, address);
                ConWHS.CallContext conContext;

                conContext = new ConWHS.CallContext();
                conContext.Company = "USMF";
                conContext.Language = "en-us";
                conContext.PartitionKey = "initial";

                var channel = client.InnerChannel;
                // we don't use the context, it is used to affect
                // the channel so that we can set the outgoing
                // message properties
                // Using is used so that it is disposed of
                // correctly.
                using (OperationContextScope context
                    = new OperationContextScope(channel))
                {
                    //Set the authentication bearer key
```

```
HttpRequestMessageProperty requestMessage;
requestMessage = new HttpRequestMessageProperty();
requestMessage.Headers[SoapUtil.OAuthHeader] =
    bearerKey;
OperationContext.Current.OutgoingMessageProperties[
    HttpRequestMessageProperty.Name] =
        requestMessage;

// setup the message
ConWHS.UpdateVehicleGroup update;
update = new ConWHS.UpdateVehicleGroup();
update._contract = _change;
update.CallContext = conContext;
ConWHS.UpdateVehicleGroupResponse response;
message = new ConWHS.ConWHSMessageContract();
response =
    ((ConWHS.VehicleService)channel).
        UpdateVehicleGroup(update);
// the response contains the current info log
// and the return result, which the return type
// we returned in the D365O method.
message = response.result;
        }
        return message;
    }
```

18. Let's see if it works. In the `Program.cs` file, write the following piece of code as the `Main` method:

```
static void Main(string[] args)
{
    AuthenticationContract authContract;
    authContract = new AuthenticationContract();
    authContract.ApplicationId = "<your application Id>";
    authContract.Resource =
"https://usnconeboxax1aos.cloud.onebox.dynamics.com/";
    Console.WriteLine("Use the O365 account that you use to log
in to Dynamics 365 for Operations");
    Console.Write("O365 Username: ");
    authContract.UserName = Console.ReadLine();
    Console.Write("O365 Password: ");
    authContract.Password = Console.ReadLine();
    Console.WriteLine("This is your tenant, and should be your
domain, such as yourdomain.com");
    string defaultDomain =
        authContract.UserName.Split('@').Last<string>();
    Console.WriteLine("O365 Domain: ");
    Console.Write("(" + defaultDomain + ") :");
```

```
        authContract.Domain = Console.ReadLine();
        if (authContract.Domain == "")
        {
            authContract.Domain = defaultDomain;
        }

        UpdateVehicleGroup update = new UpdateVehicleGroup();
        ConWHS.ConWHSVehicleGroupChangeContract change;
        change = new ConWHS.ConWHSVehicleGroupChangeContract();
        change.VehicleId = "X0002";
        change.VehicleGroupId = "Leased";

        ConWHS.ConWHSMessageContract message;
        message = update.UpdateSOAP(authContract, change);
        if (message.Success)
        {
            Console.WriteLine("Success!");
        }
        else
        {
            Console.WriteLine(message.Message);
        }
        Console.ReadLine();
    }
```

19. Build and run the project.

How it works...

When we added `Service Reference`, Visual Studio created a type for each contract the service reference uses, and a client class in order to interact with the services referenced by it. It corresponds to the Service Group within Dynamics AX 365 for Operations. This is a lot more helpful than what is provided by JSON, which is why this recipe was written before the JSON method. In the next recipe, we will see that we can deserialize SOAP types from JSON.

The `Authenticate` class is very similar to the class we wrote in `Chapter 8`, *Data Management, Odata, and Office*, just a little more elegant. We are simply getting an authentication token (known as a bearer key) that is used when the requests are made.

The `UpdateVehicleGroups` class has a little more to it. The first part is to get the authorization code, which is just a variation on the used for access data through OData. It varies more from this point on.

When we constructed the client with the code: `client = new ConWHS.VehicleServiceClient(binding, address);`, we used a binding that we constructed manually. We did this because we don't want the `App.Config` bindings to interfere. The bindings in `App.Config` are generated automatically for us when we create or update the service reference. In our case, we don't want anything special; we just want a basic binding. The authentication is done by specifying setting the Authorization header property to the bearer key (authentication token).

The next new part is a legacy from AX 2012, the `CallContext` class. This was used for setting the company, language, and also the credentials to use. This is no longer mandatory, and is filled in for completeness. `Partition` is still active, but is only used for certain testing scenarios: the client can no longer access any other partition than `"initial"`.

The next part looks complicated, but it's the only way in which we can set the request header variables. In this section, we will set up a `HttpRequestMessageProperty` instance in order to set the authorization header variable:

```
HttpRequestMessageProperty requestMessage;
requestMessage = new HttpRequestMessageProperty();
requestMessage.Headers[SoapUtil.OAuthHeader] = bearerKey;
```

This is then passed to the current outgoing message properties with the following line:

```
OperationContext.Current.OutgoingMessageProperties[
    HttpRequestMessageProperty.Name] = requestMessage;
```

We will need to ensure that this is cleaned up afterwards, so this is why we enclosed the code in the following using clause:

```
using (OperationContextScope context
            = new OperationContextScope(channel))
```

The code that does the actual work is as follows:

```
ConWHS.UpdateVehicleGroup update;
update = new ConWHS.UpdateVehicleGroup();
update._contract = _change;
```

```
update.CallContext = conContext;
ConWHS.UpdateVehicleGroupResponse response;
message = new ConWHS.ConWHSMessageContract();
response = ((ConWHS.VehicleService)channel).UpdateVehicleGroup(update);
message = response.result;
```

Within the ConWHS service, reference is a class called UpdateVehicleGroup, which is the name of the service method we wrote. The declaration was as follows:

```
public ConWHSMessageContract UpdateVehicleGroup(
        ConWHSVehicleGroupChangeContract _contract)
```

Visual Studio created this class because of the input parameter. The class contains properties for the CallContext property, which is always created, and also for the _contract method input parameter.

See also

- *Troubleshoot service authentication*
  (https://ax.help.dynamics.com/en/wiki/troubleshooting-service-authenti
  cation/).
- *Service endpoints*
  (https://ax.help.dynamics.com/en/wiki/dynamics-ax-7-services-technical
  -concepts-guide/). This is a little generic, but it contains links to some useful
  code samples.

Consuming a Dynamics 365 for Operations JSON service

In this recipe, we will extend the previous C# project to consume the service using JSON.

The primary difference is that JSON will not create the contract and client classes for us, we will need to write them. We will use a NuGet package to help with the serialization and deserialization of C# classes to JSON.

Getting ready

We are continuing the previous recipe, which must be completed and built before we continue.

How to do it...

To consume a Dynamics 365 for Operations service using JSON, follow these steps:

1. First, let's take a look at what JSON looks like; this will help the recipe make more sense as we progress. Open the following URL using Internet Explorer:

   ```
   https://usnconeboxax1aos.cloud.onebox.dynamics.com/api/servi
   ces/
   ```

2. This will ask you to open `services.json`; click on **Open**, which opens a file in Visual Studio that contains all the services exposed. The file will contain our service in the following format:

   ```
   {"ServiceGroups":[{"Name":"ConWHSServices"},{"Name":"CuesServic
   eGroup"}
   ```

   Now, open the following URL on Internet Explorer:

   ```
   https://usnconeboxax1aos.cloud.onebox.dynamics.com/api/servi
   ces/ConWHSServices
   ```

3. This time, the JSON file is called `CONWHSServices.json`, and contains the following:

   ```
   {"Services":[{"Name":"VehicleServices"}]}
   ```

4. You can do the same by adding `VehicleServices` to the URL, which will open a JSON file with the following lines of code:

   ```
   {"Operations":[{"Name":"UpdateVehicleGroup"},{"Name":"GetVehicl
   es"}]}
   ```

5. The JSON for the `GetVehicles` operation is as follows:

```
{"Parameters":[],"Return":{"Name":"return","Type":"ConWHSVehicl
eTableContract[]"}}
```

6. The JSON for `UpdateVehicleGroup` is shown here:

```
{"Parameters":[{"Name":"_contract","Type":"ConWHSVehicleGroupCh
angeContract"}],"Return":{"Name":"return","Type":"ConWHSMessage
Contract"}}
```

 The take away here is to note that we have three levels: `ServiceGroups`, `Services`, and `Operations`, which correlate to how we create services within Dynamics 365 for Operations.

7. Open the Package Manage console from **Tools** | **Nuget Package Manager**, and type the following command:

```
Install-Package Newtonsoft.Json
```

8. Create a class for the C# classes that we will use to deserialize the JSON into and name the class `JsonClient`.

9. Set up the following using declarations:

```
using System;
using System.Collections.Generic;
using Newtonsoft.Json;
using System.Net;
using System.IO;
```

10. Change the namespace to `ConServiceTest.Json` as our classes may not be unique in the `ConServiceTest` namespace.

11. Remove the default class, so that we only have a blank line inside the `namespace` braces.

12. We will first write the classes for the `ServiceGroup` JSON, which was: `{"ServiceGroups":[{"Name":"ConWHSServices"}, {etc.}"`. This is represented in C# as follows:

```
public class ServiceGroups
{
    [JsonProperty("ServiceGroups")]
    public List<ServiceGroup> ServiceGroupNames { get; set; }

public class ServiceGroup
{
    [JsonProperty("Name")]
```

```
    public string ServiceGroupName { get; set; }
}
```

 The JsonProperty decoration maps the method to the JSON property.

13. We can continue this pattern for the Services and Operations levels, as shown in the following piece of code:

```
public class Services
{
    [JsonProperty("Services")]
    public List<Service> ServiceNames { get; set; }
}
public class Service
{
    [JsonProperty("Name")]
    public String Name { get; set; }
}
public class Operations
{
    [JsonProperty("Operations")]
    public List<Operation> OperationNames { get; set; }
}
public class Operation
{
    [JsonProperty("Name")]
    public string Name { get; set; }
}
```

14. Let's write a client to access the service and deserialize the data into our new classes. In our JsonClient.cs file, create a new class called Client.

15. Start the class with the following code, in order to set up the global variables and constructor:

```
public class Client
{
    string d365OURI;
    Authenticate auth;
    public Client(string _d365OURI, Authenticate _auth)
    {
        d365OURI = _d365OURI;
        auth = _auth;
    }
}
```

16. Next, we will write two helper functions--the first to create a request for the supplier address, and the other to read the response from the request into a string. The code is as follows:

```
private HttpWebRequest CreateRequest(string _address)
{
    HttpWebRequest webRequest;
    webRequest = (HttpWebRequest)HttpWebRequest.Create(
                        _address);
    webRequest.Method = "POST";
    // the request will be empty.
    webRequest.ContentLength = 0;
    webRequest.Headers.Set(JsonUtil.OAuthHeader,
                        auth.BearerKey);
    return webRequest;
}
private string ReadJsonResponse(HttpWebRequest _request)
{
    string jsonString;

    using (HttpWebResponse webResponse =
        (HttpWebResponse)_request.GetResponse())
    {
        using (Stream stream =
            webResponse.GetResponseStream())
        {
            using (StreamReader reader = new
                    StreamReader(stream))
            {
                jsonString = reader.ReadToEnd();
            }
        }
    }
    return jsonString;
}
```

17. Let's write the methods to read the metadata (the service groups, services, and operations). The code for this is as follows:

```
public ServiceGroups GetServiceGroups()
{
    string serviceGroupAddress =
        Json.JsonUtil.GetServiceURI("", d365OURI);
    HttpWebRequest webRequest;
    webRequest =
        CreateRequest(serviceGroupAddress.TrimEnd('/'));
    // Must override the metadata request calls
```

```
        // to GET as this is not REST
        webRequest.Method = "GET";
        string jsonString = ReadJsonResponse(webRequest);
        ServiceGroups serviceGroups;
        serviceGroups =
            JsonConvert.DeserializeObject<ServiceGroups>(
                jsonString);
        return serviceGroups;
}
public Services GetServices(string _serviceGroup)
{
    string serviceGroupAddress =
Json.JsonUtil.GetServiceURI(_serviceGroup, d365OURI);

        HttpWebRequest webRequest;
        webRequest = CreateRequest(serviceGroupAddress);
        // Must override the metadata request calls
        // to GET as this is not REST
        webRequest.Method = "GET";
        string jsonString = ReadJsonResponse(webRequest);

        Services services;
        services =
            JsonConvert.DeserializeObject<Services>(
                jsonString);
        return services;
}
public Operations GetOperations(
        string _serviceGroup,
        string _vehicleService)
{
        string servicePath = _serviceGroup.TrimEnd('/')
            + "/" + _vehicleService;
        string serviceGroupAddress;
        serviceGroupAddress = Json.JsonUtil.GetServiceURI(
            servicePath, d365OURI);

        HttpWebRequest webRequest;
        webRequest = CreateRequest(serviceGroupAddress);
        // Must override the metadata request calls
        // to GET as this is not REST
        webRequest.Method = "GET";
        string jsonString = ReadJsonResponse(webRequest);

        Operations operations;

        operations =
            JsonConvert.DeserializeObject<Operations>(
```

```
                    jsonString);
            return operations;
        }
```

18. The next method is to make a call to get the vehicle list. This time, we are reusing the `ConWHS.ConWHSVehicleTableContract` type that was created in the previous recipe. The code should be written as follows:

```
public ConWHS.ConWHSVehicleTableContract[] GetVehicles(
        string _serviceGroup,
        string _service,
        string _operation)
{
        string servicePath;
        servicePath = _serviceGroup.TrimEnd('/')
            + "/" + _service.TrimEnd('/')
            + "/" + _operation;
        string serviceGroupAddress;
        serviceGroupAddress = Json.JsonUtil.GetServiceURI(
            servicePath, d365OURI);

        HttpWebRequest webRequest;
        webRequest = CreateRequest(serviceGroupAddress);
        string jsonString = ReadJsonResponse(webRequest);

        ConWHS.ConWHSVehicleTableContract[] vehicles;
        vehicles = JsonConvert.DeserializeObject
            <ConWHS.ConWHSVehicleTableContract[]>(jsonString);
        return vehicles;
}
```

 You may wonder how this could possibly work. How can the deserializer possibly know how to convert the JSON file into a class without the `JsonProperty` decoration? This is because the property methods have the same names as the property methods.

19. Let's test this now and see what happens. In the `Program.cs` file, comment out the SOAP code from `UpdateVehicleGroup update = ...` and write the following piece of code:

```
Authenticate auth = new Authenticate();
auth.Authentication = authContract;
if (auth.GetAuthenticationHeader())
{
    Json.Client client = new Json.Client(authContract.Resource,
auth);
```

```
Json.ServiceGroups serviceGroups;
serviceGroups = client.GetServiceGroups();
foreach (Json.ServiceGroup serviceGroup in
         serviceGroups.ServiceGroupNames)
{
    Console.WriteLine(serviceGroup.Name);
}
Json.Services services;
services = client.GetServices("ConWHSServices");
foreach (Json.Service service in services.ServiceNames)
{
    Console.WriteLine(service.Name);
}
Json.Operations operations;
operations = client.GetOperations(
    "ConWHSServices", "VehicleServices");
foreach (Json.Operation operation in
         operations.OperationNames)
{
    Console.WriteLine(operation.Name);
}

GetVehicles getVehicles = new GetVehicles();
ConWHS.ConWHSVehicleTableContract[] vehicles;
vehicles = getVehicles.GetVehiclesJson(authContract);
foreach (ConWHS.ConWHSVehicleTableContract vehicle
         in vehicles)
{
    Console.WriteLine(vehicle.vehicleId);
}
}
```

20. Close the code editors, build, and run the project to test it.

How it works...

The JSON method actually carries less overhead in terms of setting up the calls than SOAP. We don't need to set up any bindings; we just need to set the Authorization header property, which is easily done using this method.

The rest is generic JSON, and the code we write is the same as if we were writing for any other application that is able to use this method.

The difficult part is setting up the C# classes in which to deserialize to, or serialize from. It isn't obvious at first, especially when a simple list of names, such as `ServiceGroups`, requires two classes. Thankfully, Newtonsoft have written a great NuGet package that means a lot of the work is done for us. We can also cheat a little by using SOAP to generate classes for use, like we did for the `GetVehicles` method.

To explain this further, take the following JSON:

```
{"Services":[{"Name":"VehicleServices"}]}
```

The C# class for this was as follows:

```
public class Services
{
    [JsonProperty("Services")]
    public List<Service> ServiceNames { get; set; }
}
public class Service
{
    [JsonProperty("Name")]
    public String Name { get; set; }
}
```

The outer part of the JSON contains the `Services` property. This property is a list of `Name` properties. When the JSON is deserialized into the `Services` class, it looks for a property that is either named `Services` or has the `[JsonProperty("Services")]` decoration. In our case, `public List<Service> ServiceNames { get; set; }` has the required decoration.

This process continues. The deserializer now creates a `List` of type `Service`. It will iterate through the JSON, mapping the `Name` JSON property to the `Service.Name` property. In this case, the `JsonProperty` decoration is not actually required, as the property name is the same as the method name. The fact that it matches on name is the reason that we can use the classes created by the Service Reference.

The request is done by setting up the `HttpWebRequest` object, which sets the `Authorisation` header property to our bearer key and the `Method` property to `POST`; this is the default as most calls will be REST and these must use the `POST` method.

For metadata calls, we will set the `Method` property to `GET`, which is required for non-REST calls. We will then deserialize directly into the class.

The `GetVehicles` method deserializes into an array; we knew this because the `GetVehicles.json` file contained the following lines of code:

```
{"Parameters":[],"Return":{"Name":"return",
 "Type":"ConWHSVehicleTableContract[]"}}
```

There's more...

Let's say we want to pass data to a JSON service, as is required by the `UpdateVehicleGroups` operation.

Open the following URL in Internet Explorer:

https://usnconeboxax1aos.cloud.onebox.dynamics.com/api/services/ConWHSS
ervices/VehicleServices/UpdateVehicleGroup

The JSON file it opens contains the following lines of code:

```
{"Parameters":[{"Name":"_contract","Type":"ConWHSVehicleGroupChangeContract
"}],"Return":{"Name":"return","Type":"ConWHSMessageContract"}}
```

The actual input JSON the request needs will follow the following pattern:

```
{"_contract":{"VehicleGroupId":"New vehicle
group","VehicleId":"X0002","hideVehicleId":0,"parmCallId":"00000000-0000-00
00-0000-000000000000","parmSessionIdx":0,"parmSessionLoginDateTime":"0001-0
1-01T00:00:00"}}
```

For this, we will need to construct a class with a `JsonProperty` of `_contract`; this is done by the following class, which should be added to `JsonClient.cs`:

```
public class UpdateVehicleParameter
{
    [JsonProperty("_contract")]
    public ConWHS.ConWHSVehicleGroupChangeContract Contract
        { get; set; }
}
```

The preceding class will now serialize to the JSON that the operation needs.

We will need a new method in our client class to perform the update; this is done by writing the following piece of code:

```
public ConWHS.ConWHSMessageContract UpdateVehicleGroup(
    ConWHS.ConWHSVehicleGroupChangeContract _change,
    string _serviceGroup,
    string _service,
    string _operation)
{
```

```
                string servicePath;
                servicePath = _serviceGroup.TrimEnd('/')
                    + "/" + _service.TrimEnd('/')
                    + "/" + _operation;
                string serviceGroupAddress;
                serviceGroupAddress = Json.JsonUtil.GetServiceURI(
                    servicePath, d365OURI);

                HttpWebRequest webRequest;
                webRequest = CreateRequest(serviceGroupAddress);

                UpdateVehicleParameter parm;
                parm = new Json.Client.UpdateVehicleParameter();
                parm.Contract = _change;

                string jsonOutString = JsonConvert.SerializeObject(parm);
                webRequest.ContentLength = jsonOutString.Length;

                using (Stream stream = webRequest.GetRequestStream())
                {
                    using (StreamWriter writer = new StreamWriter(stream))
                    {
                        writer.Write(jsonOutString);
                        writer.Flush();
                    }
                }
                string jsonString = ReadJsonResponse(webRequest);

                ConWHS.ConWHSMessageContract msg;
                msg = JsonConvert.DeserializeObject
                    <ConWHS.ConWHSMessageContract>(jsonString);
                return msg;
        }
```

The complicated part was visualizing the input parameter as a class from that point in the preceding method is largely the same as before. We will just write the JSON string to the web request's request stream.

Now, add a new method in the UpdateVehicleGroup.cs file in the UpdateVehicleGroup class. The method should read as follows:

```
    public ConWHS.ConWHSMessageContract UpdateJSON(
        AuthenticationContract _authContract,
        ConWHS.ConWHSVehicleGroupChangeContract _change)
    {
        Authenticate auth = new Authenticate();
        auth.Authentication = _authContract;
        ConWHS.ConWHSMessageContract message;
```

```
    if (!auth.GetAuthenticationHeader())
    {
        message = new ConWHS.ConWHSMessageContract();
        message.Success = false;
        message.Message = auth.Authentication.Response;
        return message;
    }
    Json.Client client = new Json.Client(
            _authContract.Resource, auth);
    message = client.UpdateVehicleGroup(
        _change,
        "ConWHSServices",
        "VehicleServices",
        "UpdateVehicleGroup");
    return message;
}
```

This is to simplify usage. Finally, add a section to the `Main` method of `Program.cs`, just below the existing JSON test code:

```
ConWHS.ConWHSVehicleGroupChangeContract jsonChange;
jsonChange = new ConWHS.ConWHSVehicleGroupChangeContract();
Console.Write("Vehicle Id: ");
jsonChange.VehicleId = Console.ReadLine();
Console.Write("New vehicle group: ");
jsonChange.VehicleGroupId = Console.ReadLine();

ConWHS.ConWHSMessageContract jsonMessage;
UpdateVehicleGroup jsonUpdate;
jsonUpdate = new UpdateVehicleGroup();
jsonMessage = jsonUpdate.UpdateJSON(
    authContract, jsonChange);
if (jsonMessage.Success)
{
    Console.WriteLine("Success!");
}
else
{
    Console.WriteLine(jsonMessage.Message);
}
```

This is just the start. You can experiment further; for example, deserializing the `DataSet` objects so you can present data directly to grids in your apps.

See also...

- *Newtonsoft JSON Samples*
  (http://www.newtonsoft.com/JSON/help/html/Samples.htm)

Consuming an external service within Dynamics 365 for Operations

The technique hasn't changed substantially since Dynamics AX 2012. The key difference is that we will need to manually craft the binding. We will still need to create a C# project to consume the web service, and then use it as a reference within our Dynamics 365 for Operations project.

The example service is a weather service provided by *WebserviceX.net* (www.webservicex.net). There is no recommendation here; it was simply the first one in when I searched for weather web services. The aim is to create a recipe that you can use for your web services: the chosen service in this case isn't relevant.

 When selecting a service to use, we must check the license terms and conditions, as not all are free to use; just because the license terms aren't enforced, it does not mean that it is free to use.

Getting ready

We will need an existing Dynamics 365 for Operations project available.

How to do it...

To create the service wrapper for the service, follow these steps:

1. Create a new C# Class Library project named WeatherService.
2. Rename the class1.cs file to WeatherService.cs.
3. Create a new service reference by right-clicking on the **References** node in Solution Explorer and choosing **Add Service Reference**.

4. Enter `http://www.webservicex.net/globalweather.asmx?WSDL` in the **Address** field and click on **Go**.

5. Enter `GlobalWeather` in the **Namespace** field, and click on **OK**.

6. Open the `WeatherService.cs` file and enter the following piece of code:

```
using System.ServiceModel;
using WeatherService.GlobalWeather;
namespace Contoso.Weather
{
    public class Weather
    {
        public const string serviceAddress
        = "http://www.webservicex.net/globalweather.asmx";
        public static string GetWeatherForCity(
            string _country, string _city)
        {
            // We can't modify D365O's config file, so we
            // need to add the binding manually
            var binding = new BasicHttpBinding();
            binding.MaxReceivedMessageSize = int.MaxValue;
            var address =
                new EndpointAddress(serviceAddress);
            GlobalWeatherSoapClient client =
                new GlobalWeatherSoapClient(
                        binding, address);
            return client.GetWeather(_city, country);
        }
        public static string GetCitiesByCountry(
            string _country)
        {
            // We can't modify D365O's config file, so we
            // need to add the binding manually
            var binding = new BasicHttpBinding();
            binding.MaxReceivedMessageSize = int.MaxValue;
            var address = new
                EndpointAddress(serviceAddress);
            GlobalWeatherSoapClient client =
                new GlobalWeatherSoapClient(
                        binding, address);
            return client.GetCitiesByCountry(_country);
        }
    }
}
```

The namespace should be based on your organization's conventions, for example, `Contoso.Weather`, or `Contoso.Services`.)

7. Save all and build the project.
8. Copy the DLL from `bin/debug`, for example, `C:\Projects\TFS\WeatherService\WeatherService\bin\Debug`) to the project folder of the Dynamics 365 for Operations project (`C:\Projects\TFS\ConWHSVehicleManagement\ConWHSVehicleManagement`).
9. Add the DLL to source control using Visual Studio's **Source Control Explorer**.

The following steps show how to use the DLL created in the previous steps in order to access the service from within Dynamics 365 for Operations:

1. Close the solution, and open your Dynamics 365 for Operations project, in our case `ConWHSVehicleManagement`.
2. Right-click on the **References** node and choose **Add reference**.
3. Click the **Browse** tab, to select the DLL file that we copied to this project's project folder. Select the DLL and click on **OK**.
4. Create a new class named `ConWHSWeatherService`.
5. Create two methods so we can easily access the service, as shown here:

```
public static str GetCities(str _country)
{
    return Contoso.Weather.Weather::GetCitiesByCountry(
        _country);
}

public static str GetWeather(str _country, str _city)
{
    return Contoso.Weather.Weather::GetWeatherForCity(
        _country, _city);
}
```

6. To test this, create a form called `ConWHSWeatherTest` and use the `Dialog - Basic` form pattern.
7. Right-click on the **Methods** node, click on **New Form Method**, and enter the following piece of code:

```
str cityName;
```

```
str countryName;
Notes result;
public edit str CityName(boolean _set, str _cityName)
{
    if(_set)
    {
        cityName = _cityName;
        result = ConWHSWeatherService::GetCities(
                countryName);
    }
    return cityName;
}
public edit str CountryName(boolean _set, str _countryName)
{
    if(_set)
    {
        countryName = _countryName;
        result = ConWHSWeatherService::GetWeather(
                countryName, cityName);
    }
    return countryName;
}
public display Notes Result()
{
    return result;
}
```

8. Close the code editor and add a group control under the **Design** node.
9. Name the `MainFormGroup` control, and set the **Caption** property as desired.
10. Create three String controls as defined in the following table:

Name	Data Method	Label	Multi Line
CountryNameCtrl	CountryName	Country	No
CityNameCtrl	CityName	City	No
ResultCtrl	Result	Result	Yes

You may also wish to adjust the width and height of `ResultCtrl`.

11. Complete the pattern by adding a `Button Group` control with two `Command` buttons for OK and Cancel. They aren't needed for our test, but the form pattern

we selected requires this.

12. Save and close the form designer and create a menu item named `ConWHSWeatherTest`, labelled `Test Weather`.

13. Add the menu to the `PeriodicTasks` submenu of the `ConWHSVehicleManagement` menu.

14. Build the project and test the form.

 You may receive an error stating that the DLL or PDB file cannot be copied to `C:\AOSService\PackagesLocalDirectory\CONWHSVehicleManag ement\bin` (or similar folder). In this case, stop the `AOSService` application pool in **Internet Information Services (IIS)** Manager. You can start it once the build has completed - the recycle option may not help in this case.

15. Navigate to the menu item and enter the country name, such as `United Kingdom`.

16. The service correctly returns an XML string containing a list of cities.

17. Enter the city, and you will receive forecast data.

How it works...

The first part of the recipe is straightforward SOAP. The only variance is that we manually craft the binding.

When we added the DLL to our Dynamics 365 for Operations project, it makes the types in the DLL available to use; this is why the Intellisense worked when we wrote the two methods in X++.

The form is just a test bed, nothing really new here.

When the project is built, it copies the DLL to the bin folder of the package. In the case of the `ConWHSVehicleManagement` package, it is as follows:

```
C:\AOSService\PackagesLocalDirectory\CONWHSVehicleManagement\bin
```

This would cause a problem when a build server tries to build the project, it will need the DLL. This is why we copied it to a folder that is already in source control. There are other solutions to this but, in many cases, we may not always have the same source to a DLL.

There's more...

If we put together our knowledge of JSON, we could create a solution where we converted the XML to JSON and serialized this to C# classes. This would make the implementation much easier to use.

There are many web services out there, of which many are free to use. They can include: currency exchange rates, unit conversions, or even integration with a bot.

10
Extensibility Through Metadata and Data Date-Effectiveness

In this chapter, we will cover the following recipes:

- Using metadata for data access
- Using Interfaces for extensibility through metadata
- Making data date-effective

Introduction

In this chapter, the focus will be on providing techniques to make our solution more easily extendable by other developers and also to provide more control to users.

Using metadata for data access

All tables and fields within Dynamics 365 for Operations have an ID. The table ID can be used to generate an instance of the table, and we can work with that table as if we had declared it as a type in a method, making our code more generic and more easily extendable.

In this example, we will write a data defaulting framework to demonstrate this. Here, we will create a table and a form that allows us to store defaults for a table, and a class that will set the defaults when a record is created.

Getting ready...

We will need a settings form and table, along with a table for which we shall set the defaults for. This example will use the sample vehicle management solution developed during the course of this book.

How to do it...

First, we will create the settings table for the fields that we want to allow defaults for. To do so, follow these steps:

1. Create a new table named ConWHSVehicleTableDefaults.

This particular sample will be fixed to the vehicle table, but you should be able to extend this to work with any table you desire.

2. Locate the **Extended data types (EDT)** RefFieldName, and RefFieldLabel in the **Application Explorer** and drag them to the **Fields** node of the table. Make the RefFieldLabel field read-only.

3. Drag the EDT String255 to the **Fields** node and rename the field to DefaultValueStr. Create a label for Default value, and set the **Label** property to it.

   The pattern for this type of table would normally continue by adding a field for each base type, and the form would use a handler to show the relevant field base on the field's base type. In this case, we will stop at string, so as to not detract from the main focus of this recipe.

4. Create field groups, as shown in the following table:

Group name	Label	Fields
Overview	@ConWHS:Overview	RefFieldName RefFieldLabel
DefaultValue	@SYS40175	DefaultValueStr

5. Create a unique index for `RefFieldName` and make it the table's **Clustered index**.

6. Complete the table properties, as shown in the following table:

Property	Fields
Label	New label Vehicle table defaults
Title Field 1	RefFieldLabel
Title Field 2	DefaultValueStr
Cache Lookup	EntireTable
Clustered Index	FieldNameIdx
Table Group	Group
<Tracking fields>	As desired, it may be useful to know who last changed it.

7. Create a standard `Find` and `Exist` method, as shown in the following code:

```
public static boolean Exist(
    RefFieldName _fieldName)
{
    ConWHSVehicleTableDefaults table;

    if(_fieldName != '')
    {
        select firstonly RecId from table
            where table.RefFieldName == _fieldName;
    }
    return (table.RecId != 0);
}
public static ConWHSVehicleTableDefaults Find(
    RefFieldName _fieldName,
    boolean _forUpdate)
{
    ConWHSVehicleTableDefaults table;

    if(_fieldName != '')
    {
        table.selectForUpdate(_forUpdate);
        select table
            where table.RefFieldName == _fieldName;
    }
    return table;
```

```
}
```

8. The `RefFieldName` field will be a field name from the `ConWHSVehicleTable`; since we work with IDs, it is useful to have a helper function that returns this ID. Create the following method:

```
private RefFieldId GetFieldId(
    RefFieldName _fieldName = this.RefFieldName)
{
    return fieldName2Id(tableNum(ConWHSVehicleTable),
        _fieldName);
}
```

We will allow the field name to be passed so that we can get the field ID for a name not currently updated to the current record.

9. Next, create a new method that sets `RefFieldLabel` from the field's metadata, as shown in the following code:

```
public void InitFromFieldName()
{
    RefFieldId fieldId = this.GetFieldId();
    if(fieldId == 0)
    {
        this.RefFieldName = '';
        this.RefFieldLabel = '';
        return;
    }
    DictField dField = new DictField(
        tableNum(ConWHSVehicleTable), fieldId);
    if(dField)
    {
        this.RefFieldLabel = dField.label();
    }
}
```

10. Now, insert and override the method for `modifiedField` to call the `InitFromFieldName` method as follows:

```
public void modifiedField(FieldId _fieldId)
{
    super(_fieldId);
    switch (_fieldId)
    {
        case fieldNum(ConWHSVehicleTableDefaults,
                    RefFieldName):
            this.InitFromFieldName();
            break;
    }
}
```

11. The field selected must exist, be of type `String`, and be editable on create. To make the code easier to read, we should create a check function for this, which is written as follows:

```
public boolean CheckRefFieldName(
    RefFieldName _fieldName = this.RefFieldName,
    boolean _silent = false)
{
    boolean     ok = true;
    ErrorMsg    msg = '';

    RefFieldId fieldId = this.GetFieldId(_fieldName);
    If (fieldId == 0)
    {
        ok = false;
        //Field %1 does not exist in table %2
        msg = strFmt("@SYS75684",
                    this.RefFieldName,
                    tableStr(ConWHSVehicleTable));
    }

    DictField dField = new DictField(
        tableNum(ConWHSVehicleTable), fieldId);
    if (dField)
    {
        if(dField.baseType() != Types::String)
        {
            ok = false;
            // Type is not supported %1
            msg = strFmt("@SYS73815", dField. baseType ());
        }
        if(!dField.allowEditOnCreate())
```

```
            {
                ok = false;
                //The field %1 cannot be selected.
                msg = strFmt("@SYS70689", this.RefFieldName);
            }
        }
        If (!ok && !_silent)
        {
            return checkFailed(msg);
        }
        return ok;
    }
```

The method accepts the `_silent` parameter as we will want to use the same logic to build the lookup later.

12. We will now call the check method in the preceding code to the `validateField` form triggered event. Override the `validateField` method, as shown here:

```
public boolean validateField(FieldId _fieldIdToCheck)
{
    boolean ret;

    ret = super(_fieldIdToCheck);
    switch (_fieldIdToCheck)
    {
        case fieldNum(ConWHSVehicleTableDefaults,
                    RefFieldName):
            ret = this.CheckRefFieldName();
            break;
    }
    return ret;
}
```

13. Finally, we will need a lookup function that only allows the user to select fields that are valid. The code is as follows:

```
public static void LookupFieldName(
    FormStringControl _control)
{
    FormRun         formRun;
    Args            args;
    Map             fieldmap;

    DictTable       dTable;
    Counter         idx;
```

```
RefFieldId  fieldId;
ConWHSVehicleTableDefaults  defaultsRecord;

defaultsRecord = _control.dataSourceObject().cursor();

fieldMap = new Map(Types::String, Types::String);
dTable = new DictTable(tableNum(ConWHSVehicleTable));
for (idx = 1; idx <= dTable.fieldCnt(); idx ++)
{
    fieldId = dTable.fieldCnt2Id(idx);
    RefFieldName fieldName = fieldId2Name(dTable.id(),
                                          fieldId);
    if (defaultsRecord.CheckRefFieldName(fieldName,
                                         true))
    {
        fieldMap.insert(fieldName, fieldName);
    }
}

args = new Args(formStr(SysPick));
args.parmEnumType(enumNum(SysPickListType));
args.parmEnum(enum2int(SysPickListType::Simple));
Args.parmObject(fieldMap);
formRun = classfactory.formRunClass(args);

_control.performFormLookup(formRun);
formRun.wait();
}
```

14. Next, create a new form named `ConWHSVehicleTableDefaults` and drag the new table to its **Data Sources** node.

15. Complete the design of the form based on the `Simple List and Details - List Grid` form pattern.

16. Complete the form as per the pattern requirements, using the `Overview` group for `NavigationListGroup`. The completed design should look like the following screenshot:

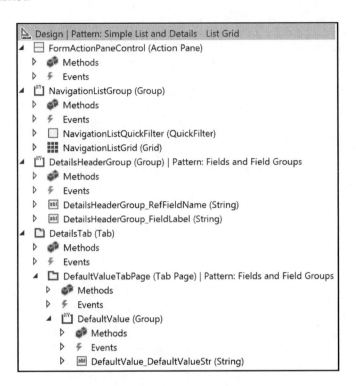

Remember to name the controls after the template name, as this makes the design easier to work with. The template will make the wrong assumptions about which control matches the template section until all the template sections have matching controls.

17. We will now need to override the lookup for the field name, expand the `Data Sources` node, and locate the `RefFieldName` field under the `ConWHSVehicleTableDefaults` data source's **Fields** node.

18. Right-click on the field's **Methods** node and select **Override | lookup**.

19. In the code editor that opens, remove the line `super(_formControl, _filterStr);` and replace it with the following line:

```
ConWHSVehicleTableDefaults::LookupFieldName(_formControl);
```

20. Create a display menu item and add it to the `Setup` submenu of

ConWHSVehicleManagement.

21. Finally, complete the **Form Ref** property of the ConWHSVehicleTableDefaults table and build the project, including database synchronization as we have added a new table.

We have now completed the set up table and form, we can now create a handler so that the table's defaults are set. To do this, follow these steps:

1. Create a new class named ConWHSVehicleTableDefaultingEngine.

2. Write the following lines of code to initialize the instance:

```
private ConWHSVehicleTable  vehicle;

public ConWHSVehicleTable Vehicle(
    ConWHSVehicleTable _vehicle = vehicle)
{
    vehicle = _vehicle;
    return vehicle;
}

public static ConWHSVehicleTableDefaultingEngine
    NewFromVehicleTable(ConWHSVehicleTable _vehicle)
{
    ConWHSVehicleTableDefaultingEngine engine;
    engine = new ConWHSVehicleTableDefaultingEngine();
    engine.Vehicle(_vehicle);
    return engine;
}
```

3. Then, write the methods that perform the update, which are as follows:

```
private void ProcessDefaults()
{
    ConWHSVehicleTableDefaults defaults;
    while select defaults
    {
        RefFieldId fieldId = fieldName2Id(
                    vehicle.TableId,
                    defaults.RefFieldName);
        if(fieldId)
        {
            DictField dField;
            dField = new DictField(vehicle.TableId,
                                fieldId);
            switch (dField.baseType())
            {
```

```
                        case Types::String:
                            vehicle.(fieldId) =
                                defaults.DefaultValueStr;
                            break;
                }
                if(vehicle.validateField(fieldId))
                {
                    vehicle.modifiedField(fieldId);
                }
                else
                {
                    switch (dField.baseType())
                    {
                        case Types::String:
                            vehicle.(fieldId) = '';
                            break;
                    }
                }
            }
        }
    }

    public boolean Validate()
    {
        if(vehicle.RecId != 0)
        {
            //Cannot default records that already exist
            return checkFailed("@ConWHS:ConWHS61");
        }
        return true;
    }

    public void Run()
    {
        if(!this.Validate())
        {
            return;
        }
        this.ProcessDefaults();
    }
```

4. The final method is the data event handler, which will trigger when the record is being initialized, and it is written as follows:

```
[DataEventHandlerAttribute(tableStr(ConWHSVehicleTable),
 DataEventType::InitializingRecord)]
public static void InitValueEventHandler(
        Common _record,
```

```
                     DataEventArgs _eventArgs)
         {
             ConWHSVehicleTableDefaultingEngine engine;
             engine = ConWHSVehicleTableDefaultingEngine::
                         NewFromVehicleTable(_record);
             engine.Run();
         }
```

5. Finally, build and run the project. Test the code by creating a set of defaults in the new `Vehicle table default values` form, and then create a new vehicle using the `Vehicles` form.

6. Try adding the `Vehicle` group as a default with a value that doesn't exist; you should get an error when a new record is created: `The value 'invalid value' in field 'Vehicle group' is not found in the related table 'Vehicle groups'`.

How it works...

There are two main new topics in this recipe. The first is to use the dictionary classes, `DictTable` and `DictField`, to gain access to the table and field properties. This was used to both validate the field and also to build a custom lookup for fields that can be edited.

The other new topic is that we can use the field ID to access the field on a record; for example, the code `vehicle.Description = "New description";` is equivalent to the following:

```
    RefFieldId fieldId = fieldNum(ConWHSVehicleTable, Description);
    vehicle.(fieldId) = "New description";
```

We have to be careful because the following code would compile, but fail with a runtime error:

```
    RefFieldId fieldId = fieldNum(ConWHSVehicleTable, Description);
    vehicle.(fieldId) = 12.345;
```

This is why we used the `DictField.baseType()` method.

You can also use this method in `where` clauses, but be very careful before you do this, in order to avoid any unpleasant runtime errors that may not present themselves at the point of failure.

We will also create a lookup using a `Map` object to create custom lookups that aren't based on data.

Although the code currently only handles fields of the `String` base type, it can be easily extended to handle other base types. You could even extend the validation on `ConWHSVehicleTableDefaults` to check if the values are valid. This would be done by creating a dummy `ConWHSVehicleTable` record, populating the field the user is adding a default for and calling the table's `validateField` method with the field ID.

To fully understand what is going on, it is useful to use the debugger to step through the code. Extending the sample in this recipe is also a great way to become comfortable with working with metadata.

One of the common modifications is to set default dates, and we could use that here, too. The default value would probably be an offset from today's date, and not a literal date.

Using Interfaces for extensibility through metadata

Interfaces enforce that all classes that implement them also implement the methods defined in the interface. This has all the traditional benefits associated with them, but in Dynamics 365 for Operations, we can go further.

We should create an interface called `MyRunnableI` with a method called `Run()` and a class that implements it called `MyRunningPerson` (which must have a method called `Run()`). We can assign an instance of `MyRunningPerson` to a variable of type `MyRunnableI` and call its `Run()` method. This allows greater flexibility and extensibility of our code.

However, in Dynamics 365 for Operations, we can create a plugin framework where the class to instantiate is configured in data. We can, therefore, control which class gets instantiated based on conditions only known at runtime.

In order to focus more on the way that we can use interfaces to create a plugin pattern, where the class to call is stored in data, the example will be simple. We will create a 'colorable' interface and allow the user to select which implementation of the colorable interface will be used. You could combine this idea with the previous chapter to determine which web service to use to get the weather, for example.

Getting ready...

In this example, we shall create a pattern based on new elements, so we will only need a Dynamics 365 for Operations project open in Visual Studio.

How to do it...

To create a plugin using interfaces through metadata, follow these steps:

1. First, create the interface, which is created as a class initially, using the following lines of code:

```
public interface ConWHSVehicleColorable
{
    public Color Color()
    {
    }
}
```

2. We will need a class that implements this interface. Create a class named ConWHSVehicleGroupColorRed, which will simply return the string literal Red, as shown here:

```
class ConWHSVehicleGroupColorRed
    implements ConWHSVehicleColorable
{
    public Color Color()
    {
        return 'Red';
    }
}
```

3. To keep logic away from the form and simplify usage, create a class named ConWHSVehicleGroupColorSetupForm.

4. Next, create a static lookup method. The pattern should be familiar from the previous chapters. This is an example of creating a lookup that is not based on data:

```
public static void LookupColorableClasses(
    FormStringControl _classNameControl)
{
    FormRun         formRun;
    Args            args;
    Map             classMap;
    List            classList;
    SysDictClass    dClass;
    ClassId         classId;
    ClassName       className;
    DictClass       implementationClass;

    dClass = new SysDictClass(
                    classNum(ConWHSVehicleColorable));
    classList = dClass.implementedBy();

    classMap = new Map(Types::String, Types::String);
    ListEnumerator le;
    le = classList.getEnumerator();

    while (le.moveNext())
    {
        classId = le.current();
        implementationClass = new DictClass(ClassId);
        if (!implementationClass.isInterface())
        {
            className = classId2Name(classId);
            classMap.insert(className, className);
        }
    }

    args = new Args(formStr(SysPick));
    args.parmEnumType(enumNum(SysPickListType));
    args.parmEnum(enum2int(SysPickListType::Simple));
    args.parmObject(classMap);
    formRun = classfactory.formRunClass(args);

    _classNameControl.performFormLookup(formRun);
    formRun.wait();
}
```

It is OK, in this case, to have this function in a case-specific class, as the usage is specific. It would usually be better to create a utility class for these functions and pass the interface as a method parameter.

5. Complete the form handler class using the standard pattern, as shown in the following code snippet:

```
FormDataSource vehicleGroupSetupDS;
protected void setVehicleGroupSetupDS(FormDataSource
_vehicleGroupSetupDS)
{
    vehicleGroupSetupDS = _vehicleGroupSetupDS;
}

public static ConWHSVehicleGroupColorSetupForm
    NewFromFormDS(FormDataSource _vehicleGroupSetupDS)
{
    ConWHSVehicleGroupColorSetupForm form =
        new ConWHSVehicleGroupColorSetupForm();
    form.setVehicleGroupSetupDS(_vehicleGroupSetupDS);
    return form;
}
```

6. Next, create a table named `ConWHSVehicleGroupColorSetup` as a group table, with the following fields:

Field	Label	EDT
VehicleGroupId	Inherited	ConWHSVehicleGroupId
Description	Inherited	Description
ColorClassName	Colorable class	ClassName

7. Ensure that the table is completed to best practices, and ensure the following:
   - The primary key is `VehicleGroupId`
   - `ColorClassName` is mandatory
   - A field group is created for the overview grid
   - The standard Find and Exist methods are created

8. Write the following static method on the table:

```
public static boolean ImplementsColorable(
```

```
                  ClassName _className)
{
    ClassId classId;
    DictClass dictClass;
    classId = className2Id(_className);
    if(ClassId == 0)
    {
        return false;
    }
    dictClass = new DictClass(ClassId);
    if(dictClass)
    {
        Counter idx;
        ClassId testClassId;
        for (idx = 1; idx <= dictClass.implementsCnt();
            idx++)
        {
            testClassId = dictClass.implements(idx);
            if (testClassId ==
                classNum(ConWHSVehicleColorable))
            {
                return true;
            }
        }
    }
    return false;
}
```

9. Now, let's validate that the class selected implements the interface. Override `validateField` and write the following code snippet:

```
public boolean validateField(FieldId _fieldIdToCheck)
{
    boolean ret;

    ret = super(_fieldIdToCheck);
    if(ret)
    {
        switch (_fieldIdToCheck)
        {
            case fieldNum(ConWHSVehicleGroupColorSetup,
                    ColorClassName):
            If (!ConWHSVehicleGroupColorSetup::
                ImplementsColorable(this.ColorClassName))
            {
                // %1 must implement %2
                ret = checkFailed(strFmt(
                    "@ConWHS:MustImplement",
```

```
                            this.ColorClassName,
                            classStr(ConWHSVehicleColorable)));
                }
            }
        }
        return ret;
    }
```

10. Create a new form for the table using the `Simple List` pattern, and follow the pattern to complete the form.

11. Complete the form handler pattern by adding the following lines of code to the form's code:

```
ConWHSVehicleGroupColorSetupForm formHandler;
public void init()
{
    super();
    formHandler = ConWHSVehicleGroupColorSetupForm::
            NewFromFormDS(ConWHSVehicleGroupColorSetup_DS);
}
```

12. To add the lookup, expand **Data Sources**, **ConWHSVehicleGroupColorSetup**, and **Fields**. Locate the**ColorClassName** field and override the `lookup` method. Write the following lines of code:

```
public void lookup(FormControl _formControl, str _filterStr)
{
    ConWHSVehicleGroupColorSetupForm::
        LookupColorableClasses(_formControl);
}
```

13. We will need a class that will execute our colorable class, name the class `ConWHSVehicleColorExecute`, and add the following piece of code:

```
ConWHSVehicleGroupId groupId;
Color    color;

public Color GetColor()
{
    return color;
}

public ConWHSVehicleGroupId ParmVehicleGroupId(
        ConWHSVehicleGroupId _groupId = groupId)
{
    groupId = _groupId;
```

```
        return groupId;
    }

    public static ConWHSVehicleColorExecute
        newFromVehicleGroupId(ConWHSVehicleGroupId _groupId)
    {
        ConWHSVehicleColorExecute execute;
        execute = new ConWHSVehicleColorExecute();
        execute.ParmVehicleGroupId(_groupId);
        return execute;
    }

    public boolean CanExecute()
    {
        If (!ConWHSVehicleGroupColorSetup::Exist(groupId))
        {
            return false;
        }
        return true;
    }

    public void Run()
    {
        If (this.CanExecute())
        {
            this.execute();
        }
    }

    private void execute()
    {
        ConWHSVehicleGroupColorSetup setup;
        setup = ConWHSVehicleGroupColorSetup::Find(groupId);

        if (!ConWHSVehicleGroupColorSetup::
            ImplementsColorable(setup.ColorClassName))
        {
            return;
        }

        DictClass dictClass;
        dictClass = new DictClass(
                    className2Id(setup.ColorClassName));
        if (dictClass)
        {
            ConWHSVehicleColorable colorable;
            colorable = dictClass.makeObject();
            color = colorable.Color();
```

```
        }
    }
```

14. Let's test this by adding a button to our setup form. Open the
    `ConWHSVehicleGroupColorSetupForm` class and add the following method:

```
public void TestColor()
{
    ConWHSVehicleGroupColorSetup setup;
    setup = vehicleGroupSetupDS.cursor();

    ConWHSVehicleColorExecute execute;
    execute = ConWHSVehicleColorExecute::
            newFromVehicleGroupId(setup.VehicleGroupId);
    execute.Run();
    info(execute.GetColor());
}
```

15. Open the `ConWHSVehicleGroupSetupForm` form and write the following
    method:

```
private void TestColor()
{
    formHandler.TestColor();
}
```

16. Close the code editor and go back to the form designer. On the
    `FormActionPaneControl` control that we created as part of completing the
    form's pattern, add an **Action Pane** tab; to this, add **Button Group** and finally a
    Button control.

17. Override the `clicked` method and write the following lines of code:

```
public void clicked()
{
    super();
    element.TestColor();
}
```

18. Create a menu item for our form and add this to the `Setup` menu for our
    `ConWHSVehicleManagement`.

19. Save everything, build the project, and synchronize the database with the project.

How it works...

This pattern achieves a safe method to allow a functional consultant (or end user) to choose the business logic based on data. This is very powerful, and allows other parties to add their own plugins, which are to be used instead of those supplied.

To understand what is going on, the first thing to know is that we can write the following code:

```
ConWHSVehicleColorable colorable;
colorable = new ConWHSVehicleGroupColorRed();
Color myColor = colorable.Color();
```

We can't instantiate an interface, but we can assign an instance of a class to a variable declared to be an interface, as long as the class implements the interface. Any errors will be handled by the compiler. We will consider the interface to be a code contract, and the `implements` keyword binds the implementation to the interface.

There is an alternative to using an interface, in that, we could write the following lines of code:

```
Object object;
object = new ConWHSVehicleGroupColorRed();
Color myObjColor = object.Color();
```

Although it would work, in this case, the code is a terrible idea. `Object` should always be a last resort, and this code is prone to regression errors. The interface is a contract; the object technique allows you to write any method name you like.

Our example is to allow the class to be defined at runtime. Using a switch or attribute-based constructor requires us to hard code the relationship between attribute or other condition and the class to construct. We want a user to be able to determine this. This is done using `DictClass`. Not only can we use `DictClass` to gain information about metadata, but we can also use them to construct an instance a class. The `DictClass` class is instantiated using a class's ID, as shown here:

```
DictClass dc = new DictClass(<MyClassId>);
```

In our case, the class name is stored in a table, allowing a class that implements `ConWHSVehicleColorable` to be selected.

The recipe can be broken down into simple steps, the first of which is to determine the class's ID from the name. This ID is an implementation specific numeric object or element identifier, so we must obtain the ID through a function call. Standard object always have the same IDs, but this should never be assumed. When we deploy a package to an environment for the first time, the ID is set; it will not change upon subsequent deployments. This is very important when you consider how extensible enumerations work, or if we decide to store IDs in setup table--if the ID changed, the code will fail in unexpected ways. The code to determine the object ID of the class name that we entered in the setup table is as follows:

```
ClassId classId = className2Id(setup.ColorClassName);
```

We can now instantiate a variable of type `DictClass`:

```
DictClass dc = new DictClass(classId);
```

Declare a variable that is of the same type as interface, `ConWHSVehicleColorable`:

```
ConWHSVehicleColorable colourable = dc.makeObject();
```

We can now call the `Color()` method. The `makeobject()` method creates an instance of the class it was constructed with: the class we entered in our setup table. Should we enter a class that does not implement the interface, we will get an error at this point, even if the class has the `Color()` method. The code contains validation on data entry and in the execution class. This must be done in order to avoid any runtime errors.

Even with validation on entry and usage, we can't completely avoid regression in this case. Using an interface, however, does help us reduce regression errors, for example, it would help us catch errors caused by refactoring.

Making data date-effective

Date effective tables allow us to create a new version whenever the data is changed, and see the date at any point in time. This sounds great, and will no doubt find requests to make all tables date effective. There is a penalty. The first is that it brings a little complexity to the process of developing the tables, reports, and user interface. The other is that it creates a new record every time, and can affect performance. We should only use this if we really need it. Great examples include the human resource tables to allow history of name changes, previous and planned positions, addresses, and so on.

In our example, we will create a new table for values such as odometer readings for a vehicle. We will create a table for this that is date effective so that we only record a new version when these key fields are changed.

Getting ready...

This recipe assumes that we have followed the chapters to create ConWHSVehicleTable, but the pattern behind this recipe can be applied to any requirement where we need to record the history of changes to a record.

How to do it...

In these steps, we create a table that puts the concept of date-effectivity into use:

1. Create a new integer EDT named ConWHSOdometer with a label Odometer.
2. Create a new table named ConWHSVehicleTableServiceData.
3. Drag the ConWHSVehicleId EDT on to the **Fields** node, and rename it to VehicleId. Configure the field's properties to be a primary key (cannot edit after creation and is mandatory). Create a foreign key relationship, but do not create an index.
4. Drag the ConWHSOdometer EDT onto the **Fields** node, and rename to Odometer.
5. We can now choose whether our changes can be updated daily, or for every change made. This is done using the table's **Valid Time State Field Type** property. We want to allow changes to be made frequently, and that every change should be saved as a new version, so choose UtcDateTime.

 This will add two fields of type UtcDateTime named FromDate and ToDate. These are used in order to time stamp each version of the apparent record.

6. Create a new primary index named VehTimeIdx using the following settings:

Property	Value
Allow Duplicates	No
Alternate Key	Yes
Valid Time State Key	Yes

Valid Time State Mode	NoGap

7. Add the `VehicleId` and `FromDate` fields to the index.

   We will need to add the `ToDate` field if we set **Valid Time State Mode** to `Gap`.

8. Set the table's **Replacement Key** property to the new index.
9. The `Find()` method must also be written in order to fetch the current version by default, which is done in the following code snippet:

```
public static ConWHSVehicleTableServiceData Find(
    ConWHSVehicleId _vehicleId,
    ValidFromDateTime _fromDateTime =
                       DateTimeUtil::utcNow(),
    ValidToDateTime _toDateTime = _fromDateTime,
    boolean _forUpdate =false)
{
    ConWHSVehicleTableServiceData serviceData;

    serviceData.selectForUpdate(_forUpdate);
    // the validtimestate is used to select
    // the version at a point in time
    select firstonly
        validtimestate(_fromDateTime, _toDateTime)
        serviceData
        where serviceData.VehicleId == _vehicleId;

    return serviceData;
}
```

10. Write the `Exist()` method using the same pattern.
11. Now, let's create a form so that we can see what happens. Name the form `ConWHSVehicleTableServiceData`.

    Since the form will be opened from a Vehicle record, and it is keyed on the `VehicleId` field, the form will usually be a dialog or details form. However, in order to demonstrate more clearly what is going on, we will use a `Simple List` pattern instead.

Extensibility Through Metadata and Data Date-Effectiveness

12. Apply the `Simple List` pattern and complete the form according to the pattern.

13. Create a menu item and add it to the `ConWHSVehicleTable` form.

14. Save everything and build the project and synchronize it with the database.

15. Open D365O in a web browser and open the `Vehicles` form. From them, open our new `Vehicle service data` form. Change the **Odometer** value, whilst saving the record for each change.

16. Open `SQL Server Management Studio`, press **Connect** on the **Connect to Server** form, and press Alt + N to create a new query window. Type the following:

```
Use AxDB
SELECT
    VEHICLEID, ODOMETER,
    VALIDFROM, VALIDTO
    FROM CONWHSVEHICLETABLESERVICEDATA
```

17. The result will be something like this:

Vehicle Id	Odometer	Valid From	Valid To
V000001	150	2017-01-31 13:42:25.000	2017-01-31 13:42:39.000
V000001	250	2017-01-31 13:42:40.000	2154-12-31 23:59:59.000

It is clearly working, but we now need to allow the user to see the records as at different times. To do this, we will need to add `DateEffectivenessPaneController` to the form.

18. Open the `ConWHSVehicleTableServiceData` form, and open `classDeclaration` from the **Methods** node and enter the code present in the next step.

19. First, we will need to implement the `IDateEffectivenessPaneCaller` interface, so alter the class declaration as follows:

```
public class ConWHSVehicleTableServiceData
    extends FormRun
    implements IDateEffectivenessPaneCaller
```

20. Now, add the following piece of code:

```
DateEffectivenessPaneController dePaneController;
// As required by the interface
```

```
public DateEffectivenessPaneController
        getDateEffectivenessController()
{
    return dePaneController;
}

private void enableAsOfDateButton()
{
    dePaneController.setDropDialogButtonEnabled(true);
    dePaneController.parmShowAllRecords(true);
}

public DateEffectivenessPaneController
    parmDatePaneController(
        DateEffectivenessPaneController _
            dePaneController = dePaneController)
{
    dePaneController = _dePaneController;
    return dePaneController;
}

public void init()
{
    super();
    dePaneController = DateEffectivenessPaneController::
        constructWithForm(
            element, ConWHSVehicleTableServiceData_ds,
            false, // show plural labels
            true, // allow show all records
            true); // use DateTime

    element.enableAsOfDateButton();
}
```

21. Build and test the form again, you should now have a new **As at date** control. Should the error `Form was called incorrectly` be thrown, it is because the `IDateEffectivenessPaneCaller` interface was not implemented.

22. This will suffice for now, but we can take it further, and this is described in the *There's more...* section.

How it works...

When D365O constructs the `ConWHSVehicleTableServiceData` data source, it automatically filters the records to the current version. The transact-SQL that does this is as follows:

```
SELECT
T1.VEHICLEID,T1.ODOMETER,T1.VALIDTO,T1.VALIDTOTZID,T1.VALIDFROM,T1.VALIDFRO
MTZID,T1.RECVERSION,T1.PARTITION,T1.RECID FROM
CONWHSVEHICLETABLESERVICEDATA T1 WHERE (((PARTITION=5637144576) AND
(DATAAREAID=?)) AND ((VALIDFROM<=?) AND (VALIDTO>=?))) ORDER BY
T1.VEHICLEID,T1.VALIDFROM OPTION(FAST 54)
```

This helps us understand why we made the property changes to the table. The index is clearly needed for performance, and the data source uses the properties on the table to decide on the query sent to SQL Server.

When working in code, we need to be sure we are selecting the correct record. `Find` methods are indispensable in this case, and it is common to write multiple `Find` methods for each type of usage scenario.

We added the date effectiveness controller to allow the user to see other versions on the record, or even to show all records. The show all option should only be used when we are viewing in a grid view, since the user couldn't see the other records anyway.

To experiment further with this, try creating a table that follows the pattern of the `HcmWorkerEnrolledBenefit` table.

There's more...

It would be a nicer interface if we could have the Odometer field on the vehicle form, which would require us to mix a non-date effective table with a date effective table. The `HcmWorker` table is a great example of this.

To implement this pattern, we would first add `ConWHSVehicleTableServiceData` to the `ConWHSVehicleTable` form, joined to the `ConWHSVehicleTable` data source as an `Outer join`. Modify `initValue` of `ConWHSVehicleTableServiceData` in order to default `VehicleId`.

Create a field group in a suitable place and add the `Odometer` field.

So far, there is nothing new. Next, we will need to construct the date effectiveness controller, but control the child data sources. This is done by subscribing to delegates on the controller. The code is similar to the code in recipe described previously.

The code is written as follows. The first part is to declare the date effectiveness controller, as we did before:

```
DateEffectivenessPaneController dePaneController;
```

Next, we will need to declare two event handler methods that we will use to subscribe the controller's events, which are delegates. We will need to filter the service data record based on the what the user did in the drop dialog, and this is done by adding the following piece of code:

```
/// <summary>
/// Event Handler for an Apply button (clicked) event in
DateEffectivenessPaneController
/// </summary>
public void datePaneController_ApplyClicked()
{
    utcdatetime asOfDateTime;
    utcdatetime nowDateTime = DateTimeUtil::utcNow();

    if (dePaneController.parmShowAsOfDate() ==
        DateTimeUtil::date(nowDateTime))
    {
        asOfDateTime = nowDateTime;
    }
    else
    {
        asOfDateTime = DateTimeUtil::newDateTime(
            dePaneController.parmShowAsOfDate(),
            Global::timeMax(),
            DateTimeUtil::getUserPreferredTimeZone());
    }

    // adjust the query for the outer joined data sources
    ConWHSVehicleTableServiceData_DS.validTimeStateAutoQuery(
        ValidTimeStateAutoQuery::AsOfDate);
    ConWHSVehicleTableServiceData_DS.query().
        validTimeStateAsOfDateTime(asOfDateTime);
}

/// <summary>
/// Event Handler for a Current button (clicked) event in
/// DateEffectivenessPaneController to
/// view the currently active version record.
```

```
/// </summary>
public void datePaneController_CurrentClicked()
{
    // adjust the query for the outer joined data sources
    ConWHSVehicleTableServiceData_DS.validTimeStateAutoQuery(
        ValidTimeStateAutoQuery::AsOfDate);
    ConWHSVehicleTableServiceData_DS.query().
        resetValidTimeStateQueryType();
}
```

The next methods are a standard part of the pattern and are the same as the recipe:

```
// As required by the interface
public DateEffectivenessPaneController
    getDateEffectivenessController()
{
    return dePaneController;
}

private void enableAsOfDateButton()
{
    dePaneController.setDropDialogButtonEnabled(true);
    dePaneController.parmShowAllRecords(false);
}

public DateEffectivenessPaneController parmDatePaneController(
    DateEffectivenessPaneController _dePaneController =
                                        dePaneController)
{
    dePaneController = _dePaneController;
    return dePaneController;
}
```

The init method is similar to the recipe, except that we don't want to show all records, and we just want to subscribe to the controller's events. The init method should read as follows:

```
public void init()
{
    super();
    dePaneController =
        DateEffectivenessPaneController::constructWithForm(
            element, ConWHSVehicleTable_ds,
            false, // show plural labels
            false, // do not allow show all records
            true); // use DateTime
    dePaneController.onApplyClicked +=
        eventhandler(this.datePaneController_ApplyClicked);
```

```
dePaneController.onShowCurrentClicked +=
    eventhandler(this.datePaneController_CurrentClicked);

element.enableAsOfDateButton();
}
```

Finally, adjust the service date form so that it has the `ValidFrom` fields. This allows the form to be used to see the history of the service data table.

11
Unit Testing

In this chapter, we will cover the following recipes:

- Creating a Form Adaptor project
- Creating a Unit Test project
- Creating a Unit Test for code
- Creating a test case from a task recording

Introduction

Unit testing helps ensure that the code both fulfills the requirement, and future changes (even in other packages) do not cause a regression. The unit test is written as a separate package that references the package it is testing. If we follow **Test Driven Development** (**TDD**), we will write the tests early in the process (some would argue first). TDD changes the way we think when writing code. Should we need to make a change to a project, we are forced to update the test case code (as the tests will otherwise fail)--this promotes a test-centric approach to development, and naturally reduces the test cycles. Regression in other packages is caught by the build process; the build server will download all checked-in code, perform a build, and then look for tests to execute. Any tests that fail are reported and the build--depending on the build's set up--will be marked as failed.

Each partner or customer may have their own policies for unit testing, some require that every piece of code is tested, and others will recommend that only key parts of the code are tested. It is common that the code of the unit tests have three times the code of the code being tested, which may seem wrong at first. Writing test cases is an investment, the benefit of which isn't always apparent at the time of writing. This is sometimes because testing whether a piece of code works is usually pretty easy, the problem is that manual tests are not repeatable, and usually neglect edge cases by testing the main scenario.

The biggest win, in my opinion, is the reduction in the risk of regression. This is where an apparent minor change (or a hotfix) is applied, which affects a seemingly unrelated part of the system. These types of regression can easily make it into production, since the testing procedures may only test that part of the system. This is compounded further by the fact that any fix will take at least a day to deploy, since we are now forced to go through test and then production.

 The following link provides some good advice on achieving balance in testing software:
`https://blogs.msdn.microsoft.com/dave_froslie/2016/02/03/achievi` `ng-balance-in-testing-software/`

Creating a Form Adaptor project

Form adaptors are used in order to create test cases for user interface events--they provide a bridge between the form interactions and code. They can be created within the main project, but this creates a lot of needless classes that we will rarely wish to see.

Getting ready

Open the project that we need form adaptors for, which, in our case, is `ConWHSVehicleManagement`.

How to do it...

To create the Form Adapter project, follow these steps:

1. Select **Dynamics 365 for Operations** | **Create model** from the top menu and complete the Create model form as follows:

Field	Value
Model name	ConWHSVehicleManagementFormAdaptor
Model publisher	Contoso IT
Layer	VAR
Model description	Form adapters for the ConWHSVehicleManagement package

Model display name	ConWHSVehicleManagementFormAdaptor

The suffix is important and should always be `FormAdaptor`.

2. Click on **Next**.

3. Select **Create new package** and click on **Next**.

4. Select `ConWHSVehicleManagement` and `TestEssentials` from the **Packages [Models]** list and click on **Next**.

5. Uncheck the default for creating a project, but leave the default option of making the new model the default for new projects. Click on **OK**.

6. Right-click on the solution node in the Solution Explorer and choose **Add** | **New project...**.

7. In the **New Project** window, ensure that the **Dynamics 365 for Operations** template is selected in the left pane, and **Operations Project** is selected in the right. Enter `ConWHSVehicleManagementFormAdaptor` as **Name** and click on **OK**.

8. Save all and close Visual Studio.

9. If the package was called `ConWHSVehicleManagementFormAdapter`, navigate to the following folder in Windows Explorer:

```
C:\AOSService\PackagesLocalDirectory\ConWHSVehicleManagementFor
mAdapter\Descriptor
```

10. Open the `ConWHSVehicleManagementFormAdapter.xml` file in Notepad and add the highlighted line in order to tell the model which model is the source to build form adapters:

```
<AppliedUpdatesxmlns:d2p1="http://schemas.microsoft.com/2003/10
/Serialization/Arrays" />
<Customization>Allow</Customization>
<Description>Form adapters for the ConWHSVehicleManament
package</Description>
<DisplayName>ConWHSVehicleManagementFormAdapter</DisplayName>
<FormAdaptorSourceModel>ConWHSVehicleManagement</FormAdaptorSou
rceModel>
<Id>895571399</Id>
```

Do not edit any other part of this file. The option to set the form adaptor source model directly in Visual Studio may be added to later versions, so this step might not be required in the future.

11. Open Visual Studio and the ConWHSVehicleManagement solution, then right-click on the ConWHSVehicleManagementFormAdaptor project, and choose **Properties**.
12. Change the **Generate Form Adapters** property to True.
13. Right-click on the ConWHSVehicleManagementForm project and choose **Properties** and change the **Generate Form Adapters** property to True.
14. Select **Build models...** from the **Dynamics 365** menu and build both models.
15. This should generate and add a class for each form, suffixed with FormAdaptor. If they don't appear, you can locate them in the Application Explorer and add them manually.

How it works...

We will create a new package in order to separate the classes from the main package. This should always be done, as we can end up with a lot of automatically generated code that would be a distraction. The key part of this process was the XML tag we entered in the form adaptor model's Descriptor file--this is what told the main package that the form adapter code should be generated in our form adaptor model.

The next part was to turn on **Generate Form Adaptors** in the properties form for both projects. The build will then generate form adapters into our form adaptor project.

We will use this later when we create a unit test for the user interface.

Creating a Unit Test project

The test project would ideally be a new project (and model) inside the package we are testing. Each package should have one test project, and, if writing user interface tests, we should have one form adapters also.

Getting ready

Open the project that we intend to write tests for.

How to do it...

To create the unit test project, follow these steps:

1. Select **Dynamics 365 for Operations** | **Create model** from the top menu and complete the **Create model** form as follows:

Field	Value
Model name	ConWHSVehicleManagementTest
Model publisher	Contoso IT
Layer	VAR
Model description	Test cases for the ConWHSVehicleManagement package
Model display name	ConWHSVehicleManagementTest

 The suffix is important and should always be `Test`.

2. Click on **Next**.
3. Select **Create new package** and click on **Next**.
4. Select `ConWHSVehicleManagement`, `ConWHSVehicleManagementFormAdaptor`, `ApplicationFoundation`, and `TestEssentials` from the **Packages [Models]** list and click on **Next**.

 Model packages may be required, depending on the code we need to write.

5. Uncheck the default for creating a project, but leave the default option of making the new model the default for new projects. Click on **OK**.
6. Right-click on the solution node in the Solution Explorer and choose **Add** | **New project...**.

7. In the **New Project** window, ensure that the **Dynamics 365 for Operations** template is selected in the left pane, and **Operations Project** is selected in the right. Enter `ConWHSVehicleManagementTest` as **Name** and click on **OK**.

How it works...

This was basically a simpler version of the steps we took to create the form adaptor project. This is done after the form adaptor, as we need to reference it; this project will contain test cases for manually crafted unit tests and those that will test the user interface.

Creating a Unit Test case for code

In this recipe, we will create a test case for the `ConWHSVehicleGroupChange` class, where we will test each part of this class. This includes when it should fail and when it should succeed. The process will involve programmatically creating some test data in order to perform the update.

Getting ready

We will just need the unit test project, which we created in the previous recipe, open. Also, on the main menu, select **X64** from **Test | Test Setting | Default Processor Architecture**.

How to do it...

To create the unit test class, follow these steps:

1. Create a new class and name it `ConWHSVehicleGroupChangeTest`. The suffix is important.
2. In the code editor, change the declaration so that it extends `SysTestCase`.
3. Next, we will need some constants for test cases that we either expect to succeed or fail; in this case, we will have the following:

```
const ConWHSVehicleGroupId groupId= '%VG01%';
const ConWHSVehicleId vehicleId  ='%V001%';
const str notFound= '%ERROR%';
```

4. The next part is to set up the test case, which is done by overriding the `setUpTestCase` method with the following code:

```
publicvoidsetUpTestCase()
{
  super();
  ConWHSVehicleGroupvehGroup;
  ttsbegin;
  vehGroup.initValue();
  vehGroup.VehicleGroupId = groupId;
  vehGroup.insert();
  ttscommit;

  ConWHSVehicleTablevehTable;
  ttsbegin;
  vehTable.initValue();
  vehTable.VehicleId = vehicleId;
  vehTable.VehicleGroupId = groupId;
  vehTable.insert();
  ttscommit;
}
```

We created a vehicle record and a vehicle group record using the constants we defined earlier. We will expect our tests to find these records to succeed.

5. To reduce the amount of repetitive code that is often found in test cases, write the following method. This will be called with different parameters from a test method. Write the code as follows:

```
private void vehicleGroupExistTest(
  ConWHSVehicleGroupId _groupId,
  boolean _shouldBeFound)
{
  boolean found;

  found = ConWHSVehicleGroup::Exist(_groupId);

  strfoundMsg;
  foundMsg = "was not found";
  if(found)
  {
    foundMsg = "was found";
  }

  strshouldBeFoundMsg;
```

```
shouldBeFoundMsg = "should be not be found";
if (_shouldBeFound)
{
  shouldBeFoundMsg = "should be found";
}

strmsg = strFmt("Vehicle group %1 was %2 when it %3",
  _groupId, foundMsg, shouldBeFoundMsg);

this.assertEquals(
  _shouldBeFound ?'Found' :'Not found',
  found ?'Found' :'Not found', msg);
}
```

The `assertEquals` method will fail if the first two parameters are not the same and show the message. If it succeeds, no message will be shown.

6. We can now write our test method. The naming is important, it describes it is a test and the element to which it is testing. The code should be written as follows:

```
[SysTestMethod]
public void testValidate()
{
  this.vehicleGroupExistTest(groupId, false);
  this.vehicleGroupExistTest(notFound, true);
}
```

We will always write the test so that it will fail first, and then alter it so that it will succeed.

7. Let's execute the tests, and check that they do, indeed, fail. To do this, build the project and choose **Test** | **Run** | **All Tests**. The result should be as shown in the following screenshot:

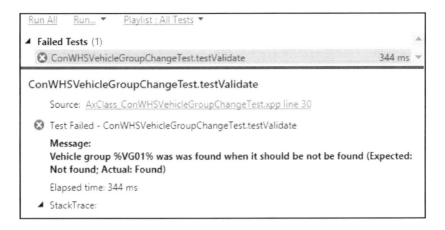

8. Change the parameters so that they should succeed; build and then click on **Run All**. The result should be as follows:

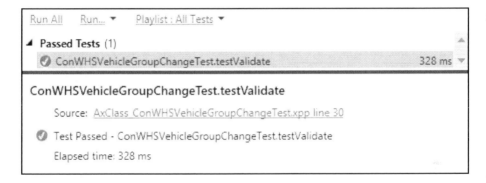

9. Do the same to test the vehicle table.

10. We will use a similar pattern for the validate method by writing the following code:

```
private void validateTest(ConWHSVehicleId _vehicleId,
ConWHSVehicleGroupId _groupId,
boolean _shouldBeValid)
{
  ConWHSVehicleGroupChangeContract contract;
  contract.VehicleGroupId(_groupId);
  contract.VehicleId(_vehicleId);

  ConWHSVehicleGroupChange change;
  change = newConWHSVehicleGroupChange();
  change.contract = contract;
```

```
boolean valid;
valid = change.Validate();
strvalidMsg = 'failed';
if (valid)
{
  validMsg = 'passed';
}
strshouldBeValidMsg;
shouldBeValidMsg = 'failed';
if (_shouldBeValid)
{
  shouldBeValidMsg = 'passed';
}
strmsg;
msg = strFmt('Vehicle %1, group %2 %3 validation ' +
  'when it should have %4',
  _vehicleId, _groupId,
  validMsg, shouldBeValidMsg);
this.assertEquals(_shouldBeValid ? 'Passed' :'Failed',
  valid ?'Passed' :'Failed', msg);
}
```

11. We can now complete our `testValidate` method, which should read as follows:

```
[SysTestMethod]
public void testValidate()
{
  this.vehicleGroupExistTest(groupId, true);
  this.vehicleGroupExistTest(notFound, false);
  this.vehicleExistTest(vehicleId, true);
  this.vehicleExistTest(notFound, false);

  // Test blank vehicle group
  this.validateTest('', '', false);
  this.validateTest(vehicleId, '', false);
  this.validateTest(notFound, '', false);
  // Test invalid vehicle group
  this.validateTest('', notFound, false);
  this.validateTest(vehicleId, notFound, false);
  this.validateTest(notFound, notFound, false);
  // Test valid vehicle group
  this.validateTest('', groupId, false);
  this.validateTest(vehicleId, groupId, true);
  this.validateTest(notFound, groupId, false);
  // Test blank vehicle
  this.validateTest('', '', false);
  this.validateTest('', groupId, false);
  this.validateTest('', notFound, false);
```

```
        // Test invalid vehicle
        this.validateTest(notFound, '', false);
        this.validateTest(notFound, groupId, false);
        this.validateTest(notFound, notFound, false);
        // Test valid vehicle
        this.validateTest(vehicleId, '', false);
        this.validateTest(vehicleId, groupId, true);
        this.validateTest(vehicleId, notFound, false);
    }
```

12. If the Test Explorer is still open, simply click on **Run All**; this will build the project for us. The result should be as follows:

 The warnings come from the target method, where it correctly failed the validation check.

13. As before, we should write the validation checks to fail first. You could also insert a runtime error to see how this is handled. On the line that defines the `ConWHSVehicleGroupChangeContract` class, comment out the line that instantiates it. When it executes, you will get a very verbose message stating `NullReferenceException`, showing us that even these types of errors will be caught through unit testing.

14. You can then continue writing the test cases for the run method, which should be done in the same pattern as the validate method check. You should also push yourself with the other assert methods.

How it works...

Most of the code we wrote is relatively straightforward. The interesting part is how the system discovers the tests and executes them.

The first part was that we referenced `ApplicationFramework` and `TestEssentials` when we created the project. The discovery works by looking for a class in the current project that extends `SysTestCase` and for methods that have the `SysTestMethod` attribute. The test method must be public, return void, and have no parameters. They should start with (or at least contain) the word test, and reference the method in the class we are testing.

Finally, what about the data we created? The test framework will automatically tear down any data we create during the testing session. This occurs between tests, so don't assume a test can use data created or updated in a previous test case.

Creating a test case from a task recording

This part of the test is to test the user interface interactions. This is done by creating a task recording from within Dynamics 365 for Operations and importing it into a project in Visual Studio.

We will test the service order creation logic by creating a task recording.

Getting ready

This continues from the previous recipes.

How to do it...

To create a unit test for the vehicle service order's form, follow these steps:

1. We must start from the main Dynamics 365 for Operations window; otherwise, the generated code may fail.
2. Once at the main menu, click on the settings icon (the cog) and choose **Task recorder**.
3. Click on **Create recording** in the **Task recorder** sidebar.
4. Enter `ConWHSServiceOrderTest` in the **Recording name** field, and a description of what we expect to happen. This will become the class name.
5. Click on **Start**.
6. Navigate to the form to test, in our case, `Vehicle service orders`.
7. Create a new service order, and add two lines. The sidebar will record each interaction with the form, so it can pay off to rehearse this first to minimize the number of steps it creates.

 To add validation, right-click on the field and choose **Task recorder** | **Validate** | **Current value**.

8. Once done, press the **Stop** button on the top left of the screen.
9. In the **Task recorder** sidebar, click on **Save as developer recording**. Save this file somewhere you can find it later.
10. Go back to Visual Studio.
11. To save time, right-click on the `ConWHSVehicleManagementTest` project and choose **Set as StartUp Project**.
12. Choose **Import Task Recoding** from the **Dynamics 365** | **Addins** menu.

13. Use the **Browse** button to find the task recording created earlier. Enter the company used to create the task recording in the **Company** field. The following screenshot is an example:

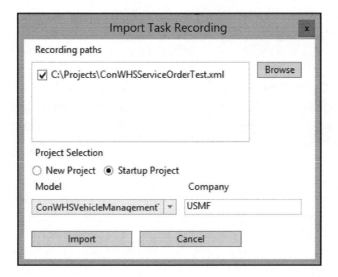

 If we used the **New Project** method, we would select the `ConWHSVehicleManagementTest` model as **Model**. When creating the project, ensure that the **Solution** drop-down is set to **Add to solution**.

14. This created a class named after the task recording name, which, in our case, is `ConWHSServiceOrderTest`.

15. In my case, I added a validation to the line number control, which resulted in the following code in the `setupData` method:

```
ConWHSVehicleServiceTable_LinesGrid_LineNum = 0;
ConWHSVehicleServiceTable_LinesGrid_LineNum1 = 0;
```

 This is clearly a bug, and we can set the expected values by editing this code. In my case, I will make them 1 and 2, respectively.

16. If we build the project now, we will get missing assembly errors. This is because the generated code references standard form adaptors. Add a reference to the following packages to the `ConWHSVehicleManagementTest` model:
    - ApplicationFoundationFormAdaptor
    - ApplicationPlatformFormAdaptor
    - ApplicationSuite
    - ApplicationSuiteFormAdaptor

17. If we hadn't corrected the line numbers, the test run would correctly state the state that the validation for the line number failed. This would then need to be corrected in code and the test rerun.

How it works...

This is a very powerful tool, where we can ask consultants and users to create the test cases based on what they expect for the developer to use as a test case.

Although there is a lot going on behind the scenes, it works by reading the XML file created by the task recording. When each step is recording, the system stores the information about the form and controls in a way that can be referenced in code. The task recoding import creates a class that uses the form adaptor in order to interact with the form programmatically, using the steps in the XML file.

Although this code is generated, we can edit it. In the case of validations, we usually have to. For example, the consultants could have added a validation for the item name. Since we can only use the current value to validate against, we will need to amend the code. In the case of an item name, we would write code to find the expected value based on the item ID the user entered.

Since these tests can be automated at the build server, the data used to create the test case and that on the build server itself must be the same. This is done by importing a backup of the database from the test database. With the technique described in this recipe we can then create integration tests that are run automatically on every build, this is much more robust that relying solely on end-user testing. It is natural for us to test what has changed, and therefore very easy to miss regression in areas that haven't been changed. The task recording is no more effort that the testing the users would have to do anyway, and with a relatively small development effort we have a repeatable set of tests that will always run, regardless of the change made in the build.

12
Automated Build Management

In this chapter, we will cover the following recipes:

- Creating a Visual Studio Build Agent Queue
- Setting up a build server
- Managing build operations
- Releasing a build to User Acceptance Testing

Introduction

In this chapter, we will cover the steps required to set up and use a build server. We touched upon some benefits with a build server in `Chapter 11`, *Unit Testing*, where unit tests can be executed to help reduce the risk of regression.

We shall cover two scenarios. These are cloud hosted customer implementation project deployed via LCS, and an on-premise build server, which is equivalent to an Azure server hosted under your own subscription.

Should the implementation be hosted in Azure deployed through a LCS customer implementation project, all we need to do is set up the Build Agent Pools and Queues and then supply the parameters to the set up form in LCS. The process of deploying a build machine is well documented and we won't duplicate this here, especially given the pace at which updates to LCS are being made. Even if we don't set up a build server manually, the information may prove useful in understanding issues that may arise with the server.

The recipes in this chapter should be used in conjunction with released Microsoft documentation. The aim (as always) is to provide practical hands-on guidance, intended to augment the already published documentation.

Creating a Team Services Build Agent Queue

Agent queues act as bridges between Visual Studio Teams Services and the build agent that is installed on the build server. We will need an agent queue before we configure the build server.

Agent Queues belong to Agent Pools, and given the way that the build servers are provisioned from LCS, we will have a one-to-one relationship for this. This is because a project will typically have its own build server (which is not limited to one) and keeping the queues and pools at one-to-one simplifies management. This is especially important for partners and ISVs who have many projects.

Getting ready

You will need to have created your Visual Studio Team Services site before you start this.

How to do it...

To create an Agent Queue, follow these steps:

1. Open the VSTS site, for example, `<your domain / tenant>.visualstudio.com`.

2. Click on the settings cog on the toolbar, and then **Agent Pools**, as shown in the following screenshot:

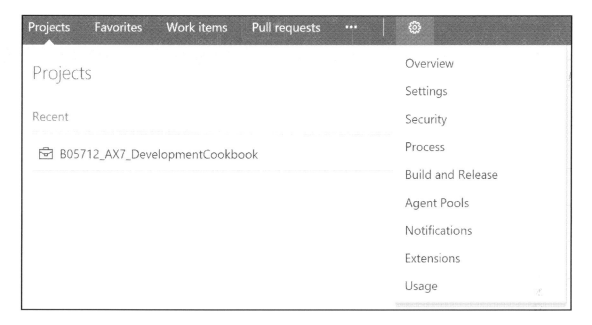

3. On the **Agents Pools** tab page, click on **New pool...**.
4. The name should relate to the project; in my case, I chose B05712AX7DevCookBook. Choose a name that is short and easy to determine which project the pool is for.
5. Uncheck **Auto-Provision Queues in all projects** and click on **OK**.

> We want each build server to have its own agent queue; if enabled, it would create the queue for all VSTS projects.

6. Click on **Projects** from the top button ribbon and select the VSTS project, and then select **Agent Queues** from the settings cog menu.
7. Click on **New queue...** and select the Agent pool we created earlier, and then click on **OK**. The Agent queue will have the same name as the pool.

How it works...

The Agent queue is used during the setup of the build server in order to associate the agent, which is installed on the build server, with the queue. This way, when a build is triggered (manually, or via a check-in), it knows which server to trigger the build to build on.

Setting up a build server

The build server is a one-box Dynamics 365 for Operations virtual machine, usually with demo data that is only ever used to produce builds. Even though it has data, and seems to have an application running in IIS, it cannot be used.

If we are creating a build server for a customer implementation project, most of the work is done for us. You will just need to specify the Agent Queue that we created in the previous recipe. This recipe will follow the ISV scenario where we may install the build agent ourselves.

Getting ready

You will need a build server VM running, with access to the internet, and the Agent Queue created against the project.

How to do it...

To configure the build server, follow these steps:

1. Open the VSTS site and select **Security** from your user options (the icon with your initials or picture).
2. Click on **Add** under the **Personal Access Tokens** tab.
3. Enter a suitable description, such as B05712_Agent.
4. Set the expiry based on the project length, usually a year for Operations projects; you can extend this should it expire.

2. Ensure that **All Scopes** is selected and click on **Create Token**.

3. Make sure you copy the token as you will not be able to see it again!

4. Open a **PowerShell** prompt (press Windows + *R* and type `PowerShell`).

5. Type the following line:

```
Cd \DynamicsSDK
```

9. Ensure that the current directory is `C:\DynamicsSDK` and type the following lines of code:

```
.\SetupBuildAgent.ps1 -VSO_ProjectCollection
https://<yourDomain>.visualstudio.com/DefaultCollection -
VSOAccessToken <your access token> -AgentName
B05712AX7DevCookBook01 -AgentPoolName B05712AX7DevCookBook
```

10. The output should be as follows:

11. Open the VSTS site, and check that the agent was added to the agent queue; it will be shown as the following screenshot:

12. We still need a build definition created for us, so go back to PowerShell and enter the following lines of code:

```
.\BuildEnvironmentReadiness.ps1 -VSO_ProjectCollection
https://<yourdomain>.visualstudio.com/DefaultCollection -
ProjectName B05712_AX7_DevelopmentCookbook -VSOAccessToken
<Your access token>
```

13. Open the VSTS site again and open your project. Select **Build & Release** from the top and then **Builds** from the button ribbon, just below the main button ribbon. You should see the following:

14. Click on the three dots and choose **Clone...** as we will create a definition for continuous integration: every check-in will perform a build and run our tests.

15. After a few seconds, the page will show the definition, and we should name it based on the original, suffixed with continuous. The default page is the **Tasks** page, and will show the tasks that the build definition will process. This is shown in the following screenshot:

16. Select the **Triggers** page and enable **Continuous Integration**. The defaults are otherwise correct.
17. Select the **Options** page and change the **Default agent queue** setting to the correct queue (the one we created earlier and which now contains our new agent).
18. Select **Save** from the **Save & queue** option button.
19. Click on **Builds** again to see the list of build definitions, then click on the three dots icon on AX7 - Build Main, and, this time, select **Edit**.
20. Click on **Variables** and select **+ Add** at the bottom of the page.
21. Enter **Build.Clean** in the **Name** column and All in the **Value** column.

This forces the agent to perform a clean build.

22. Select **Triggers** and enable **Scheduled**. This is based on your company's procedures, and most companies wish to run a clean build (complete fetch from TFS) nightly. The default schedule is usually correct.
23. Click on **Options** and change the **Default agent queue** setting to the correct queue.
24. Save your changes and queue a new build (**Save and Queue**)--this will take anything from 15 minutes to 2 hours, depending on the hardware the VM is running on.
25. On the **Query build for AX7 - Build Main** option, click on **Queue**.
26. You should now see a console window showing the progress (very verbosely as the build is performed).

How it works...

There were five parts to this recipe:

- Getting a Personal Access Token
- Installing the build agent
- Configuring the build agent
- Uploading a build definition to the VSTS project
- Configuring a build agent for clean and continuous integration

We could have downloaded the build agent manually from the Agent Queue form (you may have noticed the **Download agent** button), and then configured it using the agent's `config.cmd` script. This would be OK, but we wouldn't have been able to deploy a build definition to the project if we did. The next part, `BuildEnvironmentReadiness.ps1`, assumes that the agent is installed in a particular place on the drive, and will therefore fail to run.

We ran each command with parameters rather than entering them at runtime because the script doesn't ask for the optional parameters and it will use defaults.

The result of the configuration is that we have an Agent linked to our Agent queue through its configuration, and two build definitions that are both linked to the Agent queue.

Once all these are linked, and we have set up the build definitions, the build server is ready for operation.

There's more...

We configured both build definitions to execute any test that the project may contain, which is the default behavior. If the project does not contain tests, we will need to disable the test steps on the build definitions.

To disable the test execution, select **Builds** from the **Build & Release** section of the VSTS project site. Click on the three dots icon and select **Edit**. You will see the list of tasks on the **Tasks** tab page. The test tasks are as follows:

- Test Setup
- Execute Tests
- Test End

For each of these tasks, uncheck **Enabled** from the **Control Options** section.

Of course, we would always have tests for our projects!

See also

- Developer topology deployment with continuous build and test automation:

  ```
  https://ax.help.dynamics.com/en/wiki/developer-topology-deployment
  -with-continuous-build-and-test-automation/
  ```

- Development and continuous delivery FAQ:

  ```
  https://ax.help.dynamics.com/en/wiki/development-and-continuous-de
  livery-faq/
  ```

Managing build operations

This recipe focusses on what happens when a build is triggered, and how to deal with some common issues. We will trigger a build and then monitor its progress.

Getting ready

We must have a fully functional build server, and a build definition that will trigger on check-in.

How to do it...

To manage the build operations, follow these steps:

1. Make a minor change to any code in your project and check-in the changes.
2. Then open the VSTS project and select **Build** from the **Build & Release** menu. You should see something like the following screenshot:

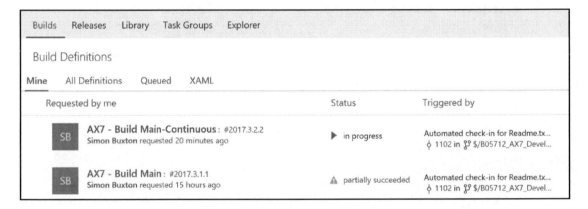

3. The #<build number> link will take us to the details of the build; click on this link.
4. This will open the details of the build operation with the Console open by default. This verbosely lists every detail of the operation as it happens. Any errors or warnings are also listed here.
5. Once complete, check for errors and look at the Summary section (click on the root of the progress tree on the left). You may find that you will receive the following message:

```
EXEC(0,0): Warning : 1:22:57 PM: No Models returned by model
info provider from metadata
```

6. You may also notice that even though no error was shown, no tests were run. The console will provide another clue:

```
No test assemblies found matching the pattern:
'C:\DynamicsSDK\VSOAgent\_work\2\Bin\**\*Test*.dll'.
```

It is looking for DLLs that contain `Test`! We can see that naming conventions are important, albeit seemingly a little ugly; there is no way the build agent can see that the class in the DLL extends `SysTestCase`.

7. Why did it fail? Open Visual Studio and select **Team Explorer**. From there, select **Source Control Explorer**.

8. The first check is to check if the `Descriptor` folder is added; in the following screenshot the `Descriptor` folder is not listed under the `ConWHSVehicleManagementTest` folder:

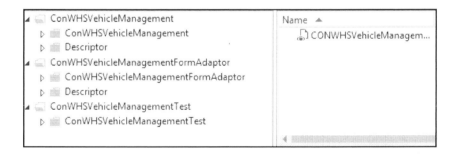

9. We add the `Descriptor` file added by right-clicking on the package (the first **ConWHSVehicleManagementTest** node in this case) and selecting **Add Items to Folder...**. Add the **Descriptor** folder, but nothing else.

When hotfixes are applied, which will need to be added to source control so that the build server builds them, it will only add the source files. You will manually have to add the models' description file (a package can have more than one model, and there is a descriptor for each model). Only add the descriptor file for the models that have elements added to source control.

10. The other reason is that the mapping of TFS is wrong. The build agent will assume (and create) the structure `Trunk\Main\Metadata` and download changes from this folder. If we mapped the metadata differently, the build agent will not find any source code to build. Do this by editing your workspace (it will usually be the server name) and mapping as follows:

Name:	MININT-TE88M28		
Working folders:			
Status	Source Control Folder ▲		Local Folder
Active	$/B05712_AX7_DevelopmentCookbook/Trunk/Main/Metadata	...	C:\AOSService\PackagesLocalDirectory
Active	$/B05712_AX7_DevelopmentCookbook/Projects		C:\Projects\TFS

Before you make this change, make sure everything is checked-in and that you have moved the existing folders against the 'wrong' folder to the correct folder in TFS (`Trunk\Main\Metadata`). Failure to do this will result in errors checking code in and out, and you could lose code.

12. Trigger a build either manually or via a check-in. Open the build details from the VSTS site and look at the **Get Sources** node. You should see entries similar to the following code snippet:

```
2017-03-02T13:43:47.6277906Z
C:\DynamicsSDK\VSOAgent\_work\2\s\Metadata:
2017-03-02T13:43:47.6287911Z Getting ConWHSVehicleManagement
2017-03-02T13:43:47.6287911Z Getting
ConWHSVehicleManagementFormAdaptor
2017-03-02T13:43:47.6297916Z Getting
ConWHSVehicleManagementTest
2017-03-02T13:43:47.6498150Z
2017-03-02T13:43:47.6507910Z
C:\DynamicsSDK\VSOAgent\_work\2\s\Metadata\ConWHSVehicleManagem
ent:
2017-03-02T13:43:47.6517934Z Getting ConWHSVehicleManagement
2017-03-02T13:43:47.6517934Z Getting Descriptor
```

13. Once the build has finished, you should see the following on the build's summary page:

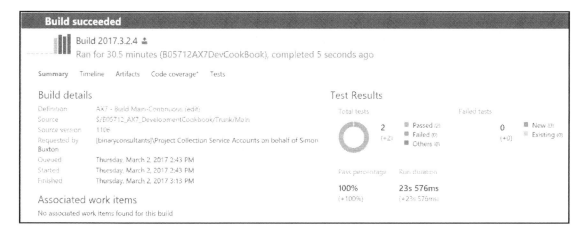

14. You can then click on the detailed report, usually in the case of failures, to view the detailed test results:

The default is to show only failed tests; to view all, click on the outcome (for example, `Failed`) next to the label **Outcome** and choose `All`.

How it works...

When the build agent is installed, it creates a TFS workspace that is hardcoded to be `Trunk\Main\Metadata`, the agent assumes a mapped server's local packages folder. It starts by downloading all changes from this folder in TFS to a local working folder. It then uses the descriptor file to determine what to build.

Once the files have been downloaded, the following happens:

- Check if the `DynamicsBackup` folder exists on the C drive--this will be on a specific drive if it is an LCS deployed build server, and will not be on the C drive.
- If it does not exist, a SQL backup is made to the `DynamicsBackup\Databases` folder and the local packages folder is copied to the `DynamicsBackup\Packages` folder.
- If the folder exists, the SQL database is restored from this backup and the local packages folder is recreated from this folder.
- The system will then start a full build of the system, and process each step in the build definition. Most call PowerShell scripts stored in the `C:\DynamcisSDK` folder.
- Once complete, it uploads the source and resultant deployable package to the build. This will then be applied to our test server, and eventually production.

It is possible, as at Update 6 of Operations, to include a partner's or ISV's package directly on the build server, and to configure the build agent to include that package in the build's artifacts.

This is referenced in the following link:

What's new or changed in Dynamics 365 for Operations platform update 6 (April 2017) (`https://docs.microsoft.com/en-us/dynamics365/operations/dev-itpro/get-started/whats-new-platform-update-6`)

The actual details are to hand at this point, and even with this functionality Microsoft do encourage that ISV packages are installed on the development machines and pushed through VSTS. This is a complicated subject, as ISVs naturally want to protect their intellectual property and customers often desire to have source code in order to protect their investment.

Releasing a build to User Acceptance Testing

At the end of the build process, a deployable package file was uploaded to the build. This file can then be applied to your user acceptance test or sandbox server.

We can apply the package manually on the test server, but for LCS deployed **User Acceptance Testing** (**UAT**) environments, this is always done via LCS. Any release to production must first be deployed to a sandbox server and marked as a release candidate.

Getting ready

In order to follow this recipe, we need to have an LCS Operations server deployed through LCS.

How to do it...

To apply the build to a test server, follow these steps:

1. Open the VSTS site, and then open your project and select **Explorer** from **Build & Release**.
2. Double-click on the build that you wish to deploy to UAT.
3. On the page that opens, select **Artifacts**, and click on **Explore** for the `Packages` artifact, as shown in the following screenshot:

4. In the **Artifacts Explorer** tab, expand the `Packages` node and click on the arrow icon next to the file starting with `AXDeployableRuntime`. Click on **Download**. The icon only appears when you move the mouse over it, as shown in the following screenshot:

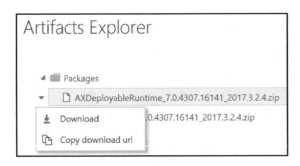

5. Download the file and then open LCS (`https://lcs.dynamics.com/`).

6. Open your LCS project and then open the Asset Library. Depending on the type of project, this will be under the burger icon or a tile on the project. Do not use the Shared Asset Library.

7. In **Asset library**, select **Software deployable package** from the left, and then press the plus symbol. In the dialog, enter the build name, (for example, Build-2017-03-02), a description, and then click on **Add a file**.

8. Locate the deployable package we just downloaded and click on **Upload**. Once complete, click on **Confirm** on the **Upload Software deployable package file** dialog.

9. Open the environment to which this should be deployed to and choose **Maintain | Apply updates**. This will show a list of `Software deployable package` assets. Select the asset and click on **Apply**.

 The update process will start immediately. This will take the server offline and apply the update. This will take several hours to complete.

10. After testing is complete, go back to the sandbox environment and you will be prompted to confirm that the update was successful. After that, go back to the Asset library, select the deployable package, and then click on **Release candidate**. This is so that it will be available to be deployed to the production environment.

How it works...

The application of deployable packages is performed by a PowerShell script on the target server. There are agents installed on LCS deployed servers that allow LCS to perform this task.

The processes are as follows:

- Download the deployable package to the target server or servers (test and production environments have multiple servers and the components installed on each may vary)
- Extract the deployable package
- Apply the update to the server using the PowerShell scripts included in the package
- At the end of the process, the servers' services are restarted

This process is best used, and is, in fact, mandatory for applying updates to customer implementation environments. You can't apply an update to production servers that hasn't been applied to the sandbox server through LCS.

13
Servicing Your Environment

In this chapter, we will cover the following recipes:

- Applying metadata fixes
- Applying binary updates
- Servicing the Build server
- Servicing the Sandbox - Standard Acceptance Test environment

Introduction

This chapter focuses on the services of the various environments used in a customer implementation project. We will also cover the servicing of environments typically used by ISVs.

The important part of this chapter is the process. The actual details of the tasks can be found in the Operations documentation. The recipes are written to help this process make more sense as to why, which is mainly to help manage how updates are applied and to minimize the risk of regression.

For general information on the update process and the update policies please see the following link:

Dynamics 365 for Operations versions and update policy
(`https://docs.microsoft.com/en-us/dynamics365/operations/dev-itpro/migration-upgrade/versions-update-policy`)

Applying metadata fixes

Metadata fixes are updates to the source code of Operations. For over-layering we would use the These are used to code-merge over-layered code, but they are still needed on extension projects as this is part of the process to push updates downstream to the build, test, and eventually, the production environment.

The process of applying the updates is straightforward; it is the process that is the most important aspect to take away from this.

LCS can see which metadata fixes are available for each environment connected to the project. When working on a customer implementation project, use the Sandbox (test) environment as the reference VM to check for updates. When working on internal or ISV projects, use a reference VM hosted in Azure for this. On-premise implementations will be connected to LCS and will be handled in the same way as Azure-based implementation projects.

The cycle is as follows:

- Check the availability of metadata fixes required against a reference VM or environment
- Download the desired fixes to a development VM
- Apply the hotfixes so that they are placed in TFS
- Check-in so that a build is triggered (and other developers can bring down the hotfixes applied, maintaining the same code base across developers)
- Deploy the resultant package to the test environment (or reference VM)

When moving to the latest update release, where new VMs are deployed with the new update, we remove the hotfixes from source control before connecting the new dev VMs back to the source control project with the upgraded code. This process may change, and the standard documentation covers this very well. The process is described in the following link:

Overview of moving to the latest update of Dynamics 365 for Operations
(https://docs.microsoft.com/en-us/dynamics365/operations/dev-itpro/migration-upgrade/upgrade-latest-update)

Getting ready

You need access to an LCS project that allows the download of metadata hotfixes. LCS deployed VMs and Customer implementation LCS projects can do this. Ensure that Visual Studio is connected to the correct TFS project.

How to do it...

To apply a metadata hotfix to a development VM, please follow these steps:

1. Within the desired development VM, open `https://lcs.dynamics.com` and navigate to your implementation project (or the project that hosts your Azure hosted VM).
2. Click on **Full details** on the **Sandbox: Standard acceptance test** environment (or the VM if this is not a customer implementation project).
3. There are two tiles for metadata hotfixes, which are called X++ updates on this page: **Application x++ updates** and **Platform x++ updates**.

The number indicates the number of fixes to be applied.

4. Click on the first tile.
5. You will now see a list of the fixes, and you can choose which to apply. They are linked, which will force us to add sets of hotfixes where a dependency has been identified. Click on **Select all** and press **Add**.

Take note of the fixes included in the update, so that these can be tested for regression in process of code that we have extended.

6. Click on **Download package** from the top left of the window, and then **Download** on the next page.

There is no need to select them; these buttons are to allow you to remove fixes from the download list.

7. On the file that is downloaded, right-click on it, choose **Properties**, and unblock the file. Rename the file so that it reflects the tile used to download the updates, such as AppXpp20170309.zip, and extract the file contents.

8. Within Visual Studio, select the **Addins | Apply hotfix** from the **Dynamics 365** menu.

9. Select **Apply Metadata Hotfix**, and use the **Browse** button to select the file extracted from the update package.

10. The other three text boxes are taken from Visual Studio; check if these are correct and click on **Apply**.

11. Once complete, you will see many pending changes ready to be checked into TFS.

12. Before checking in, we need to check that each affected model's descriptor file is also added. Open **Source Control Explorer** from the **Team Explorer** home tab.

13. Expand **Trunk**, **Main** and then **Metadata**.

14. The following screenshot shows the structure of models Electronic Reporting Application and Foundation sit within the ApplicationSuite package:

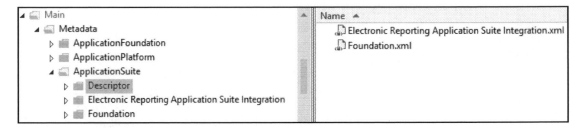

15. We need to ensure that there is a model descriptor file for both of these models; if one is missing, add it by right-clicking on the package's folder and choosing **Add Items to Folder....**

16. Add the files by double-clicking on the Descriptor folder from within the **Add to Source Control** dialog and selecting the missing files for the models already added to source control. **Do not add any model descriptor files for models that are not added to source control**. In the following screenshot, the Foundation Update and SCMControls files must not be added:

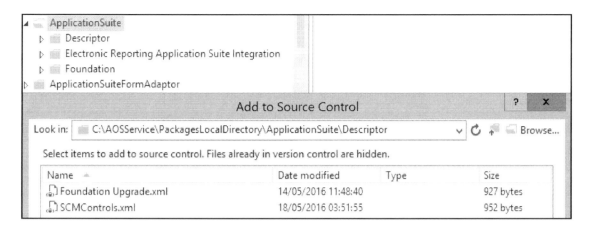

17. Once all required model descriptor files are added, perform a full build and check-in the changes. This build will execute out test script, which is especially important as they will help us identify regression before the users start testing.

 If any over-layering has been done, these changes must be merged prior to build and check-in.

How it works...

The update works by checking the local packages folder for updates, and applying those that are not yet applied. The change is made using delta changes, which is why the files are so small.

The reason that we add the changes to source control is so that they are pushed to other developers and also to the build. Once a hotfix has been added to TFS, the resulting deployable package increases in size from a few megabytes to around 600 MB. This is because packages must be deployed in total.

We have to manually add the model descriptor file to TFS if we want the build server to build the package. This is used by the build server to work out what needs to be built, and what will end up as a build artefact against the build. Should we add model descriptor files for models that are not in TFS, errors will be produced; this is solved by removing the file from TFS.

There's more...

These updates can also be added using a command line, which is done as follows:

```
c:\AOSService\PackagesLocalDirectory\bin\SCDPBundleInstall.exe
-packagepath=<path>HotfixPackageBundle.axscdppkg
-metadatastorepath=c:\AOSService\PackagesocalDirectory
-tfsworkspacepath=C:\AOSService\PackagesLocalDirectory
-tfsprojecturi=https://<your company site>.visualstudio.com
```

This is typed as one line, and is split in the preceding code so that it is easier to read.

You may wonder how it knows which project it should use, and you may have thought that Visual Studio autocompleted this parameter when we used the GUI method.

It does this using the workspace mapping that was configured in Visual Studio. This is what the `tfsWorkspacePath` parameter does--it tells the command to look up the mapping from the current TFS workspace. The fact that we specify the paths for the local packages folder and TFS workspace path separately seems to be legacy, and these must always be the same.

See also

- *Installing a metadata hotfix*
  (https://docs.microsoft.com/en-us/dynamics365/operations/dev-itpro/migration-upgrade/install-metadata-hotfix-package)
- *Download hotfixes from Lifecycle services*
  (https://docs.microsoft.com/en-us/dynamics365/operations/dev-itpro/migration-upgrade/download-hotfix-lcs)

Applying binary updates

Binary updates contain replacement binary updates to the target VM. The binary updates downloaded from LCS are merged deployable packages containing updates to one (and usually) more packages.

They also contain updated Visual Studio tooling, which has to be installed separately.

Getting ready

You need access to an LCS project that allows the download of metadata hotfixes. LCS deployed VMs and Customer implementation LCS projects can do this.

How to do it...

To apply a binary hotfix to a development VM, follow these steps:

1. Within the desired development VM, open `https://lcs.dynamics.com` and navigate to your implementation project (or the project that hosts your Azure-hosted VM).
2. Click on **Full details** on the **Sandbox: Standard acceptance test** environment (or the VM if this is not a customer implementation project).
3. There is one tile for binary updates, named **Binary updates**; click on this first tile.
4. You will now see a list of the fixes, and you can choose which to apply. They are linked, which will force us to add sets of hotfixes where a dependency has been identified. Click on **Select all** and select **Add**.
5. Click on **Download package** from the top left of the window, and then **Download** on the next page.
6. On the file that is downloaded, right-click, choose **Properties**, and unblock the file. Rename the file so that it reflects the tile used to download the updates, such as `Bin20170309.zip`, and extract the file contents.
7. Within Visual Studio, select **Addins | Apply hotfix** from the **Dynamics 365** menu. Select the **Apply Binary Hotfix** tab, and then browse to the file before clicking on **Apply**.
8. Select **Extension and Updates...** from the **Tools** menu.
9. Click on **Dynamics 365 for Operations Visual Studio Tools** and then click on **Uninstall**.
10. Close Visual Studio.
11. In Windows Explorer, navigate to the folder extracted from the downloaded deployable packaged.
12. Navigate through the `DevToolsService` folder, and then `Scripts`. Double-click on the `Microsoft.Dynamics.Framework.Tools.Installer.vsix` file (the `.vsix` extension may not be visible) and follow the prompts to install the updated extension.

How it works...

The binary update package is a merged deployable package, which usually contains a merged set of packages that can be (technically) applied directly to any Operations environment.

The dialog, just like the metadata hotfixes, is optional, and we can use a command line to apply the update.

This is done in the *Servicing the build server* recipe.

See also

- *Install a deployable package*
  (https://ax.help.dynamics.com/en/wiki/installing-deployable-package-in -ax7/)

Servicing the build server

Although we could use the same process to apply binary updates to the build server as we did on the development VMs (albeit using the command version), the build server is a little special.

The process of applying a build is that the environment (local packages folder and data) is restored from a backup and merged with objects from TFS. If we simply applied the update, the next build will, effectively, remove it.

Getting ready

You need access to an LCS project that allows the download of metadata hotfixes. LCS deployed VMs and Customer implementation LCS projects can do this.

How to do it...

To apply binary updates to the build server, follow these steps:

1. Within the build server, open https://lcs.dynamics.com and navigate to

your implementation project (or the project that hosts your Azure-hosted VM).

2. Click on **Full details** on the **Sandbox: Standard acceptance test** environment (or the VM if this is not a customer implementation project). Do not use the Development/build server tile.

3. Click on the **Binary updates** tile.

4. In the list of fixes, click on **Select all** and then **Add**.

5. Click on **Download package** from the top left of the window, and then **Download** on the next page.

6. On the file that is downloaded, right-click, choose **Properties**, and unblock the file. Rename the file so that it reflects the tile used to download the updates, such as `Bin20170309.zip`, and extract the file contents.

7. Open Services (Windows + *R* and type `services.msc`).

8. Stop the following services:
   - World Wide Web Publishing Service
   - VSTS Agent
   - Microsoft Dynamics AX Batch Management Service

9. Rename `J:\AosService\PackagesLocalDirectory` to `J:\AosService\PackagesLocalDirectory_OLD`.

10. Rename `I:\DynamicsBackup` to `I:\DynamicsBackup_OLD`.

11. Open a command prompt as administrator and type the following command:

```
robocopy I:\DynamicsBackup_OLD\Packages
J:\AosService\PackagesLocalDirectory /E
```

 The backup is the baseline that is used to merge with TFS on each build, so we need to copy this to our main packages folder before the update is applied.

12. Start the following services:
    - World Wide Web Publishing Service
    - Microsoft Dynamics AX Batch Management Service

13. Navigate using `CD` to the root of the extracted files, for example, `CD C:\Updates\Bin20170309\`.

14. Run the following commands:

```
AXUpdateInstaller.exe generate -runbookid=Build<YYYYMMDD>
 -runbookfile=Build<YYYYMMDD>
 -topologyfile=DefaultTopologyData.xml
 -servicemodelfile=DefaultServiceModelData.xml

AXUpdateInstaller.exe import -runbookid=Build<YYYYMMDD>
 -runbookfile=Build<YYYYMMDD>

AXUpdateInstaller.exe execute -runbookid=Build<YYYYMMDD>
```

The run book is stored internally, so you must use unique names for each update; we use the following schemas:

Update type	Naming scheme
Binary platform update	BinPlatform<YYYYMMDD> For example, BinPlat20160219 Do not use DDMMYYYY or MMDDYYYY as this can cause confusion between those in the USA and outside.
Binary application update	BinApp<YYYYMMDD>
New build (a release of your code)	Build<YYYYMMDD>: this doesn't have to match your version numbering system; it just needs to be unique.

15. Start the VSTS Agent service and trigger a new build. This package will then be used to service the Sandbox (standard acceptance test) environment.
16. You can delete the folders we renamed as OLD.

How it works...

The application of the update is the same as before; the only change is that we need to re-baseline the build server's clean environment. The baseline is actually created when the next build runs. Since we renamed the backup folders, the build agent thinks that this is a new server and will recreate a new baseline backup from the updated files in the local packages folder.

Servicing the Sandbox - Standard Acceptance Test environment

This process is now done entirely within Visual Studio Online and LCS, and we don't need to be logged into a Operations server.

The process is to take the latest build from the build server and merge it with a binary update before applying it to the test server.

Getting ready

You need access to LCS and the Visual Studio Online site from which the builds are executed and stored.

How to do it...

To apply the updates to the Sandbox - Standard Acceptance Test environment, follow these steps:

1. Navigate to your Visual Studio online project and locate the latest build.
2. Within the build details, click on **Artifacts** and download the file starting with `AXDeployableRuntime`.
3. The size of the file varies; once it includes hotfixes to the base application, it can inflate to over 600 MB.
4. Next, download the binary updates to a folder; this should be taken from the development server that started this process in order to ensure that the updates are the same as applied to developer and build servers.
5. Open `https://lcs.dynamics.com/`.
6. Open **Asset library** from the "burger".
7. Select **Software deployable package**.
8. If any are marked **Release candidate**, select them and click on **Not release candidate**.
9. Click on the + icon.
10. Name the package as `Build20170306`.
11. Enter the build number and version in the description, and select `AOT deployable package` as **Package type**.
12. Upload the file.

13. Repeat this for the binary update, for example, `Binary20170306`.

14. Select both updates and click on **Merge**. Use the `Merge20170306` pattern, and click on **Confirm**.

15. Click on the project name at the top to return to the project details page.

16. Click on **Full details** on the **Sandbox: Standard Acceptance Test** option.

17. Click on **Maintain** and then **Apply updates**. Select the merged package from the list and click on **Apply**. This starts immediately and all Operations services will be stopped. You can use **Message online users** to warn them in advance of this.

How it works...

Although you can technically use the command-line method for this by connecting to the server through a remote desktop, the sandbox environments involved more than one server. The LCS method applies the update to all servers.

This method does take longer (several hours at present) to process, so this should be timed with that in mind.

The actual technical process is the same as the binary update we used when applying the updates to the development server.

There's more...

Sometimes, this can fail. It is usually a file permission issue. LCS first downloads the update to a folder on each server, and then executes the runbook as we did when we serviced the build server.

This is usually in `F:\DeployablePackages`.

Inside the folder, there is a folder called `RunBookWorkingFolder`; if you navigate down through the folders, finally expanding `AOSService`, you will see a list of numbered folders.

In these folders are the logs produced by the update. The failure, if any, will be in the last folder. You can open the logs and search for the `error` or `fail` keywords to help diagnose the problem.

If it is a file access issue, it was probably locked by a process. Locate the file and simply rename it. Check that the file was correctly created once the update completes.

Servicing production

In order to apply any update to live, the package must first be deployed to the Standard Acceptance Test environment (LCS enforces this rule). If the new update passes user acceptance testing, go back to the Asset library and locate the merged package. Select it and click on **Release candidate**.

Then, use the same process as we did for the sandbox server to apply the update. The difference in this case is that it can be scheduled. Since this requires Microsoft's DSE (a team of engineers that help maintain the cloud environments) to be on call for this, they need notice which is currently 8 hours. The update window is 5 hours, and it will take 5 hours. It can take longer, so plan this carefully with the customer.

See also

- *Upgrade Dynamics 365 for Operations to the latest platform update*
  (https://docs.microsoft.com/en-us/dynamics365/operations/dev-itpro/migration-upgrade/upgrade-latest-platform-update)
- *Process for upgrading a sandbox environment*
  (https://docs.microsoft.com/en-us/dynamics365/operations/dev-itpro/migration-upgrade/upgrade-sandbox-environment)

14
Workflow Development

In this chapter, we will cover the following recipes:

- Creating a workflow type
- Creating a workflow approval
- Creating a manual workflow task
- Hooking up workflow to the user interface
- Creating a sample workflow design

Introduction

Workflow in Microsoft Dynamics 365 for Operations have two main types of element, **approvals** and **tasks**, centered on a document. This is the center of the workflow where tasks are triggered based on what the user decides. By a document, it means a record with a form that maintains it. For example, a **New customer creation** workflow would be based on the customer table using the customer details form as the document.

The workflow designer can then use conditions based on fields and display methods on the tables used in the workflow in order to decide what happens. This solves many requirements where a great deal of configurability is required, but can also be misunderstood and used inappropriately. The submission of a workflow is usually started with the user pressing a Submit button on the form, which is then processed within a minute by the batch server. The minimum time it can take for a workflow to complete, if the conditions for automatic completion are met, is three minutes: up to one minute for submission, one minute for evaluation, and one minute per subsequent workflow step. This, therefore, can't be used when the user is expected feedback as part of the data entry.

In this chapter, the workflow design is to control the approval of a new vehicle, including a task to inspect the vehicle as part of the workflow.

Creating a workflow type

The workflow type can be considered a template or a document definition. The workflow type acts like an umbrella for the associate workflow elements, such as approvals and tasks. When the designer starts to design a workflow, they actually select a workflow type, and the design surface will allow them to select workflow elements we have associated with it.

We create the workflow type first because the workflow type creation tooling will create elements used in other workflow elements. We just come back to this in order to add them to the list of supported types by the workflow type.

 Be careful with the naming, as this process automatically creates menu items and classes. They are all prefixed with the workflow type's name. If we have a class that exists already, it will add a 1 to the name, which is unpleasant. For this reason, the maximum length is 20 characters for all workflow types, approvals, tasks, and automated tasks.

We will create a Base Enum to persist the workflow status. In this recipe, we will only use one of the status fields to handle the started and canceled events. The Base Enum was designed with the whole workflow in mind, which includes handling the status of the workflow approval.

Getting ready

This recipe can apply to any record that has a main form managing its data--these are typically main or worksheet table types. In this example, we will use the vehicle table.

How to do it...

To create the workflow type, follow these steps:

1. If we are creating a workflow for a new module, or one that currently doesn't have a workflow, we need to create a new workflow category, which means we need to add a module to `ModuleAxapta`. Locate the `ModuleAxapta` Base Enum and choose **Create extension** from the right-click context menu. Rename as usual; change the `.extension` or add a prefix to make it unique.

2. To create the workflow category, we need to add a new item to our project and choose **Workflow Category** from the **Business process and Workflow** list. Enter the name `ConWHSVehicleManagement` before clicking on **Add**.

3. Complete the **Label** and **HelpText** properties; these will be visible to the workflow designer in the user interface. Set the **Module** property to the module name, which is `ConWHS` in our case.

4. Before we create the actual workflow type element, we need to create some base elements required by the workflow approval element. First, create a new query called `ConWHSVehWF`. To this query, add the `ConWHSVehicleTable` table, and set the **Dynamics Fields** property to `Yes`.

5. We can now go and get into creating the workflow type, choose to add a new item to the project, and select **Workflow Type** from the **Business process and Workflow** list. Name the new element `ConWHSVehWF` and click on **Add**.

6. Complete the **Workflow Type** dialog as shown in the following screenshot:

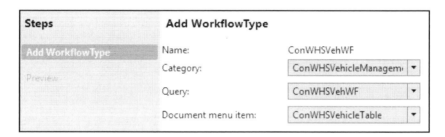

7. Click on **Next**.

8. You will see the elements that will be created; check that none are suffixed with 1 (which means that the preferred element name already exists), and click on **Finish**.

9. Since we used a prefix, locating the elements will be relatively easy for all menu items. Complete the **Label** and **Help Text** properties, creating labels as required using named label identifiers.

10. Next, open the `ConWHSVehWFDocument` class, the workflow document class, and alter as shown by the following code:

```
/// <summary>
/// The ConWHSVehWFDocument workflow document class.
/// </summary>
[WorkflowDocIsQueueEnabledAttribute(true,
 "@ConWHS:VehicleApproval")]
class ConWHSVehWFDocument extends WorkflowDocument
{
```

```
/// <summary>
/// Returns query name for the workflow document.
/// </summary>
/// <returns>
/// Name of the query <c>ConWHSVehWF</c>.
/// </returns>
public queryName getQueryName()
{
  return querystr(ConWHSVehWF);
}


/// <summary>
/// Provides days since acquired on workflow
/// condition editor in workflow configuration form.
/// </summary>
/// <param name="_companyId">
/// The company on which the workflow is running.
/// </param>
/// <param name="_tableId">
/// The table ID of the table which is associated
/// with the workflow.
/// </param>
/// <param name="_recId">
/// The record ID of the table which is associated
/// with the workflow.
/// </param>
/// <returns>
/// The days since the vehicle was acquired.
/// </returns>
public Days parmDaysSinceAcquired(
    CompanyId _companyId,
    tableId _tableId,
    recId _recId)
{
    Days days;
    if(_tableId == tableNum(ConWHSVehicleTable))
    {
        ConWHSVehicleTable vehicle;
        select crosscompany AcquiredDate
            from vehicle
            where vehicle.DataAreaId == _companyId
                && vehicle.RecId == _recId;
        days = vehicle.AcquiredDate - systemDateGet();
    }
    return days;
}
}
```

We added the `parm` method as an example of how to add display methods that can be used in the workflow expression builder and as a placeholder in the workflow text presented to the user.

11. There will be two new Action Menu Items created, prefixed with the approval name, `ConWHSVehWF`. These are suffixed with `CancelMenuItem`, and `SubmitMenuItem`. For each of these, set the **Label** and **Help Text** properties with a suitable label, for example:

Menu item	Label	Help Text
CancelMenuItem	Cancel	Cancel the vehicle workflow
SubmitMenuItem	Submit	Submit vehicle to workflow

Create the labels using names and not numbers, as we will reuse these labels in other elements.

12. We need to handle the state change, so first we need to create a Base Enum name, `ConWHSVehApprStatus`, with the following elements:

Element	Label	Description
Draft	@SYS75939	Draft--the workflow has not yet been submitted to workflow
Waiting	Waiting	The workflow has been submitted, but has not yet been allocated an approver
Inspection	Inspection	The vehicle is being inspected
InReview	In review	The workflow has been allocated one or more approvers
Approved	Approved	The workflow has been approved
Rejected	Rejected	The workflow was rejected by the approvers
Revise	Revised	A change was requested by an approver

These labels should be created using named label identifiers, as we did for the menu items as we will reuse them on other elements.

13. Use the @SYS101302 label (**Approval Status**) in the Base Enum's **Label** property. Add the new Base Enum to the ConWHSVehicleTable table as Status, and add it to the Overview field group. Make the field read-only.

14. Open the ConWHSVehWF workflow type and complete the **Label** and **Help Text** fields. These are to assist the workflow designer in selecting the correct workflow type when creating a new workflow.

15. Next, create a class called ConWHSVehicleStatusHandler, and write the following piece of code:

```
class ConWHSVehicleStatusHandler
{
    /// <summary>
    /// Sets the vehicle's approval
    /// status
    /// </summary>
    /// <param name = "_vehicleRecId">
    /// The vehicle record id
    /// </param>
    /// <param name = "_status">
    /// The new status
    /// </param>
    public static void SetStatus(RefRecId _vehicleRecId,
        ConWHSVehApprStatus _status)
    {
        ConWHSVehicleTable vehicle;

        ttsbegin;
        select forupdate vehicle
            where vehicle.RecId == _vehicleRecId;
        if (vehicle.RecId != 0
            && vehicle.Status != _status)
        {
            vehicle.Status = _status;
            vehicle.update();
        }
        ttscommit;
    }
}
```

Create common select statements, such as the preceding one, as a static Find method, for example, FindByRecId. When writing any select statement, check that the table has a suitable index.

16. Save and close the class.

17. Create a new class named `ConWHSVehWFBase` and add the following method:

```
public boolean ValidateContext(WorkflowContext _context)
{
    If (_context.parmTableId() !=
        tableNum(ConWHSVehicleTable))
    {
        //Workflow must be based on the vehicle table
        throw error("@ConWHS:ConWHS72");
    }
    ConWHSVehicleTable vehicle;
    select RecId from vehicle
        where vehicle.RecId == _context.parmRecId();
    if (vehicle.RecId == 0)
    {
        //Vehicle cannot be found for the workflow instance
        throw error("@ConWHS:ConWHS73");
    }
    return true;
}
```

 We throw an error in case of a validation error, as we need the workflow to stop with an error should it fail; the workflow cannot continue with an invalid context.

18. Next, add a method so that the workflow type's handler class knows whether or not the supported elements actually ran. Since that final result will be approved or rejected, we can't use the same field to state that the workflow is completed. In fact, if the workflow type completed, but nothing was done, the document should reset back to `Draft` (not submitted). Write the method as follows:

```
public boolean CanCompleteWF(WorkflowContext _context)
{
    ConWHSVehicleTable vehicle;
    select RecId from vehicle
        where vehicle.RecId == _context.parmRecId();
    if (vehicle.RecId != 0)
    {
        // Code to check if the workflow can be completed,
        // i.e. nothing in progress
        return true;
    }
    return true;
}
```

19. Save and close this class, and open the `ConWHSVehWFEventHandler` class and alter the class declaration so that it extends `ConWHSVehWFBase`.

20. Add the following methods in order to handle the workflow type's events:

```
public void started(WorkflowEventArgs _workflowEventArgs)
{
    WorkflowContext context;
    context = _workflowEventArgs.parmWorkflowContext();
    if(this.ValidateContext(context))
    {
        ConWHSVehicleStatusHandler::SetStatus(
            context.parmRecId(),
            ConWHSVehApprStatus::Waiting);
    }
}

public void canceled(WorkflowEventArgs _workflowEventArgs)
{
    WorkflowContext context;
    context = _workflowEventArgs.parmWorkflowContext();
    if(this.ValidateContext(context))
    {
        ConWHSVehicleStatusHandler::SetStatus(
            context.parmRecId(),
            ConWHSVehApprStatus::Draft);
    }
}

public void completed(WorkflowEventArgs _workflowEventArgs)
{
    WorkflowContext context;
    context = _workflowEventArgs.parmWorkflowContext();
    if(this.ValidateContext(context))
    {
        If (!this.CanCompleteWF(context))
        {
            ConWHSVehicleStatusHandler::SetStatus(
                context.parmRecId(),
                ConWHSVehApprStatus::Draft);
        }
    }
}
```

The status changes here are that we move from Draft to Waiting when the workflow engine starts, and back to Draft if canceled. Should the workflow complete, but fail the CanCompleteWF check, reset it back to Draft.

21. Finally, open the ConWHSVehWFSubmitManager class and complete the main method, as shown here:

```
public static void main(Args _args)
{
    RefRecId              recId;
    CompanyId             companyId;
    RefTableId            tableId;
    WorkflowComment       comment;
    WorkflowSubmitDialog  dialog;
    WorkflowVersionTable  version;

    recId = _args.record().RecId;
    tableId = _args.record().TableId;
    companyId = _args.record().DataAreaId;

    // The method has not been called correctly.
    if (tableId != tablenum(ConWHSVehicleTable)
        || recId == 0)
    {
        throw error(strfmt("@SYS19306", funcname()));
    }

    version =
        _args.caller().getActiveWorkflowConfiguration();
    dialog = WorkflowSubmitDialog::construct(version);
    dialog.run();

    if (dialog.parmIsClosedOK())
    {
        comment = dialog.parmWorkflowComment();

        Workflow::activateFromWorkflowConfigurationId(
            version.ConfigurationId,
            recId,
            comment,
            NoYes::No);
    }
    // Set the workflow status to Submitted.
    ConWHSVehicleStatusHandler::SetStatus(
        _args.record().RecId,
        ConWHSVehApprStatus::Waiting);
```

```
if(FormDataUtil::isFormDataSource(_args.record()))
{
    FormDataUtil::getFormDataSource(
        _args.record()).research(true);
}

_args.caller().updateWorkflowControls();
}
```

22. Open the `ConWHSVehSubmitMenuItem` menu item and change the **Object** property to `ConWHSVehWFSubmitManager`.

23. Close all code editors and designers and build the project. The compiler will highlight code we forgot to handle by showing the TODO comments as warnings.

How it works...

The workflow type required a few elements before we created the actual workflow type. The document is defined by a query, which has a main table. This could be a query of sales orders and sales order lines, where the sales order is the main table, and lets the workflow designer use fields from the query to define messages to the user, and also control how the workflow behaves. The workflow has special application element types for workflow, which point to classes that implement specific interfaces.

The workflow type is a higher level than the workflow elements. Workflow elements are the tasks assigned to the user, and they handle states such as Review, Reject, Approve, and so on. The workflow type is at a higher level, and controls whether the workflow is started, cancelled, or completed.

It may seem odd that we don't map the workflow event types directly to the Base Enum elements. The workflow engine doesn't read this field; it knows within itself the status of the workflow. The status field is to allow us to easily read the status or act on a particular workflow event. For this reason, we don't actually need to handle all of the events that the workflow provides.

The `ConWHSVehWFEventHandler` class was tied to the workflow type, and is used to persist the workflow's state in the target document record--the vehicle record, in our case.

The `parm` method on the workflow document class, `ConWHSVehWFDocument`, adds a calculated member that can be used by the workflow designer to either make decisions in the workflow design, or displayed in messages to the users.

The `parm` methods have to be written with the same input parameters as shown in the example method, and we are free to write any code we like, and return data of any base type that can be converted to a string, such as strings, dates, and Base Enum. We cannot, therefore, return types such as records, objects, or containers. Consider how the method will perform, as this will be run whenever it needs to be evaluated by the workflow engine.

See also...

Check out the following links for help setting up workflows and for further reading:

- *Workflow system architecture*
  (`https://docs.microsoft.com/en-us/dynamics365/operations/organization-administration/workflow-system-architecture`)
- *Creating a workflow*
  (`https://docs.microsoft.com/en-us/dynamics365/operations/organization-administration/create-workflow`)
- *Overview of the workflow system*
  (`https://docs.microsoft.com/en-us/dynamics365/operations/organization-administration/overview-workflow-system` and `https://ax.help.dynamics.com/en/wiki/overview-of-the-workflow-system/`)

- *Workflow elements*
  (`https://docs.microsoft.com/en-us/dynamics365/operations/organization-administration/workflow-elements`)

Creating a workflow approval

A workflow approval is an element that allows approval tasks to be routed, which can be approved or rejected. The design can then use this outcome in order to trigger tasks, or simply inform the user. The workflow approval status is persisted as a field on the document record (that is, the vehicle record in our case), in the same way that the workflow type does.

As a result of this, there are often two fields on the workflow's main table, one for workflow document state, and another for workflow element state. In some cases, such as human resource workflows, the Base Enum is combined into one field. This can seem confusing, but when the workflow status field is properly defined, it simplifies the process.

 We cannot create extensions for workflow elements, so we cannot use workflow types created by other parties without customization (over-layering).

Getting ready

We just need to have created a workflow type, or have a suitable workflow type to add the approval to.

How to do it...

To create a workflow approval, follow these steps:

1. Add a new item to the project by selecting **Business Process and Workflow** from the left-hand list, and then **Workflow Approval** from the right. Enter `ConWHSVehApprWF` as the **Name** and click on **Add**.

2. Complete the **Workflow Approval** dialog as shown here:

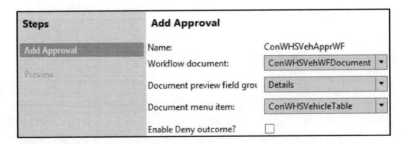

3. Click on **Next**.

4. You will be presented with all of the elements the wizard will create for us, reminding us again why the limit is 20 characters and also why the naming is important. Click on **Finish**.

5. Open the new `ConWHSVehApprWF` workflow approval, expand the **Outcomes** node, and note that the system has associated a workflow event handler class

with **Approve**, **Reject**, and **RequestChange**. To complete this element, complete the **Label** and **HelpText** properties on the root `ConWHSVehApprWF` node element. The workflow designer will need this to identify the correct workflow.

6. There will be five new Action Menu Items created, prefixed with the with approval name, `ConWHSVehApprWF`. These are suffixed with `Approve`, `DelegateMenuItem`, `Reject`, `RequestChange`, and `ResubmitMenuItem`. For each of these, set the **Label** and **Help Text** properties with a suitable label, for example:

Menu item	Label	Help text
Approve	Approve	Approve the new vehicle request
DelegateMenuItem	Delegate	Delegate this approval to a colleague
Reject	Reject	Reject the new vehicle request
RequestChange	Revise	Send the request back for revision
ResubmitMenuItem	Resubmit	Resubmit the new vehicle request

Create the labels using names and not numbers, as we will reuse these labels in other areas.

As well as menu items, it also created an event handler class, which is named based on the workflow approval, suffixed with `EventHandler`. This class will implement seven interfaces, which enforce that a method is implemented, one per event type.

7. Open the work event handler class, `ConWHSVehApprWFEventHandler`, and alter the class declaration so that it extends `ConWHSVehWFBase`.

8. This class implements the `WorkflowElementDeniedEventHandler` interface, even though we chose not to in the creation dialog; remove this from the list.

9. Then, locate the `denied` method and delete it.

10. We now need to write some code for each method that was generated for us with a `TODO`. The sample code to write for each method is as follows:

```
public void started(WorkflowElementEventArgs
_workflowElementEventArgs)
{
    WorkflowContext context;
    context =
```

```
        _workflowElementEventArgs.parmWorkflowContext();
    if(this.ValidateContext(context))
        {
            ConWHSVehicleStatusHandler::SetStatus(
                context.parmRecId(),
                ConWHSVehApprStatus::InReview);
        }
    }
```

11. Follow this pattern for each method using the following table to determine which status to set:

Element	Method
Waiting	started
InReview	created
Approved	completed
Rejected	returned
Revise	changeRequested
Draft	cancelled

12. For the created method, the input parameter is a different type; simply change the method as follows:

```
public void created(WorkflowWorkItemsEventArgs
_workflowWorkItemsEventArgs)
{
    WorkflowContext context;
    WorkflowElementEventArgs workflowArgs;
    workflowArgs =
_workflowWorkItemsEventArgs.parmWorkflowElementEventArgs();
    context = workflowArgs.parmWorkflowContext();
    if(this.ValidateContext(context))
        {
            ConWHSVehicleStatusHandler::SetStatus(
                context.parmRecId(),
                ConWHSVehApprStatus::InReview);
        }
    }
```

13. In the previous recipe, we wrote a method to determine if the workflow did anything that was used to reset the workflow should nothing have been done when the workflow type completed. Open the `ConWHSVehWFBase` class and alter the method as follows:

```
public boolean CanCompleteWF(WorkflowContext _context)
{
    ConWHSVehicleTable vehicle;
    select RecId from vehicle
    where vehicle.RecId == _context.parmRecId();
    boolean canComplete;
    if (vehicle.RecId != 0)
    {
        switch (vehicle.Status )
        {
            case ConWHSVehApprStatus::Approved:
            case ConWHSVehApprStatus::Rejected:
                canComplete = true;
            default:
                canComplete = false;
        }
    }
    return canComplete;
}
```

14. The final piece of code to write is the resubmission code. A template was created for us, so open the `ConWHSVehAppWFResubmitActionMgr` class.

15. In the main method, remove the `TODO` comment and write the following code snippet:

```
public static void main(Args _args)
{
    // The method has not been called correctly.
    if (_args.record().TableId !=
            tablenum(ConWHSVehicleTable)
        || _args.record().RecId == 0)
    {
        throw error(strfmt("@SYS19306", funcname()));
    }
    //Resubmit the same workflow, Workflow handles
    // resubmit action
    WorkflowWorkItemActionManager::main(_args);
    // Set the workflow status to Submitted.
    ConWHSVehicleStatusHandler::SetStatus(
        _args.record().RecId,
        ConWHSVehApprStatus::Waiting);
```

```
                    _args.caller().updateWorkflowControls();
            }
```

16. Open the `ConWHSVehApprWF` workflow approval, select the **Deny** outcome, and change the **Enabled** property to `No`.

17. Finally, open the workflow type and then right-click on **Supported Elements** node. Select **New Workflow Element Reference** and set the properties as follows:

Field	EDT / Enum	Description
Element Name	ConWHSVehApprWF	This is the element's name
Name	ApprovalVehicle	This is a short version of the name, prefixed with the type
Type	Approval	This is the workflow element's type

18. Save and close all code editors and designers and build the project. Don't forget to synchronize, as we have added a new field.

How it works...

The workflow approval is set up with outcomes, which are referenced to an event handler class that implements an interface for each outcome it handles. Each outcome is tied, internally, to that interface. When the outcome occurs, it will construct the referenced event handler class using the interface as the type. It then calls the appropriate method. This pattern of instantiating a class using the interface as the type is common pattern, and we have used this ourselves in `Chapter 10`, *Extensibility Through Metadata and Data Date-Effectiveness*.

There are some events (`Started` and `Cancelled`, for example) that are set on the work approval's main property sheet. All this was created for us when we created the workflow approval element.

The class that the code generated for us implements all required interfaces with `TODO` statements where we need to write code. The code is usually simple, and, in our case, we are just updating the vehicle's status field. The generated code will always implement all interfaces that the workflow element can support, so it is common to remove methods and interfaces from the event handler class.

Creating a manual workflow task

A manual task is a task that is assigned to a user in order to perform an action. The action can be any task, such as Inspect vehicle, and the user will then state that the task was complete.

This workflow will be used to instruct the vehicle to be inspected, and record whether it was inspected in a new field on the vehicle table.

Getting ready

This follows from the *Creating a Workflow Type* recipe, as we need a workflow document class.

How to do it...

To create the manual workflow task, follow these steps:

1. We need a new Base Enum for the inspection status, as this will be used both to see whether a vehicle has been inspected and also to control the state of the workflow task; name it `ConWHSVehInspStatus` and create the elements as shown in the following table:

Element	Label	Description
NotInspected	Not inspected	This vehicle has not yet been inspected
Waiting	Waiting	This workflow has been submitted, but has not yet been allocated an approver
InProgress	InProgress	This workflow has been allocated to one or more workers to perform the task
Completed	Completed	This workflow has been completed

2. Create a new Date EDT for `ConWHSVehInspDate`, setting the properties as follows:

Field	EDT/Enum	Description
Extends	TransDate	This EDT should be used for all dates.
Label	Date inspected	Create a named label for this, such as `@ConWHS:DateInspected`.
Help Text	The date the inspection was carried out	This is left generic and not tied to its eventual implementation in order to make the EDT reusable. The help text does not reference the vehicle for this reason.

3. Add the following fields to the vehicle table and set the **Allow Edit** and **Allow Edit On Create** to `No`:

Field	EDT / Enum	Description
InspStatus	ConWHSVehInspState	This is the status Base Enum created in the previous step
InspComment	WorkflowComment	This will hold the last note when the task is completed
InspDate	ConWHSVehInspDate	This is the date on which the workflow task was completed

4. Create a field group named `Inspection` and set the **Label** property to a label for Inspection. Add the fields to this group and then add the field group to a suitable place in the `ConWHSVehicleTable` form.

5. Next, let's add a status handler class; create a new class name, `ConWHSVehicleInspStatusHandler`. Create a method to handle the status change, and set the `InspComment` and `InspDate` fields from the method's parameters. The code is written as follows:

```
/// <summary>
/// Handle the inspection date change
/// </summary>
/// <param name = "_vehicleRecId">
/// The record id of the vehicle
/// </param>
/// <param name = "_status">
/// The new status
```

```
/// </param>
/// <param name = "_comment">
/// Comment is set when the status
/// is complete
/// </param>
/// <param name = "_inspDate">
/// InspDate is set when the
/// status is complete
/// </param>
public static void SetStatus(RefRecId _vehicleRecId,
    ConWHSVehInspStatus _status,
    WorkflowComment _comment = '',
    ConWHSVehInspDate _inspDate = dateNull())
{
    ConWHSVehicleTable vehicle;

    ttsbegin;
    select forupdate vehicle
        where vehicle.RecId == _vehicleRecId;
    if(vehicle.RecId != 0)
    {
        vehicle.InspStatus = _status;
        // if the inspection is complete set
        // the comment and inspection date fields
        // otherwise clear them, as the workflow
        // may have been cancelled.
        switch (_status)
        {
            case ConWHSVehInspStatus::Complete:
                vehicle.InspComment = _comment;
                vehicle.InspDate = _inspDate;
                break;
            default:
                vehicle.InspComment = '';
                vehicle.InspDate = dateNull();
        }
        vehicle.update();
    }
    ttscommit;
}
```

6. Against the project, add a new item and choose **Workflow Task** from the **Business process and Workflow** list. Use the `ConWHSVehWFInspect` name and click on **Add**.

7. Configure the **Workflow Task** dialog as shown in the following screenshot:

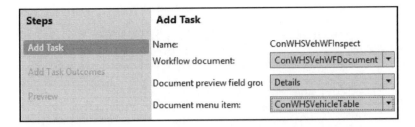

8. Click on **Next**.
9. On the next page, choose **Complete** in the **Type** drop-down list, and enter `Complete` in the field before clicking on **Add**.

> You can add further outcomes, which will follow the same pattern when implemented.

10. Click on **Next** and then **Finish**.
11. For each action menu item created by the wizard, complete the **Label** and **Help Text** properties.

> You may recognize that the code generated by this process is very similar to the Workflow approval. We will follow that pattern again by handling the required methods in the `ConWHSVehWFInspectEventHandler` class.

12. Since we don't handle all of the possible outcomes, we should only implement the required interfaces. Also, in order to have access to the `ValidateContext` method, we should extend `ConWHSVehWFBase`. The class declaration should read as shown here:

```
public final class ConWHSVehWFInspectEventHandler
    extends ConWHSVehWFBase
    implements WorkflowElementCanceledEventHandler,
    WorkflowElementCompletedEventHandler,
    WorkflowElementStartedEventHandler,
    WorkflowWorkItemsCreatedEventHandler
```

13. Also, remove the methods linked to the interface that we removed. Change the started method as shown here. It maintains the vehicle status and inspection status fields:

```
public void started(
    WorkflowElementEventArgs _workflowElementEventArgs)
{
    WorkflowContext context;
    context =
        _workflowElementEventArgs.parmWorkflowContext();
    if(this.ValidateContext(context))
    {
        ConWHSVehicleInspStatusHandler::SetStatus(
            context.parmRecId(),
            ConWHSVehInspStatus::Waiting);

        ConWHSVehicleStatusHandler::SetStatus(
            context.parmRecId(),
            ConWHSVehApprStatus::Inspection);
    }
}
```

14. The `canceled` method should reset both status fields back to their initial states:

```
public void canceled(
    WorkflowElementEventArgs _workflowElementEventArgs)
{
    WorkflowContext context;
    context =
        _workflowElementEventArgs.parmWorkflowContext();
    if(this.ValidateContext(context))
    {
        ConWHSVehicleInspStatusHandler::SetStatus(
            context.parmRecId(),
            ConWHSVehInspStatus::NotInspected);

        ConWHSVehicleStatusHandler::SetStatus(
            context.parmRecId(),
            ConWHSVehApprStatus::Draft);
    }
}
```

15. The completed method needs to get the current system date, and also fetch the last comment from the workflow. This is done in the following code:

```
public void completed(WorkflowElementEventArgs
_workflowElementEventArgs)
{
    WorkflowContext context;
    context =
        _workflowElementEventArgs.parmWorkflowContext();
```

```
WorkflowCorrelationId correlationId;
correlationId = context.parmWorkflowCorrelationId();

WorkflowTrackingTable trackingTable;
trackingTable =
    Workflow::findLastWorkflowTrackingRecord(
    correlationId);

WorkflowTrackingCommentTable commentTable;
commentTable = trackingTable.commentTable();

WorkflowComment comment = commentTable.Comment;
Timezone timezone =
    DateTimeUtil::getUserPreferredTimeZone();
if(this.ValidateContext(context))
{
    ConWHSVehicleInspStatusHandler::SetStatus(
        context.parmRecId(),
        ConWHSVehInspStatus::Complete,
        comment,
        DateTimeUtil::getSystemDate(timezone));
}
}
```

16. Finally, write the `created` method. This is when the task is assigned to one or more users. The code should be written as follows:

```
public void created(
    WorkflowWorkItemsEventArgs _workflowWorkItemsEventArgs)
{
    WorkflowContext context;
    WorkflowElementEventArgs workflowArgs;
    workflowArgs = _workflowWorkItemsEventArgs.
        parmWorkflowElementEventArgs();
    context = workflowArgs.parmWorkflowContext();
    if(this.ValidateContext(context))
    {
        ConWHSVehicleInspStatusHandler::SetStatus(
            context.parmRecId(),
            ConWHSVehInspStatus::InProgress);

        ConWHSVehicleStatusHandler::SetStatus(
            context.parmRecId(),
            ConWHSVehApprStatus::Inspection);
    }
}
```

17. We should also update the `CanComplete` method on the `ConWHSVehWFBase` class, but what we do here is dependent on what we want to control. We are in danger of hardcoding a business rule, which is ironically what workflows are designed to avoid. As a result of this, we just want to ensure that the document (vehicle record) is always left in a consistent state when the workflow type completes. The following piece of code will only return false if either the approval or task is in progress:

```
public boolean CanCompleteWF(WorkflowContext _context)
{
    ConWHSVehicleTable vehicle;
    select RecId from vehicle
    where vehicle.RecId == _context.parmRecId();
    boolean canComplete = true;
    if (vehicle.RecId != 0)
    {
        switch (vehicle.Status )
        {
            case ConWHSVehApprStatus::Revise:
            case ConWHSVehApprStatus::Waiting:
            case ConWHSVehApprStatus::InReview:
            case ConWHSVehApprStatus::Inspection:
                canComplete = false;

            default:
                canComplete = true;
        }
        switch (vehicle.InspStatus)
        {
            case ConWHSVehInspStatus::InProgress:
            case ConWHSVehInspStatus::Waiting:
                canComplete = false;
        }
    }
    return canComplete;
}
```

18. Next, complete the `ConWHSVehApprWFResubmitActionMgr` class as follows:

```
public static void main(Args _args)
{
    // The method has not been called correctly.
    if (_args.record().TableId !=
            tablenum(ConWHSVehicleTable)
        || _args.record().RecId == 0)
    {
        throw error(strfmt("@SYS19306", funcname()));
```

```
        }
        //Resubmit the same workflow, Workflow handles resubmit
action
        WorkflowWorkItemActionManager::main(_args);
        // Set the workflow status to Submitted.
        ConWHSVehicleInspStatusHandler::SetStatus(
            _args.record().RecId,
            ConWHSVehInspStatus::Waiting);

        _args.caller().updateWorkflowControls();
    }
```

19. Finally, open the workflow type and then right-click on the **Supported Elements** node. Select **New Workflow Element Reference** and set the properties as follows:

Field	EDT / Enum	Description
Element Name	ConWHSVehWFInspect	This is the element's name
Name	TaskInspect	This is a short version of the name, prefixed with the type
Type	Task	This is the workflow element's type

20. Copy and paste the task name into the **Element Name** and **Name** properties.
21. Save and close all designers and code editors and build the project, followed by synchronizing the database with the project.

How it works...

The concept is the same as for the workflow approval in the previous recipe. The Workflow task element is a definition that the designer will use when creating a workflow. The code we wrote simply handles the events as we need to.

The complicated part to understand is the status handling. It seems natural to have a status field for each workflow element (the type, approval, and task), and with this paradigm, we would be left thinking why there isn't a standard Base Enum we could simply use. The status of the document, and the statuses the document can be defined by us--what makes sense to the business, and not what makes sense in code. For the inspection task, we want to know if a vehicle is waiting inspection, is in progress, or if it is complete.

Hooking up a workflow to the user interface

This is the final step in designing our workflow, and involves setting a property on the form referenced by the document menu item, ConWHSVehicleTable, and adding the option to design workflows to the menu.

Getting ready

The minimum we need to have completed for this is create a workflow type.

How to do it...

In order to be able to design and process workflows, follow these steps:

1. Expand **User interface**, **Menu items**, and then **Display** from the **Application Explorer**. Located WorkflowConfgurationBasic, right-click on it and choose **Duplicate in project**.
2. Locate the new menu item in the **Solution explorer**, and rename it to ConWHSWorkflowConfiguration.

 Depending on the version of the development tools, you will need to undo the change to WorkflowConfigurationBasicCopy and then add the renamed element to source control.

3. Open the new menu item in the designer and set the **Enum Parameter** property to ConWHS, and then create labels for the **Label** and **Help Text** properties. The label should be the module name, followed by the word workflows, Vehicle management system workflows, for example.
4. Add this menu item to the Setup submenu of our menu. This should usually be the second option in the list.
5. Open the ConWHSVehicleTable form in the designer.

6. Select the Design node of the form design and locate the following properties:

Property	Value
Workflow Data Source	ConWHSVehicleTable
Workflow Enabled	Yes
Workflow Type	ConWHSVehWF

7. Right-click on the **Methods** node of the form and select **Override** | **canSubmitToWorkflow**. Alter the code so that it reads as follows:

```
public boolean canSubmitToWorkflow()
{
    If (ConWHSVehicleTable.Status ==
        ConWHSVehApprStatus::Draft)
    {
        return true;
    }
    return false;
}
```

We may need this to be more elaborate in some cases, but the minimum is that we can't allow a workflow to be submitted that is already in progress.

8. Save and close all designers and build the project.

How it works...

The workflow configuration is a generic form that builds based on the ModuleAxapta Base Enum. We linked ConWHS to the workflow category, which was then linked to the workflow type. This will, therefore, allow the workflow designer to create and modify workflows for this module.

The form changes were simply to link the workflow type to the form, and which data source is the document data source. This is then used to query if there are any active workflows for that type, and will show the option to submit the vehicle for approval if there is an active vehicle workflow design.

Creating a sample workflow design

Let's test the elements we have created. The following workflow design is only intended to test the workflow we have created, and omits many of the features that we would normally use. We will also use the same user for submission and approval, and you will see that appear to be waiting for the workflow engine as we test. This seems a problem at first glance, but in real-life scenarios, this is fine. In practice, the tasks and approvals are performed by different users and are not done as a series of tasks. They will receive a notification, and they can then perform that action and pass the ball back to the workflow engine.

Getting ready

Before we start, ensure that the project is built and synchronized with the database.

How to do it...

To create the workflow design, follow these steps:

1. Open the following URL, and from there, open **Vehicle management** | **Setup** | **Vehicle management workflows**:

   ```
   https://usnconeboxax1aos.cloud.onebox.dynamics.com/?cmp=usmf
   ```

   You can navigate directly to the configuration form using the following URL:
   ```
   https://usnconeboxax1aos.cloud.onebox.dynamics.com/?cmp
   =usmf&mi=ConWHSWorkflowConfiguration
   ```

2. Click on **NEW**, and you should see the workflow type in the list, and is listed using the **Label** and **Help Text** properties that we set.

3. Select the workflow type link, as shown in the following screenshot:

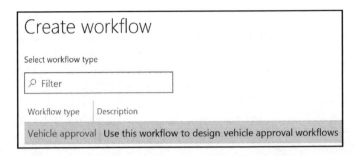

4. You will then be asked to log in, which you should do as the same user you used to log in to Operations. You will then be presented with a new window, with the two workflow elements that we wrote and some flow control options in the left-hand pane.

5. Drag the **New vehicle approval workflow** and **Inspect vehicle** elements onto the design surface, as shown in the following screenshot:

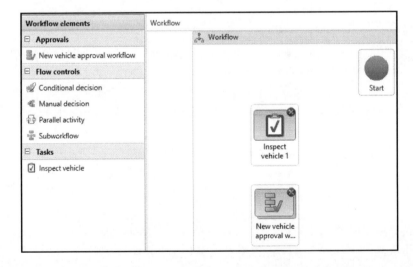

6. As your mouse hovers over the **Start** element, you will see small handles appear-- drag one of these handles so that it connects the Start element to the **Inspect vehicle 1** element. Connect all elements, as shown in the following screenshot:

7. Select the **Inspect vehicle 1** element, and click on **Basic Settings** from the action pane. Configure it as shown in the following screenshot:

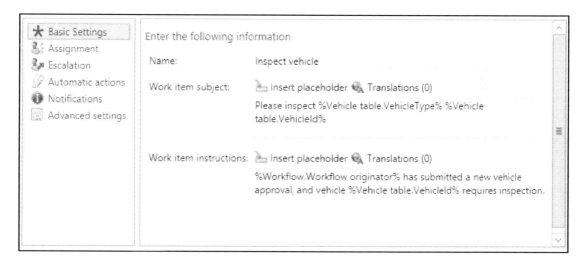

The text within % symbols was added using the **Insert placeholder** button; click on this and you will see that our `parm` method was added and the `parm` prefix was automatically removed.

8. Click on **Assignment** from the left, and choose **User** from the **Assign users to this workflow element** list. Select the **User** tab, and manually assign this to `Admin`. This is the default administration user. Since we are simply testing our code works, we will assign all tasks and approvals to our user.

9. Click on **Close**.

10. Double-click on the **New vehicle approval workflow 1** element and click on **Basic Settings** from the action pane. Change **Name** to `New vehicle approval workflow` and click on **Close**.

We would normally configure the notifications; for example, we would usually notify **Workflow Originator** if the approval was rejected.

11. Then, select **Step 1**, press **Basic Settings**, and configure as shown here:

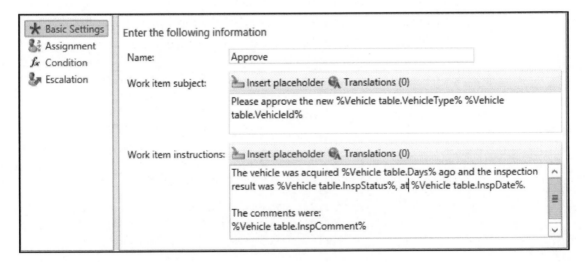

12. Click on **Assignment** and assign this to our user as we did before. Press **Close**. There is a bread crumb at the top of the workflow designer's design surface, which shows **Workflow | New vehicle approval**. Click on the word **Workflow** from the bread crumb.

13. Finally, we must give submission instructions to the person who submitted the vehicle approval. Right-click on an empty area of the workflow designer's design surface and click on **Properties**. Enter suitable instructions in the **Submission instructions** field and click on **Close**.

14. Click on **Save and close**, and then the **OK** on the **Save workflow** dialog. Select **Active the new version** on the **Activate workflow** dialog and click on **OK**.

Let's now test if the workflow works:

1. Open the vehicle form, and you should see the **Workflow** button as shown in the following screenshot:

2. Click on the button and select **Submit**, which is the label we assigned to the `ConWHSVehWFSubmitMenuItem` menu item. Enter a comment and click on **Submit**.

3. The options should change to **Cancel** and **View history**. You can choose **View history** to see the progress of the workflow engine. If the tasks aren't assigned within a minute, check that the `Microsoft Dynamics 365 for Operations - Batch Management Service` Windows service is running. Also check that there are batch jobs for `Workflow message processing`, `Workflow due data processing`, and `Workflow line-item notifications`. If not, open **Workflow infrastructure configuration** from **System administration | Workflow**, and click on **OK**.

4. After approximately two minutes, having pressed the refresh icon, you should see the **Complete**, **Delegate**, and **Cancel** options. These are the options for the inspection task. Select **Complete**. Enter an inspection comment and click on **Complete**. View the vehicle details and wait for about a minute. Click on the refresh button. You should see information similar to the following:

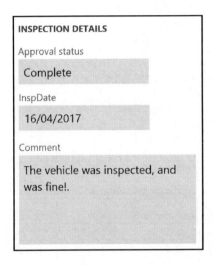

5. After a further minute, refresh the form, and the options will change to the approval options. Choose **Approve** from the list.

How it works...

The workflow design has many options available to us, and is used to tell the workflow engine how the approvals and tasks should be processed. When we develop workflows, we do so as generically as possible in order to leave the business logic to the workflow designer. This means that we reduce the need for changes to the code as the business evolves.

The test was to help demonstrate what happens to the status fields as the workflow is processed. This should help us in our own workflow development in understanding the link between events and status changes.

15
State Machines

In this chapter, we will cover the following recipes:

- Creating a state machine
- Creating a state machine handler class
- Using menu items to control a state machine
- Hooking up the state machine to a workflow

Introduction

State machines are a new concept in D365O, and a very welcome feature. Previously, the control of status fields was handcrafted in code, which could be often hard to read as there was no obvious pattern to follow; having said that, we will always look at a similar standard example to our case and use that idea. This is not plagiarism, it is good practice. It is a good general rule to seek examples in standard code, as there is a much higher chance that another developer will understand the code we've written.

State machines allow us to define in metadata how the status transitions from an initial state to its final state. These rules are then enforced by code that the state machine will generate.

There is a restriction though. There must be one initial state and one final state. When we are at the final state, there is no going back. If we take the sales order status, we have two final states: **Invoiced** and **Cancelled**. There is another reason why we wouldn't use a state machine on this type of status. The sales order status is a reflection of actual order state; it is system controlled. State machines are designed to enforced status change logic when the state is asserted by a user.

Creating a state machine

This first recipe is to create a state machine for vehicle inspection. In Chapter 14, *Workflow Development*, we created a workflow task and an inspection status field. In this recipe, we will use a state machine to handle the inspection status change logic.

Getting ready

We need to have a table with a status field with an initial and final status, such as the InspStatus field we added to the ConWHSVehicleTable table in Chapter 14, *Workflow Development*.

How to do it...

To create a state machine, follow these steps:

1. Open ConWHSVehicleTable in the designer. Right-click on the **State Machines** node and choose **New State machine**.

2. Rename the new state machine InspStateMachine and complete the properties as shown in the following table, creating labels for the **Description** and **Label** properties:

Property	Value
Description	Use this to control the inspection status
Label	Inspection status
Data Field	InspStatus

3. Right-click on the new state machine definition and select **New State**.

4. Complete the properties of this state using the following table:

Property	Value
Enum Value	NotInspected - change this to Waiting, and then back again to default the **Label** property.
Description	The vehicle has not yet been inspected
Label	Not inspected

State Kind	Initial

We will create a state for each element in the `ConWHSVehInspStatus` Base Enum, so it is a good idea to create description labels in advance and just paste them in. Use named labels for this, not numeric. I use a suffix of HT, which is short for `Help Text`, for labels that are used for both help text and descriptions of elements.

5. Create the remaining states using the following table as a guide:

Enum Value	Name	State Kind	Description
Waiting	Waiting	Intermediate	The vehicle is awaiting inspection
InProgress	InProgress	Intermediate	The vehicle inspection is in progress
Complete	Complete	Final	The vehicle inspection is complete

6. The result should look like the following screenshot:

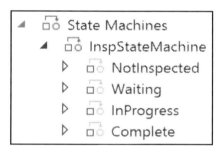

7. We will now need to tell the state machine the transition rules. We will define the rules as follows:
   - `NotInspected` can only transition to `Waiting`
   - `Waiting` can only transition to `InProgress`
   - `InProgress` can transition to both `Waiting` and `Complete`
   - `Complete` is the final state and cannot transition backwards

8. Again, create labels in advance. The following table explains the type of wording we should use:

Label ID	Label
VehTransWaiting	Add to waiting list
VehTransWaitingHT	Add the vehicle to the list of vehicles awaiting inspection
VehTransInProgress	Start inspection
VehTransInProgressHT	Start the vehicle inspection process
VehTransBackWaiting	Revert to waiting
VehTransBackWaitingHT	Place the vehicle back onto the waiting list
VehTransComplete	Complete inspection
VehTransCompleteHT	Complete, and finalize the vehicle inspection

9. To do this, right-click on the `NotInspected` state and select **New State transition**. This time, the **Label** and **Description** properties define the action, not the state. Set the properties to define the transition to the `Waiting` state as follows:

Property	Value
Description	@ConWHS:VehTransWaitingHT
Label	@ConWHS:VehTransWaiting
Name	TransitionToWaiting
Transition To State	Waiting

10. Add a new transition state to the `WaitingState` state using the following table:

Property	Value
Description	@ConWHS:VehTransInProgressHT
Label	@ConWHS:VehTransInProgress
Name	TransitionToInProgress
Transition To State	InProgress

11. Next, add two transition states to the `InProgress` state. The first is to revert back to waiting:

Property	Value
Description	@ConWHS:VehTransBackWaitingHT
Label	@ConWHS:VehTransBackWaiting
Name	TransitionToWaiting
Transition To State	Waiting

12. The second state to add to the `InProgress` state completes the state machine, and should be configured as follows:

Property	Value
Description	@ConWHS:VehTransCompleteHT
Label	@ConWHS:VehTransComplete
Name	TransitionToComplete
Transition To State	Complete

13. Save your changes, the result should look like the following screenshot:

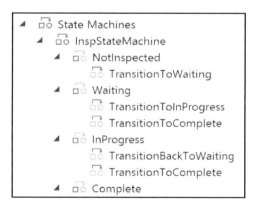

14. The final step is to right-click on the `InspStateMachine` state machine, and click on **Generate**. This generates the code that will be used to control the inspection status progression.

 If you get the error **Given key does not exist in the dictionary**, it is because the name of the state did not match the **Enum Value** property. This may be changed in future releases so that it can be named differently.

15. The generated classes may not be added to your project; to do so, locate the classes that start with `ConWHSVehicleTableInspStateMachine` and drag them on to the **Classes** node of your project. Do not modify these classes; these are shown in the following screenshot:

```
+ ConWHSVehicleTableInspStateMachine
+ ConWHSVehicleTableInspStateMachineEnterEventArgs
+ ConWHSVehicleTableInspStateMachineExitEventArgs
+ ConWHSVehicleTableInspStateMachineTransitionEventArgs
```

How it works...

What this process actually does is generate four classes. The main class is named `ConWHSVehicleTableInspStateMachine`, which is a concatenation of the table's name and the state machine's name. The other three classes are all prefixed with this class, and allow typed date to be passed to the delegates that were written into this class.

The fact we have a state machine does not prevent the user from manually changing the status field's value. It also does not stop us from manually changing the status in code. So the restriction on the final status being final is only true when using the state machine.

There are two ways in which we can use the state machine:

- Attach to workflow events
- Use with menu items added to a form

We will explore these in the following recipes.

Creating a state machine handler class

The state machine provides control over the transition rules, but, sometimes, we want to ensure that other validation rules are obeyed in order to validate whether the transition can be done.

This is done by subscribing to the `Transition` delegate of the `ConWHSVehicleTableInspStateMachine` class that was generated by the state machine.

The code in this recipe refactors the `ConWHSVehicleInspStatusHandler` class that we created in `Chapter 14`, *Workflow Development*. The code written in this recipe will tie it programmatically to the state machine. Should you wish to attach the statement to the workflow directly (which is a great idea), the status will be set by the state machine. Therefore, the event handlers must not set the status. Furthermore, should the validation written in this recipe fail, we must ensure that the workflow's internal status matches the state machine's status. This could be by canceling the workflow by throwing an error.

Getting ready

We created a class named `ConWHSVehicleInspStatusHandler`; we will extend this class so that we can use it with the state machine.

How to do it...

To create a handler class to add further validation to the state machine, follow these steps:

1. Open the `ConWHSVehicleInspStatusHandler` class and add the following piece of code:

```
public ConWHSVehInspStatus fromStatus;
public ConWHSVehInspStatus toStatus;
public ConWHSVehicleTable vehicle;

public boolean Validate()
{
    switch (toStatus)
    {
        case ConWHSVehInspStatus::Complete:
            if (vehicle.InspComment == '')
            {
                DictField field = new DictField(
                    tableNum(ConWHSVehicleTable),
```

```
                            fieldNum(ConWHSVehicleTable,
                                    InspComment));

                    //The field %1 must be filled in"
                    return checkFailed (strFmt(
                                    "@SYS110217",
                                    field.label()));
            }
            break;
        }
    return true;
}

public void run()
{
    if(toStatus == fromStatus)
    {
        return;
    }
    if(this.Validate())
    {
        switch (toStatus)
        {
            case ConWHSVehInspStatus::Complete:
                Timezone tz = DateTimeUtil::
                                getClientMachineTimeZone();
                ConWHSVehInspDate inspDate;
                inspDate = DateTimeUtil::getSystemDate(tz);
                vehicle.InspDate = inspDate;
                break;
        }
    }
    else
    {
        vehicle.InspStatus = fromStatus;
    }
}
```

There is nothing new about the preceding code, except that we don't (and must not) call update on the record. It is just a validation class that will stop the transition if the comment is blank.

2. The code to tie it to the transition delegate is as follows:

```
[SubscribesTo(classStr(ConWHSVehicleTableInspStateMachine),
 delegateStr(
```

```
        ConWHSVehicleTableInspStateMachine, Transition))]
    public static void HandleTransition(
        ConWHSVehicleTableInspStateMachineTransitionEventArgs
        _eventArgs)
    {
        ConWHSVehicleInspStatusHandler handler;
        handler = new ConWHSVehicleInspStatusHandler();

        handler.vehicle = _eventArgs.DataEntity();
        handler.fromStatus = _eventArgs.ExitState();
        handler.toStatus = _eventArgs.EnterState();
        handler.Run();
    }
```

How it works...

When the state machine generated the classes, it added a delegate that is called whenever the state changes. This delegate is called before the changes are committed. The table is passed by reference, which means that we can revert the status back without calling `update`. If we did call `update`, we could cause concurrency issues within the standard code.

There's more...

When working with a handler class, also be careful with transaction state. We could update data in a table, for instance, a manually crafted status history table. We can nicely handle any potential exception with a `try...catch` statement within our handler class, but we can't control what happens when control returns back to the state machine. For example, if we update a history table, but the code fails later on, we could end up with a non-durable transaction if the code handles the exception and continues to commit the transaction.

Using menu items to control a state machine

In this section, we will actually add the state machine to the form, so we can use it. Using menu items for this is a nice concise way to control the state machine, and follows the UI patterns found in other areas, such as the projects module.

Getting ready

The prerequisite for this recipe is that we have a table with a state machine that has been generated.

How to do it...

To create the state machine menu items, follow these steps:

1. Add a new action menu item to the project named ConWHSVehInspStatusWaiting. Complete the property sheet as follows, in the order stated in the following table:

Property	Value
State Machine Data Source	ConWHSVehicleTable
State Machine Transition To	Waiting
Label	The label you use in the Waiting state's **Label** property
Help Text	The label you use in the Waiting state's **Description** property
Needs Record	Yes

2. Create the menu items for the remaining states (InProgress and Complete) following the same pattern.
3. Open the ConWHSVehicleTable form in the designer.
4. Under the form's **Design** node, expand the ActionPaneHome control, and then ActionPaneActionButtonGroup. Right-click on this control and choose **New |
Menu Button**.
5. Rename the new control InspStatusMenuButton. Set the **Text** and **Help Text** properties to the same as we used on the state machine, for example, @ConWHS:InspectionStatus and @ConWHS:InspectionStatusHT respectively.
6. Then, drag the three menu items onto this menu button. Set the **Data Source** property to ConWHSVehicleTable--the table that the state machine operates on.
7. If you can't add them directly, drag them first onto the ActionPaneActionButtonGroup button group, and then drag them from there to the correct place.

8. Save and close all code editors and design windows and build the project.

How it works...

When we created the menu items, the system defaulted many properties for us. If the table only has one state machine, all we had to do was set the label properties. You may notice that it changes the menu item's properties so that it referenced the state machine class that was generated by the table's state machine.

When we test the buttons, you can see that if we choose a transition that is not valid, we get this error:

 Invalid operation - the state transition from NotInspected state to Complete state is invalid.

We can't change this message, as it is controlled by a protected method, and we shouldn't edit the generated classes, as the code changes will be lost should the state machine be regenerated. This is a little odd, as the generated code does gather the user friendly labels we added.

Hooking up the state machine to a workflow

In this recipe, we will hook up our state machine to the `ConWHSVehWFInsp` workflow task.

Getting ready

We need to have a workflow task and have completed the recipes in this chapter.

How to do it...

To hook up the state machine to a workflow task, follow these steps:

1. Open the `ConWHSVehWFInsp` workflow task.
2. Set the **Canceled State Machine** property to `InspStateMachine`.

Yes, this is spelled `Canceled`, but it is more than compensated by the clever way it has determined the list of valid state machines.

3. Set the **Canceled State Machine Target State** property to `Waiting`; we won't be allowed to use `NotInspected`. Due to this being the state machine's initial state, it will let you set this value, but the state machine will reject the change.
4. Set the **Started State Machine** property to `InspStateMachine`, and the **Started State Machine Target State** property to `Waiting`.

You will also need to allow the `Waiting` state to transition directly to `Complete`. Don't forget to click on **Generate** to regenerate the state machine class.

5. Select the **Completed** outcome, set the **State Machine** property to `InspStateMachine`, and the set **State Machine Target State** property to `Complete`.
6. Since we now have two ways to set the status, we will (as a short term fix) disable the status update code that set the status in the `SetStatus` method of the `ConWHSVehInspStatusHandler` class. Open this class and remove the line that set the `InspStatus` field.

We will update this code properly in the *There's more...* section.

7. Upon testing this, we will find that the task completed sets the comment correctly, but the status doesn't change to completed. The reason is because the workflow events fire last, so the state machine validation rejected the update because the comment was not yet set. We need to update our validation logic so that it only runs when triggered from the form. Alter the `Validate` method of the `ConWHSVehInspStatusHandler` class so that it reads as follows:

```
public boolean Validate()
{
    switch (toStatus)
    {
        case ConWHSVehInspStatus::Complete:
            if (vehicle.InspComment == ''
```

```
              && FormDataUtil::isFormDataSource(vehicle))
      {
          //The field %1 must be filled in"
          DictField field = new DictField(
              tableNum(ConWHSVehicleTable),
              fieldNum(ConWHSVehicleTable,
                      InspComment));
          return checkFailed(strFmt(
                  "@SYS110217",
                  field.label()));
      }
      break;
  }
  return true;
}
```

 The highlighted code checks if the record buffer is a form data source;
if the code was called from within workflow, the table will not be
linked to a form's data source.

8. Build and test the workflow; all should work correctly.

How it works...

The change we have made was to simply tie the events on the workflow task to a state of
the state machine. This means that the event handler methods we normally write should
not update the status, but they can perform actions that should happen when the event
happens.

The state machine is called by the workflow engine, just before the events are called. This is
why we had to remove the validation on the comment--the state is changed before the
completed event was called, which means that the comment was empty. There isn't much
we can do in this case but to allow the workflow to continue. We could use the workflow
designer to check for this event and resubmit the task to the user.

There's more...

This seems to greatly simplify the workflow development. We don't need all of the event
handler methods, since most of them only update the record's status. There is some thought
required, if we consider the following scenario.

The workflow is cancelled by the user, which means that the status will go back to `Waiting`. We chose `Waiting`, for when the workflow task was cancelled, because the state machine will throw an error if we try to set it to the initial state. The problem is that we can't change the status to the same status; we will still get an error. The error is not just a message to the user; it will place the workflow in a failed state, which will require an administrator to cancel, resubmit, or resume it.

 The problem is that we should not have a scenario where a user action can cause a failure that requires an administrator to rescue them; we need to handle this eventuality elegantly within our code.

The first thing we could do is add an internal state to the status Base Enum and to the state machine, for example, "Internal processing". We would not create a menu item for this as it is only for internal use. On the state machine, we would allow any transition from this state; it can transition freely from and to this state.

This is the state we use for the `Cancelled` event. This means that the workflow can set the status to Waiting after the workflow was canceled.

The next part of the changes we would make would be to remove all calls to `ConWHSVehiInspStatusHandler::SetStatus(...)`. We would write a new method called `SetComment`, which is called from the `Completed` event on the workflow task event handler class.

Index

using, for extensibility 306, 307, 309, 310, 311, 313, 314, 315
Internet Information Services (IIS) 292
Intrinsic Functions [AX 2012]
  reference 66

K

key performance indicators (KPIs)
  about 176
  creating 178
  using 179, 181, 183

L

label file
  creating 28, 29
latest update, of Dynamics 365 for Operations
  reference 360
Lifecycle Services (LCS)
  about 10
  reference 10, 15
lookup
  replacing, form event handler used 217, 219, 221, 222

M

main data tables
  creating 58, 59, 60, 61, 62, 63, 64
manual workflow task
  creating 389, 390, 391, 392, 393, 395, 396
menu items
  about 90
  creating 90, 91
  used, for controlling state machine 413, 414, 415
menu structure
  about 78
  creating 78, 79, 80, 81
metadata fixes
  about 360
  applying 360, 361, 362, 363
metadata hotfix
  reference 364
metadata
  interface, using for extensibility 306, 307, 309, 310, 311, 313, 314, 315

using, for data access 295, 296, 298, 299, 300, 301, 302, 303, 304, 306
methods
  copying 57
  pasting 57
Microsoft / Dynamics-AX-Integration
  reference 257
Microsoft Connect 11
Microsoft Dynamics 365 9
Microsoft Dynamics 365 for Operations for Developers and IT Pros
  reference 10
Microsoft Dynamics 365 for Operations
  about 9, 227
  application updates 10
  options 26
  platform updates 9
  reference 10
Microsoft Dynamics AX 2012 9
Model
  about 24
  creating 20, 21, 23

N

naming conventions 25
Newtonsoft JSON Samples
  reference 287
Non-Clustered Column Store Indexes (NCCI) 66
number sequence
  hooking up 134, 136, 138, 140, 142, 144, 146
  setting up 145

O

OData
  data, reading through 246, 247, 248, 250, 252, 253
  data, updating through 246, 247, 248, 250, 252, 253
  data, writing through 246, 247, 248, 250, 252, 253
  references 239, 257
Odometer field
  using, on vehicle form 320
On Delete property 71
Optimistic concurrency (OCC) 57

Made in the USA
San Bernardino, CA
27 November 2019